Table of Cases

AN INTRODUCTION TO
ADMINISTRATIVE
LAW

PETER CANE

CLARENDON PRESS · OXFORD
1986

Oxford University Press, Walton Street, Oxford OX2 6DP
Oxford New York Toronto
Delhi Bombay Calcutta Madras Karachi
Petaling Jaya Singapore Hong Kong Tokyo
Nairobi Dar es Salaam Cape Town
Melbourne Auckland
and associated companies in
Beirut Berlin Ibadan Nicosia

Oxford is a trade mark of Oxford University Press

Published in the United States
by Oxford University Press, New York

British Library Cataloguing in Publication Data
Cane, Peter
An introduction to administrative law.—
(Clarendon law series)
1. Administrative law—Great Britain
I. Title
344.102'6 KD4879
ISBN 0-19-825484-9
ISBN 0-19-825485-7 Pbk

Library of Congress Cataloging in Publication Data
Cane, Peter.
An introduction to administrative law.
(Clarendon law series)
Includes index.
1. Judicial review of administrative acts—Great Britain.
I. Title.
KD4902.C36 1986 342.41'06 86-732
ISBN 0-19-825484-9 344.1026
ISBN 0-19-825485-7 (pbk.)

Set by Hope Services, Abingdon, Oxon
Printed in Great Britain
at the University Printing House, Oxford
by David Stanford
Printer to the University

Preface

STUDENTS of administrative law are now well served by a number of full-length textbooks and volumes of cases and materials. This book aims to provide a relatively short statement of the most important rules and principles of administrative law; but also to provide a constitutional and political context in which to view the legal rules and principles. In this respect I have taken inspiration from Atiyah's volume on the law of contract and Fleming's on the law of torts in this series: both of these authors seek to clothe the bones of the legal rules with 'garments of a different hue'.

I am grateful to Jack Beatson, Carol Harlow, and Martin Matthews, who have read various parts of the book at various stages of its production and made very valuable criticisms; and to Simon Lee, who read the whole for OUP and made some penetrating comments. I remain solely responsible for the shape and contents of the final result.

In recent years some writers on administrative law have been calling for less concentration on the rules and more on theories which explain them. The best approach is a balance between the two—theory which is too abstract is as arid as rule formalism. I hope that I have struck a reasonable balance.

Oxford
14 October 1985

PETER CANE

Contents

Table of Statutes and Statutory Instruments

Abbreviations

AC	Appeal Cases (1890–)
ALR	Australian Law Reports
All ER	All England Law Reports
App. Cas.	Appeal Cases (1875–1890)
Brit. J. of Law & Society	British Journal of Law and Society
CBNS	Common Bench New Series (Court of Common Pleas 1856–65)
CJQ	Civil Justice Quarterly
CLA	Commission for Local Administration
CLJ	Cambridge Law Journal
CLP	Current Legal Problems
CLR	Commonwealth Law Reports (Australian)
CMLR	Common Market Law Reports
Ch.	Chancery Division Reports
Cmnd	Command Papers (HMSO)
HC	House of Commons
Harvard LR	Harvard Law Review
ICR	Industrial Cases Reports
J	Mr Justice
J. of Law & Society	Journal of Law and Society
KB (or QB)	King's (or Queen's) Bench Division Reports
LGR	Local Government Reports
LJ	Lord Justice
LR HL	House of Lords Appeals (1866–75)
LR Ir.	Reports of Irish Cases
LS Gaz.	Law Society Gazette
LQR	Law Quarterly Review
MLR	Modern Law Review
MR	Master of the Rolls
Monash LR	Monash Law Review (Australian)
NSWR	New South Wales Reports
OJLS	Oxford Journal of Legal Studies
PCA	Parliamentary Commissioner for Administration
P&CR	Property and Compensation Reports
PL	Public Law

Parl. Aff.	Parliamentary Affairs
Pol. Q.	Political Quarterly
QB (or KB)	Queen's (or King's) Bench Division Reports
RSC	Rules of the Supreme Court
RTR	Road Traffic Reports
Sydney LR	Sydney Law Review
TLR	Times Law Reports
U. of NSWLJ	University of New South Wales Law Journal
U. of Penn. LR	University of Pennsylvania Law Review
WLR	Weekly Law Reports

PART I

INTRODUCTION

I

The Constitutional Perspective

1. WHAT IS ADMINISTRATIVE LAW ABOUT?

COULD a private citizen obtain a court order to prevent post office workers boycotting mail to South Africa? Could the Greater London Council lawfully cut tube fares? Could a local authority be sued for damages for negligently inspecting or failing to inspect the foundations of a house to ensure that they complied with building regulations? Could a taxi driver be deprived of his licence to operate at Heathrow because of misconduct, without being given a chance to put his side of the story? Could the Secretary of State for Education force a local authority to go ahead with its predecessor council's plan to 'comprehensivize' schools in its area? Could parents force a local authority to keep schools open during a strike of ancillary workers? When is the Home Office entitled to change policy guidelines concerning the release of prisoners on licence or the admission to Britain of immigrant children wanted for adoption here? Must a local authority keep lanes free of snow and ice in the winter? Could the government be liable for damage done by escaping prisoners? Could the Bank of England be required to disclose records of discussions between it and the Department of Trade about the price at which Burmah Oil shares were to be bought by the government?

These are just a few of the issues which arose in cases that will be discussed in this book. They show how diverse and important are the matters with which the rules and principles of administrative law deal. Many administrative law cases concern situations of immediate importance to ordinary people—whether the Home Office could prevent people buying a new TV licence before their current one had expired in order to avoid a licence fee increase; whether an immigrant will be allowed to enter Britain or will be sent back whence he came; whether a landowner will be allowed to build on his land. But many cases also raise constitutional and political issues of the most fundamental importance. Take the case about cheap fares on the London Underground. Was the GLC entitled to cut fares and subsidize travellers out of rate revenue and central government grants? Among the issues raised by this case were how a court was to go about deciding exactly what powers Parliament had intended to give to the GLC in relation to London Transport; whether the GLC owed a duty to its ratepayers not to spend the rates on large subsidies for travellers; whether the GLC was entitled to implement its cheap fares policy just because it had been a major issue in the recent GLC elections; the extent to which central government ought to control local authority spending; whether and to what extent public transport ought to be treated as a public service or, on the other hand, as a business which has to break even or make a profit. These questions raised not only legal points but also constitutional and political issues of great complexity. We will discuss some of them in the course of this chapter. But before doing so we should make some attempt to define more precisely what is meant by administrative law.

2. THE DISTINCTION BETWEEN PUBLIC LAW AND PRIVATE LAW

Administrative law is part of what is often called 'public law'. Public law can, of course, be contrasted with private law. Some writers argue that it is undesirable to draw *any* distinction between public law and private law partly because the distinction is often used to accord legal privileges and immunities to governmental bodies. I do not subscribe to this view, as will be clear throughout this book, and I shall show that there are sound reasons for drawing such a distinction.

Private law might be defined as law regulating the relations of private persons, whether individuals, corporations, or unincorporated associations, with one another. This definition suggests that public law concerns the activities of governmental agencies; it regulates relations between governmental agencies and private individuals on the one hand, and between different governmental agencies on the other. Further, just as private law defines what is meant in law by a 'person', so public law regulates the creation and organization of governmental agencies.

Let us rest content for the moment with this definition of public law, and ask why a distinction is drawn between public and private law. The obvious, but not very informative, reply is: because we want to subject activities of governmental agencies to a different legal regime from that which regulates the activities of private individuals. There are a number of reasons for this. First, since the government has the job of running the country it must have some functions, powers, and duties which private individuals do not have; obvious examples are the waging of war and the issuing of passports. Private law has nothing to say about these. Secondly, because of the very great power which the government can wield over its citizens the law has traditionally imposed on governmental agencies special duties of procedural fairness (embodied in the rules of natural justice discussed in Chapter 5) which do not normally apply to dealings between private citizens. The courts have also developed a set of rules embodied in the doctrine of *ultra vires* (see Chapters 3 and 4) which impose certain limitations on the substance of governmental actions and decisions. Thirdly, the activities of governmental agencies are often subject to forms of public accountability, notably to Parliament, to which the activities of private individuals are not subject.

Fourthly, the view the courts take of their proper role when dealing with the exercise of governmental power is different from the way they view their role in relation to purely private matters. In relation to the affairs of private citizens the courts are the primary organs for interpreting, applying, and enforcing the law. But when they are dealing with matters involving other branches of government the courts take a more restrained view of their role. The legislature is almost entirely free of judicial control and, under the doctrine of *ultra vires*, the executive enjoys a considerable degree of autonomy and immunity from judicial control. This judicial restraint is partly a function of the doctrine of separation of powers which will be considered shortly.

A fifth reason for distinguishing between public and private law arises out of the fact that, although some of the functions of government are uniquely governmental, not all are: governments make (and sometimes break) contracts just as private individuals do; governments own property in the same way as private citizens; governments also commit torts on occasion. The law of contract, torts, and property are central areas of private law. Should the unmodified rules of private law apply equally to government contracts, government property, and government torts, or should there be a law of public contracts, public property, and public torts? The answer which the courts have given to this question is, as we shall see, neither an unqualified 'yes' nor an unqualified 'no'. There are, for example, some 'public law' rules of liability in contract and tort.

The argument against having a special regime of rules to regulate the activities of government which are not uniquely governmental was most famously put by the eminent Victorian jurist, A. V. Dicey.[1] In his view, it was a great strength of English law that governmental officials were subject to exactly the same laws as private citizens, to the extent that these covered the activities of government. In this way the law ensured that the government was given no unfair privileges or advantages over its citizens. An argument which pulls in the opposite direction is this: even when the government (or a governmental agency such as a nationalized industry) is, for example, making contracts, it is doing so in some sense as representative of the citizenry at large and must bear the interests of the community as a whole constantly in mind. It might sometimes harm the public interest to subject the government to rules designed to deal with cases in which the peculiar responsibilities of government are not at issue. On the other hand, the government is a very powerful institution, and in some cases there may be an argument for protecting private citizens, in their dealings with government, against the operation (even in the absence of abuse) of this power, by modifying the rules which govern the citizen's dealings with other citizens, when these rules are applied to dealings between citizens and government. The distinction between public and private law can, therefore, be used either to accord government special privileges, or to impose on it special responsibilities and duties, and to subject it to special controls.

This discussion suggests that the question we ought to be asking is not a descriptive one—what *is* public law?—but a prescriptive or formative one: when *ought* public law rules apply, or, what is the proper scope of public law? The fact that some of the activities and functions of governmental agencies are subject to the rules of private law shows that we cannot (contrary to the tentative definition of public law suggested earlier) answer this question solely in terms of whether we are dealing with a governmental agency. In order to give a full account of the scope of public law, it is necessary to add to the institutional criterion (are we dealing with a public body?) a functional criterion—is it performing a public (or governmental) function? But once we add this functional criterion we create a different problem: sometimes private non-governmental bodies perform functions which we might consider to be public in nature. For example, private

---

[1] *An Introduction to the Study of Law of the Constitution* (10th edn., Wade), chapter 4.

professional bodies such as the Law Society or the British Medical Association perform licensing functions designed to protect the public generally against unqualified practitioners. Sometimes the government delegates public administrative functions to private bodies: for example, the Rowntree Trust (a private charitable organization) administers the Family Fund (a public fund to assist families of severely handicapped children). It may not be satisfactory to control and regulate private bodies exercising 'public' functions just by applying private law rules and concepts to their activities.

Perhaps, therefore, we should say that public law ought to govern the exercise of public functions whether by public or private persons, or bodies. But how are we going to decide whether a function is a public one or not? The discussion so far might suggest the following definition: a public function is a function peculiar to government, or a function not peculiar to government, the performance of which has an important impact on society at large. This definition, however, does not enable us to say which functions are public functions but only to give a reason why certain functions are classified as public. In the end, the question of whether a function is a public one is a political question which may not always be answered in the same way. This can be appreciated by considering how, in different countries and at different times, the provision of health care, education, and other essential services, such as electricity and transport, has been subject to varying degrees of public control.

It is also worth noting that a number of techniques are available for giving legal force to the judgment that an activity is in some sense 'public'. One is to bring it into the public sector by nationalizing it. Another is to leave it in private hands, but to invest public money in it. A third technique is to leave the activity in the private sector but to regulate it by legislation or common law. Examples of the latter are provided by cases which have held that the licensing of a racehorse trainer[2] or the dismissal of a union official[3] should be done in conformity with the public law rules of natural justice.[4] The choice between these techniques is itself to some extent a question of political ideology.

Furthermore, contrary to my earlier assumption, the distinction between public and private bodies is neither easy to draw, nor

[2] *Nagle* v. *Fielden* [1966] 2 QB 633.
[3] *Stevenson* v. *URTU* [1977] 2 All ER 941.
[4] On these rules, see Chapter 5, below.

irrelevant to the question of the proper scope of public law. Some offices and bodies are clearly governmental and public; for example, Ministers of State and their Departments, the National Health Service, local authorities. But there are more difficult cases. What about the BBC, or a nationalized industry such as British Gas, or, bodies (sometimes called quasi-autonomous non-governmental organizations—QUANGOS—or non-departmental bodies) such as the Manpower Services Commission, the Health and Safety Executive, the Arts Council or the Welsh Development Agency? The status of such bodies is less clear, because the extent of their links with, and the extent to which they are controlled and supported by, governmental agencies varies a great deal and is often somewhat problematic in legal and political terms.

The basic dilemma presented by such bodies is that on the one hand they are often created exactly in order to distance their activities from government; and yet at the same time, because they perform important public functions, or are funded wholly or partly by public money, or both, we may say that their activities cannot be left regulated only by private law. The nationalized industries illustrate the difficulties very clearly. To the extent that nationalized industries are meant to operate commercially then private law rules of contract, and so on, might be thought to be appropriate regulators of their activities. On the other hand, as they enjoy a monopoly, or near monopoly, of a particular service as well as government patronage and funding, it might be argued that they ought to be subject to some degree of public control.

This discussion should have made it clear that no sharp distinction can be drawn between public and private. It also suggests that the classification of functions or institutions as public or private by nature is not the best way of deciding the scope of public law. Rather we should begin by asking why we have a distinction between public and private law. Earlier, five reasons were suggested. There are, as we will see, yet other reasons for the distinction. For example, procedural reasons are discussed in Chapter 10; reasons associated with imposing liability in tort and contract are discussed in Chapters 15 and 16; and reasons associated with the free flow of information in society are considered in Chapter 19. We should then ask whether any of these reasons are relevant to the case with which we are concerned, and classify the agency or activity in question in such a way as to achieve the desired level and type of control. In other words, we can only understand the difference between the public and the private by understanding the reasons for drawing the distinction. Furthermore, it appears that the distinction is not drawn in the same way in all areas where it is used. The reasons for which it is drawn influence the way it is drawn.

3. ADMINISTRATIVE LAW

The field of public law is a large one, and there is no universally accepted way of dividing it up for the sake of exposition. However, just as the definition of public law contains both institutional and functional elements, so also we find institutionally and functionally based 'subject divisions' within public law. Examples of the latter are social security law, housing law, planning law, immigration law, the law relating to civil liberties, and so on. Institutional divisions within the study of public law tend broadly to follow the traditional tripartite division of government into the Legislature, the Executive, and the Judiciary.

Works on administrative law vary widely in their concerns. Some are primarily institutional, such as studies of the functions of local government, of the Civil Service, or of tribunals. Other works choose to consider the role of each of the branches of government, including the administrative, in a particular area of public law, such as immigration. Many books on administrative law concentrate on the legal control of administrative action, especialy by means of judicial review.

Writers on administrative law are not all in agreement about the best way of approaching the study of the legal control of administrative action. Some people think that the law of judicial review, for example, cannot be properly understood unless it is studied against the background of a particular area of governmental activity, such as housing or immigration. On the other hand, some people think that general rules, such as the rules of natural justice, which apply across the whole range of administrative activities, can usefully be examined and discussed in their own right. An analogy can be drawn with study of the law of contract: books are written both on particular types of contract, such as contracts of agency or sale, but also on the general principles of the law of contract. This book is based on the view that the general principles of judicial review of administrative action are worth studying. This does not mean that the context in which the general rules operate can be ignored, and sometimes it will be crucial. But there is much that can be usefully said about the way in which *all* administrative activities are controlled by law, particularly in the consideration of the relationships between different branches of government, where we will often be dealing with matters of general constitutional and political import. One of the main assumptions underlying this book is that a sound understanding of public law generally requires attention to be paid to the interaction between the different branches of government.

This book is chiefly about *control* of governmental activities and the redress of grievances against government. It concentrates on legal control by the courts, but certain non-legal controls will also be considered. Legal control by the courts is basically retrospective—it is concerned primarily with cure (dispute resolution), not prevention (dispute avoidance); but prospective methods of regulating government activities will also receive some discussion. Nearly all of the techniques considered in this book for controlling government and redressing grievances are formal and institutionalized. In one sense this presents a misleading picture because only a small fraction of complaints against government is handled through these formal channels.[5] Many more are dealt with by direct complaint to the official or department concerned by the aggrieved citizen or by some body on his behalf such as an MP,[6] local councillor, union, pressure or interest group, or other voluntary organization.[7]

But the techniques discussed in this book are more important than the frequency of their use would suggest, for a number of reasons. First, because formal institutionalized procedures generally attract more publicity than informal ones, the outcome of individual cases can influence the outcome of a large number of other complaints (or potential complaints). Secondly, as we will see in the final chapter, decisions about the legality or propriety of past administrative action may influence the way administrators deal with similar cases in the future; and the threat of publicity may contribute further to the deterrent effect of formal complaint procedures. Thirdly, the respect in which the courts are held gives their decisions an influence quite out of proportion to the number of cases they deal with. Fourthly, because decisions of the courts are often elaborately reasoned and reported in

[5] For some statistics about judicial review, see Harlow & Rawlings, *Law and Administration* (London, 1984), pp. 257–63; an account of a number of non-judicial grievance-handling mechanisms will be found in P. Birkinshaw, *Grievances, Remedies, and the State* (London, 1985).

[6] Norton (1982) 35 Parliamentary Affairs 59.

[7] See Ridley (1984) 37 Parliamentary Affairs 1; Birkinshaw [1985] CJQ 15.

law reports, such decisions are crucially important in developing the concepts and rules of common law which define the limits of lawful administrative action. The courts do not hear a large number of cases, but they are the major source, apart from Parliament, of the legal rules governing administrative action. Legal rules are a very important part of the 'instructions' according to which administrators exercise their powers. Legal rules are not the whole of the instructions—departmental policy guidelines, for example, also play a part (see Chapter 4 and Chapter 6)—but the legal rules are of central importance because they are binding and authoritative.

4. THE CONSTITUTIONAL BACKGROUND TO ADMINISTRATIVE LAW

Administrative law is concerned to a considerable extent with the relationships between different branches of government. In the first place, it is concerned with the position of administrative authorities *vis-à-vis* Parliament, since nearly all of the functions of administrative authorities are conferred and defined by statute, and Parliament exercises a certain amount of control over the exercise of these functions. At the same time, the importance of judicial review, as a mechanism for supervising the activities of administrative agencies, makes the question of the proper relationship between the legislative and the administrative branches of government, on the one hand, and the judicial branch, on the other, central to administrative law. There are several so-called 'constitutional doctrines' which have a bearing on these relationships and it is worthwhile spending some time considering these. They are: the supremacy (or sovereignty) of Parliament; ministerial responsibility; the separation of powers; and the rule of law. All of these doctrines are to a greater or lesser extent concerned with a central issue in constitutional theory, namely that of responsibility or accountability: how can those who wield governmental power best be made accountable for the way in which they exercise it? Accountability is a form of control. The courts are concerned mainly with control by the use of law, whereas Parliament is concerned with control by means of the exercise of political power. It is with the interaction between legal and political control that this section mainly deals.

(a) *The Supremacy of Parliament*

This doctrine is contained in four main propositions, namely: (1) in case of conflict between statute law and common law, statute law prevails; (2) Parliament is free to enact whatever law it chooses; (3) Acts of Parliament cannot be challenged in the courts on the grounds of invalidity or lack of constitutionality; and (4) Parliament cannot bind its successors. For present purposes, the first proposition alone demands our consideration.

Nearly all of the powers and duties of administrative agencies, whether they are part of central or of local government, are laid down by statute; there are only a few non-statutory administrative functions of importance. It follows from the first proposition about parliamentary supremacy that courts are bound to apply statutes according to their terms. Traditional theory also says, although this does not follow from the first proposition, that ambiguities in the language of statutes should be resolved and gaps in them filled by reference to the intention of the legislature. Thus, it is often said that the enforcement of statutory duties and the control of the exercise of statutory powers by the courts is ultimately justifiable in terms of the doctrine of parliamentary supremacy: even though Parliament has not expressly authorized the courts to supervise governmental activity, it cannot have intended breaches of duty by governmental agencies to go unremedied (even if no remedy is provided in the statute itself), nor can it have intended to give administrative agencies the freedom to exceed or abuse their powers, or to act unreasonably. It is the task of the courts to interpret and enforce the provisions of statutes which impose duties and confer powers on administrative agencies. In so doing they are giving effect to the will of Parliament.

There are two main weaknesses in this theory of the basis of judicial review. The first is relevant to statutory interpretation generally: it is unrealistic to treat the process of interpreting statutes, resolving ambiguities, and filling gaps, as always being a matter of discerning and giving effect to the intentions of Parliament. Even assuming that we can make some sense of the notion of intention when applied to a multi-member body following simple majoritarian voting procedures, there will be many cases in which Parliament did not think about the question relevant to resolving the ambiguity, or filling the gap. In such cases the courts must act creatively in deciding what the statute means.

A second weakness of this theory of judicial review is that it gives an account of the role of the courts which is at variance with the actual conduct of the courts. The principles which form the basis of judicial review—the doctrine of *ultra vires*[8] and the rules of natural justice[9]—are common law principles created and developed *by the courts* as means of controlling administrative activities. The courts have shown themselves prepared to go a very long way to preserve their jurisdiction to supervise administrative action by applying these principles. Perhaps the most striking modern example of this is the case of *Anisminic Ltd.* v. *Foreign Compensation Commission.*[10] The main question in this case was whether a section in the Foreign Compensation Act purporting to oust the jurisdiction of the court to review 'determinations' of the Commission was effective to that end. The House of Lords held that the word 'determination' must be read so as to exclude *ultra vires* determinations; it then went on to extend considerably the notion of *ultra vires* as it applied to decisions on questions of law, the final result being to reduce the application of the ouster clause almost to vanishing point, despite the fact that Parliament had fairly clearly intended it to have wide effect.

A second example is provided by the attitude of the courts to the exclusion, by statute, of the rules of natural justice. In the face of legislative silence on the question of whether an applicant before an administrative body is entitled to the protection of these procedural rules, two approaches are possible. It could be said that the rules of natural justice will apply only if there is evidence of a legislative intention that they should; alternatively, it could be argued that silence should be construed as an invitation to the courts to apply common law procedural standards of natural justice. On the whole the courts, especially in recent years, have tended to the latter view, thus asserting the independent validity of the rules of natural justice.

A third example is provided by cases, which we will examine later,[11] concerning powers given to a Minister, for example, 'to act as he sees fit'. Such phraseology appears to give the Minister unfettered discretion, but the courts tend to hold that such powers must be exercised reasonably, given the aims and purposes of the legislation conferring the power, and in the light of the relevant facts. In reality, the terms of the legislation may give very little guidance as to the way Parliament wished the power to be exercised, even assuming that it did not intend, as the phrase itself indicates, to leave the Minister

---

[8] See Chapters 3 and 4, below.   [9] See Chapter 5, below.
[10] [1969] 2 AC 147.
[11] See pp. 83–4, below.

free to exercise his own best judgment. In effect, the courts are imposing their own standards of reasonable conduct on the Minister, irrespective of the question of legislative intent.

How is this independent attitude of the courts to be justified? Two lines of argument suggest themselves. First, despite the second proposition of parliamentary supremacy stated above, there are certain features of our constitutional and political arrangements which are so basic to our system of government that it is not seriously thought that they could ever be subject to the whim of Parliament—for example, the right to vote in free elections. Parliament could, of course, pass legislation inimical to this right, but attempts to enforce it, whether in the courts or outside would, no doubt, precipitate a national crisis. Similarly, the rights to apply to the courts for judicial review of administrative action and to receive a fair hearing before administrative bodies, are of such fundamental importance in a democratic society that it is vital that some independent body has the power to protect these rights from any but the most limited statutory abridgement. A second line of argument which might support the refusal of the courts to be too subservient to Parliament is this: a vital underpinning assumption of parliamentary supremacy is that Parliament is the most democratic governmental institution in our system. But the political reality is that, when the party in government has a comfortable majority in the House of Commons, the House is almost as much under the control of the government as is the administration. The implications of this line of argument will be considered more later.

The autonomy of judicial review has an important implication which ought to be made explicit, namely that, in controlling administrative activity, the courts are asserting and exercising, in their own right and in their own name, a power to limit and define the powers of other governmental agencies. Parliament allocates decision-making powers to governmental agencies by virtue of its unlimited legislative power. The courts, by virtue of their inherent (i.e. self-conferred) common law power of judicial review of administrative action, decide the exact legal limits of those allocations of power. In so doing they can not only castigate governmental agencies for abuses or excesses of power, but, equally importantly, they can legitimize controversial exercises of power by holding them to have been lawful. The courts, in short, perform an indirect power-allocation function. Once this is realized it can be seen how important it is to understand the exact nature of this function and the justification for it, since it is clear that the courts are not detached umpires in the governmental process, but that they play an integral part in deciding how it will operate.

(b) Ministerial Responsibility

This doctrine is theoretically of great importance in administrative law because it provides the mechanism through which Parliament can exercise political control over those activities of central government which are under the ultimate supervision of a Minister. The mechanism also provides a limited means of control over local government and agencies such as nationalized industries, in so far as Ministers have powers over and responsibilities for the activities of these bodies.[12]

The political responsibility of Ministers for activities under their control is designed basically to protect the anonymity of Civil Servants and their independence from political pressure, while at the same time ensuring a degree of democratic supervision of the unelected part of the government machine. The most serious sanction theoretically attaching to ministerial responsibility is resignation from office. 'Responsibility' can bear a number of different meanings: a Minister might be responsible in the sense that he was the author of a criticized action; or in the sense that he (accepts that he) is morally blameworthy for it; or in the much less significant sense that he is prepared to answer questions about it and to make sure that it does not happen again but not to defend it.[13] The sanction of forced resignation will not attach to responsibility in the third sense, but this is the most commonly used sense of the three because, in practice, Ministers are personally involved in only a very small proportion of the activities of their departments. Therefore, whereas, ideally, ministerial responsibility would provide a channel of communication between Parliament and administrators, to convey information and explanations in one direction, and praise or blame in the other, it tends to operate as a shield—the harmless buck stops with the Minister, who gives only enough information to satisfy critics as to what happened, rather than as to how or why.

A device adopted to help overcome this blockage in the lines of

---

[12] de Smith, *Constitutional and Administrative Law* (5th edn., Street & Brazier, London, 1985), pp. 183–4; Walkland & Ryle (edd.), *The Commons Today* (1981), pp. 186–90.

[13] Marshall & Moodie, *Some Problems of the Constitution* (rev. edn., London, 1961), chapter 4; Marshall, *Constitutional Conventions* (Oxford, 1984), chapter 4.

responsibility is that of the Ombudsman or Parliamentary Commissioner for Administration. Through him, members of the public can make complaints (via their MPs) about the operation of government departments and other public authorities. This can be an effective method, both of obtaining redress, and of providing Parliament with detailed information about, and explanations of, maladministration. Parliamentary Select Committees also play a part in scrutinizing administrative conduct. These devices will be considered later.

Ministerial responsibility is a mechanism for securing political accountability of the administrative branch of government and of other governmental bodies. The important point to make at this stage is this: the weaker the mechanisms of political accountability are, the more important, potentially at least, are the mechanisms of legal control of administrative action, even though in theory the two types of control are directed to different ends. The role of judicial review and of legal control generally should not be considered in isolation from methods of securing political accountability.

(c) Separation of Powers

This doctrine has received a wide variety of interpretations in different periods of history and in different systems. The basic idea, which underlies all versions of the doctrine, is that excessive concentration of power in the hands of a single official or agency is to be avoided, because it encourages, or at least facilitates, abuse of power. For example, it is undesirable that the same body should make the laws and also adjudicate disputes about their appliction. To this end, powers are usually divided into legislative, administrative, and judicial.[14]

According to a strict version of separation theory, any one authority should wield powers of only one of these three types. This version of separation is not a feature of the British governmental system. A rather different interpretation distinguishes between different branches of government—the legislature, the executive, and the judiciary—according to the type of power which is most prominent in the functions of each branch, and then forbids interference by any branch in the activities of any other branch. This version has not been adopted in Britain either. On the contrary, the British system, at least in its classic form, could be said to be a system of checks and balances. Under such a system, abuse of power is guarded against, not by

---

[14] See further, p. 18 below.

avoiding the conferral of powers of different types on the one authority, but by giving some other body, usually belonging to one of the other branches of government, the power to scrutinize the activities of the authority and to invalidate acts done in abuse or excess of power. This interpretation of separation underlies the doctrine of ministerial responsibility and also, as we shall see, the notion of the rule of law.

The most prominent application of the separation of powers theory in the British system is that which dictates the preservation of the independence of the judiciary from control or influence by the political branches of government. Independence is protected in part by giving judges security of tenure in office; this minimizes the risk of direct interference. But equally important to the preservation of independence is that the judiciary should not appear to be politically biased or partial. Crucial in this respect is the extent to which judges are asked to decide politically controversial issues in the course of litigation, and the way judges react when confronted with such issues. The essence of the judicial function is the resolution of disputes by the application of law. But in many cases, especially in superior courts, the application of existing law will not provide an answer to the questions confronting the court. In administrative law, as we have seen, the appeal to the intention of the legislature will not always relieve the court of the need to make its own decisions as to whether an administrative authority has exceeded or abused its powers. In public law matters, in particular, courts will often be faced with the need to decide whether an administrative authority has given due weight to competing public and private interests, or competing public interests. This is a delicate task, not only when the issues involved are controversial from a party-political point of view, but also when there are controversies about issues which cross party lines.

It is pointless and dangerous to deny that judges sometimes make political decisions. At the same time, the more highly controversial the decisions and choices which the courts are required or prepared to make are, the more their independence will be brought into question. Attack is likely from two angles: first, it will be suggested that judges are allowing political factors to influence their decisions, thus endangering their reputation for impartiality; and secondly, it will be argued that if judges make political decisions they ought to be politically answerable. These attacks are likely to be less loud and less effective when the only policy judgments which courts make are relatively uncontroversial in nature.

The courts have developed a number of devices designed to keep them out of highly controversial areas. In particular, the general principle on which the exercise of discretionary powers is reviewed is that of 'unreasonableness' understood in a rather strict sense which allows judicial intervention only when an administrative authority has acted so unreasonably that no reasonable authority could so act. The court, it is said, will not interfere just because, if it had been the authority, it would have acted differently. This principle of restraint is, of course, very vague and leaves judges considerable freedom to decide, in particular cases, the degree of interference with the exercise of discretionary powers which it allows.

The doctrine of separation of powers encourages us to view the courts as independent and impartial third party adjudicators of disputes between citizen and citizen, or between citizen and government. But the doctrine also draws our attention to the fact that the courts are themselves a branch of government, and that judicial power is governmental power. The courts are part of the machinery of government; they are not external to it nor unconnected with the governmental system. This is one reason why we draw a distinction between public law and private law—the courts see their role differently according to whether they are dealing with a purely private dispute or not. We must bear in mind, therefore, that the role of the courts in reviewing governmental action is inevitably affected by the fact that the courts themselves are a branch of government.

(d) Digression on Classification of Functions

It might be useful at this stage to say a little more about the tripartite division of governmental functions—legislative, administrative, and judicial. Legislation might be defined as the making of general rules to govern future conduct; under this definition, Public Acts of Parliament are the central case of legislation. Administration is considerably more difficult to define briefly, but for our purposes may be taken to mean the application of general rules to particular cases by the making of some order (for example, a demolition order), or some decision (for example, that an immigrant's entry certificate was obtained by fraud in contravention of some statutory regulation), or by performing some action (for example, making a payment of supplementary benefit). The central case of the judicial function is the final and binding resolution of bipartite (i.e. two-party) disputes as to facts, or as to the existence or scope of legal rights or duties, by means of the ascertainment of facts and the application of law.

None of these definitions is entirely straightforward because borderline cases can easily be found. For example, Private Acts of Parliament are treated as legislation even though they may regulate the conduct of only a single individual. Again, it is not easy to be dogmatic in answer to the question whether a court is exercising a judicial function when it entertains a reference from the Attorney-General. Another complication arises from the fact that the same term may have different meanings in different contexts. For example, the definition of the judicial function may vary according to whether we are concerned with rules about contempt of court, absolute privilege in the law of defamation, judicial immunity from actions in tort, or the availability of judicial review in administrative law.[15]

Despite these complications, each of these types of function has a relatively clear central core, and the distinction between them is of importance in several areas of administrative law. It should be noted, however, that it is by no means true that each function is performed only by the branch of government with the corresponding name. In particular, the administration exercises all three types of function. For example, a great deal of legislation is made by administrators in the name of Ministers under statutory powers delegated by Parliament.

Another point to note is that, at certain times in the history of administrative law, a distinction has been drawn between judicial and quasi-judicial functions. The distinction was drawn in the following terms: both types of function involved the resolution of a dispute, but whereas the former involved resolution by recourse to law, the latter allowed and often required recourse to considerations of public policy. Quasi-judicial functions, it was thought, were best committed to politically responsible Ministers rather than to courts because ultimately the required decision had to be made on policy grounds.

This distinction was heavily criticized, chiefly on the ground that courts, when exercising judicial functions, often cannot resolve a dispute simply by applying the law but must sometimes exercise discretion on policy grounds to fill gaps in the law; so the need to have recourse to policy was no reason not to commit a decision to a body which would deal with it in a fully 'judicial' way. This criticism is part of a wider attack on the use of classification of functions as a criterion

[15] See pp. 149–52 below.

for deciding issues in administrative law, such as the availability of
judicial remedies to control administrative action (the remedy of
certiorari was at one time said to be available only if the decision-maker
was under a duty to act 'judicially'),[16] or the applicability of the rules of
natural justice in particular circumstances (sometimes said to apply
only to 'judicial functions').[17] Classification of functions fell
into disrepute because the classifications were often applied mechani-
cally and without it being asked whether judicial review *ought* to be
available, or whether the rules of natural justice *ought* to apply as a
matter of justice or policy. Such mechanical use of classification by the
courts is now quite rare, but the distinction between types of function
is not without its uses, and it will be discussed in more detail in the
chapters on natural justice and remedies.

(e) The Rule of Law

Once again, we are here dealing with a phrase of vague meaning which
has received a wide variety of interpretations. The interpretation most
relevant to the study of administrative law is that of the nineteenth-
century jurist A. V. Dicey.[18] The two features of Dicey's theory which
are of importance to administrative law theory are first, the idea that
discretionary governmental power should be subject to legal control;
and secondly, that such control ought to be exercised by courts of law
applying the same law to governmental officials and bodies as that
which applies to private individuals.

The principle that all discretionary power should be subject to legal
control lies at the heart of judicial review of administrative action. Very
few of the discretionary powers wielded by governmental authorities
are not subject to review—examples of these few are the 'prerogative'
power of conducting war and foreign relations, and the powers of the
Attorney-General to control criminal and other proceedings by
refusing his consent to what are called 'relator actions'[19] and by
entering a '*nolle prosequi*'.

The major power in our system not subject to legal control is the
legislative power of Parliament. Those who argue for an entrenched
Bill of Rights argue for just such legal control of legislative power. The

---

[16] See p. 149 below.   [17] See p. 96 below.
[18] op. cit. n. 1 above, chapters 4 and 13.
[19] See p. 158 below; whether a 'prerogative' power is reviewable or not depends on
whether its subject matter is suitable for judicial control: *CCSU* v. *Minister for the Civil
Service* [1984] 3 WLR.

fact that the legislative programme is controlled in large measure by the government might be thought to add extra weight to this argument. Dicey's resolution of the conflict between parliamentary supremacy and the rule of law is not very satisfactory. The reconciliation, he believed, lay in the facts that the legislative process is formal and elaborate, that Parliament does not take part in the day-to-day running of government or appoint members of the executive branch, and that legislation is subject to potentially restrictive judicial interpretation. Furthermore, but somewhat inconsistently with the last point, Parliament enacts the law the rule of which the courts enforce and this enforcement, in turn, reinforces the spirit of legality. There are some today who are not satisfied with such a complacent acceptance of 'parliamentary dictatorship' which allows the majority to trample over the rights of minorities, and allows the government, restrained only by public opinion and periodical elections, to impose its views on citizens through its control of the Parliamentary machine.

The second feature of Dicey's account which we should consider is that it requires that administrative action should be subject to review in the ordinary courts of law, primarily the High Court. This was an unnecessary stricture, and today there are many bodies other than courts of law (for example tribunals) which perform important functions in ensuring that administrative authorities do not abuse or misuse their powers.

Finally, Dicey felt that the best way to control administrative action was to subject it to the same law as that which governed the activities of private citizens. So, for example, if an authority demolished a house in pursuance of an illegal order it should be liable in trespass in the ordinary way. There are three points to be made about this view. The first is that this approach will only work in cases where the action of the administrative authority is of a type which citizens can and may do. If it is not, then there will be no relevant rules applying to private citizens which can be used against the administrative authority. Some, at least, of the activities of government are unique to it. These, too, must be subjected to legal control and for this purpose 'public law' rules are needed. Secondly, however, a lot will depend on how we characterize the particular activity. For example, should the purchase of submarines be treated as providing for the defence of the realm—clearly a uniquely governmental activity, for the control of which special public law rules would be appropriate; or as 'contracting', in which case ordinary rules of contract law could be applied.

Thirdly, it is often assumed that special public law rules will be more generous to the government than the rules of private law, because the government will always be able to excuse itself from liability by saying that it was acting in the public interest. But we should not accept the validity of this assumption too quickly. There may be room for an argument that special rules of public law ought to be developed to take account of the fact that the government is very powerful and that the private citizen needs *more* protection in his dealings with it than he would need if he were dealing with another citizen. On the other hand, it does seem true as a matter of history that special public law rules are more often vehicles of governmental privilege than of governmental responsibility. At all events, it is clear that the issue of the application of private law rules of liability to public bodies is a difficult and complex one which will demand detailed consideration later.

(*f*) *Central and Local Government*

A final general point should be made about the constitutional doctrines we have been discussing, namely that they are concerned almost exclusively with central government. Governmental power is, in fact, considerably decentralized and administrative law is as much concerned with the activities of local as of central government. In strictly legal terms the control of the activities of local authorities presents no constitutional issues different from those raised by the control of government activity generally. This is because, like administrative powers and duties generally, the powers and duties of local authorities are statutory in origin. On the other hand, the position of local authorities is somewhat special. Although local authorities are subordinate in the governmental hierarchy to Parliament and to central government, they are nevertheless popularly elected and they carry out functions of national importance such as providing housing and education. If these activities were conducted by central government it could, within the limits of the law as laid down by Parliament and the courts, conduct them as it wished. Central government could integrate these activities into its management of the social and economic life of the nation as a whole. Local authorities are, by contrast, obviously concerned primarily to further the interests of their own areas. Many local authorities are under the control of political parties which do not form the government at Westminster, and local authorities spend very considerable amounts of money (much of it raised by general taxation and provided by central government in the form of block grants) largely according to their own priorities, rather than those of central government. For these reasons, local government presents central government with co-ordination problems, problems of integrating the activities of local government into the running of the nation as a whole.

Tensions and conflicts between central and local government can and do easily arise, and there has been an increasing tendency in recent times for central government to assume tight control over local government. Real local devolution of governmental functions is not a prominent feature of modern English political life. The main *legal* tool for the exercise of central control over local government is legislation coupled with common law rules of judicial review, which require local authorities not to exceed their statutory powers or neglect their statutory duties. Central government also exercises considerable political, administrative, and financial control over many local authority activities. Given that twenty-five per cent of public expenditure is by local authorities, and that many of the services provided by them are basic social services which it is desirable should be uniform throughout the country, a high degree of control is inevitable. But the desire for and the desirability of local autonomy remain and argue against excessively tight central control. Local authorities are, after all, democratically elected, and political theorists in the past 150 years have put forward a variety of arguments, mostly emphasizing the educative and socializing value of participation in community decision-making, in favour of 'local democracy'.

So far as administrative law is concerned, the most radical proposal for increasing local autonomy would be to loosen the fetters of judicial review on local authorities, and permit them more freedom in giving practical effect to the statutes under which they operate. Local authorities would be required to show that they were pursuing a defensible plan for local development in their area, within the broad spirit of the empowering legislation, but not necessarily to show that they were complying with the letter of the statute. In other words, whereas under the present system local government has to cut its cloth to meet the demands of central government, under this radical proposal central government would more often have to accommodate local government and run the nation in such a way as to leave people freer to do what they wanted in their local area. But even within the confines of the present law, if the courts were to adopt a presumption that statutes should be, if possible, interpreted so as to promote local autonomy, they could do much for the independence of local government. In the end, however, radical change could only be achieved if central government were prepared to relinquish more control of local affairs and to pass legislation to this effect. In the current political climate this seems an unlikely development.

5. THE POLITICAL BACKGROUND TO ADMINISTRATIVE LAW

Loosely speaking, constitutional and administrative law provide a framework for the exercise of political power. However, law provides *only* a framework and, in any system, the exercise of high political power and its distribution between different governmental institutions tend to be regulated to a greater or lesser extent by conventions, understandings, or practices of no legal force. The most commonly advanced reason for this is that these non-legal standards are more flexible than legal rules would be (although this argument is more compelling in respect of statutory than in respect of common law rules). It might also be argued that it is very difficult and of little use, to attempt by law to prevent changes in the distribution of ultimate political power, because, at the end of the day, the pattern of distribution of such power will operate satisfactorily only if it is acceptable to those competing for and wielding power, and to the nation generally. Conventions are rather like moral rules—when those whose conduct they regulate no longer find them acceptable, they are changed.

It is important, therefore, to give some thought to the impact of political realities and political theory on the constitutional theory we have considered, and on administrative law. Both law and constitutional theory are primarily concerned with the structure of governmental institutions and the distribution of power between them, whereas political theory is more concerned with the conduct and behaviour of actors on the political stage, and with the aims of the exercise of political power, such as furthering the public interest. All three are concerned with issues of control over and accountability of governmental officials and bodies, and with legitimizing (i.e. rendering acceptable to those subject to them) their existence and activities.

(a) *The Nature of the Political Process*

The classic doctrine of parliamentary supremacy seems to rest on the view that Parliament is the effective legislative power in our system, and is truly representative of the people. However, there are features of the legislative process which render this view untenable. First, the government has almost complete control over the legislative activities of Parliament. If the government has a clear majority in the House of Commons then, by and large, its legislation (and it is the major initiator of legislative proposals) will be passed; party discipline ensures this. Legislative proposals initiated by private members are unlikely to succeed without government support (or neutrality, at least). And, because of the strength of the party system within Parliament, MPs are viewed not as relatively independent representatives of their constituents, but more as 'lobby fodder' for their party.

Secondly, persons and groups outside Parliament (including Civil Servants and, perhaps most importantly, the non-parliamentary wings of the political parties) are probably much more important than individual MPs in the process of moulding and formulating government policy, and in influencing the final shape of legislation. The importance of this for the nature of representative democracy can be seen in recent debates in the Labour Party over its constitution: to what extent should trade union members and constituency party members have control over the contents of the party's manifesto; should MPs be bound by the manifesto, as opposed to being free to exercise their own best judgment in the light of the manifesto; should constituency parties be able to 'sack' MPs whose views or performance in the House do not meet with their approval? Those who advocate greater accountability of MPs to the non-parliamentary wing of their party seek to strengthen the role of MPs as representatives of the views of the people. Critics of such change might argue that MPs must be freer to exercise their own independent judgment than such change would allow, because their constituents include many who are not supporters of their party and did not vote for them, but whom they must nevertheless represent. In reply it could be argued that, given the size of modern electorates, the representative model is inappropriate, and that elections are really a means not of choosing representatives, but of choosing between policies. It would follow from this that reforms which increased the number of people with a say in the formulation of the policies, for which the parties and their electoral candidates stand, would be highly desirable. Whatever view is taken on these issues it is clear that they raise crucial questions about the nature of the political process.

More generally, both of the main parties, when in government, now tend to justify their legislative programmes not by reference to the principle of representative democracy as embodied in the classic picture of the constitution, but by appealing to their 'mandate' from the people based on their manifesto. It is clear, then, that the activities of Parliament represent only the tip of the legislative iceberg.

But it is not only on the legislative process that the policy-making activities of political parties impinge. The policies adopted and given effect to in the day-to-day running of government will often be predetermined party policies. This is as true of local as of central government. For example, a major justification put forward by the GLC for reducing fares on London Transport, was that fare reduction had been a plank òf the Labour Party's platform in the previous election. Such evidence as there is suggests that the courts are unwilling, in judging the legality of administrative action, to take account of the claim that the action was in accordance with publicly announced party policy. The notion of legality is treated as being quite distinct from that of political propriety.

The very considerable influence of pressure and lobby groups on government policy, and on the process of initiating and settling the content of new legislation, both parliamentary and delegated (including by-laws of local authorities), also raises important issues about the nature of the political process. This influence is relevant not only to the legislative process; interest groups influence the exercise of administrative as well as of legislative power. This influence is sometimes formalized: the government may establish (and perhaps fund) an 'advisory committee' representative of what the Minister thinks are properly interested groups, and give it a statutory right to be consulted. Even more importantly, non-governmental interest groups may be entrusted with administrative power (for example, the Law Society administers the Legal Aid Scheme), and even with powers of law enforcement (for example, in order to be exempted from the operation of Sunday trading laws on the grounds of being a Jew, a trader needs a certificate from the Jewish Board of Deputies).

The influence of such groups places emphasis in the political system on consultation with interest groups (such as trade unions and business or professional associations) and groups espousing particular causes (such as child or animal welfare) rather than on the representation of individuals on a geographical basis. Under a system of universal adult suffrage a major justification of geographical representation is that everyone has an equal voice in government by virtue of being able to elect parliamentary representatives. So the importance in our political system of interest consultation raises the question of whether the groups consulted represent the interests of everyone. It might be argued that the interest consultation system, as it works at present, is, on the whole, not sufficiently structured or controlled to ensure a proper voice to all; rather, by its frequent informality it offers much to those who have bargaining strength and 'loud voices', but little to the ordinary citizen. Some interests are not sufficiently well-organized to put their case forward, and anyway it is, in the end, up to the government to decide which groups they will consult on any particular matter. Of course, many pressure groups represent significant sections of the public, but nevertheless their function is to promote interests which are, by definition, sectional rather than broadly based in the community at large. This may not matter so long as the courses of conduct urged by these sectional interests are weighed properly against all other options, but it might be argued that the influence of certain lobby groups means that they can effectively discourage consideration of courses of action other than that which they propose. The importance of interest consultation has, it might be argued, considerably reduced the responsiveness and accountability of the government to ordinary, unorganized people, at least between elections.

Furthermore, entrusting administrative powers to non-governmental, sectional interest groups might be thought to raise fundamental issues of accountability and control. To what extent should such bodies be treated as if they were part of government and subjected to public control?

(b) The Function of Judicial Review and the Role of the Courts

(i) Group and interest representation

It is, of course, a difficult question (on which opinions can and do differ) as to what extent this picture of our modern democratic processes is accurate, but for present purposes it is enough to note that such arguments can be and have been used, especially in the United States, as a basis for suggesting that the primary role of the courts in reviewing governmental activity should be the protection of significant sectional interests, particularly when the political system works in such a way as to deny them an effective voice in the legislative and governmental process. According to this view, the role of the courts is not primarily to ensure that government makes the 'right' decisions, but to ensure that the decisions it makes are made in response to all the arguments and points of view that it ought to have considered. Thus, the role of judicial review is to ensure that all properly interested parties are given a chance to participate effectively in the administrative decision-making process. This approach implies that decisions made without some interested party being heard would be invalid.

Several points should be made about this approach. First, the prevalence of interest consultation in our system suggests that the political process is seen in part as a mechanism for reconciling competing and conflicting interests. Because such interests are often not concentrated in a particular locality they may not be represented in Parliament and so they seek other methods of influencing government. To some extent they do this *through* Parliament by lobbying and briefing MPs, by providing secretarial and research assistance to 'all party' committees of MPs and by 'sponsoring' MPs as their spokesmen. Some form of proportional representation might facilitate greater interest representation *in* Parliament, although the advocates of PR tend to be small political parties rather than interest groups. But the main method by which interest groups seek to infuence government is by direct communication with Ministers and Civil Servants. This method is subject to very little publicity or outside control. Interest groups are not accountable to the public for their lobbying activities, nor does the law have anything much to say about the internal structure of interest groups, or their accountability to those whom they represent. Nor is the government usually answerable, either at law or in Parliament, for the way it consults interest groups. The proposed interest protection function of the courts would deal with only one of these issues—that of ensuring that all interests were properly consulted. Whether the law in general, and the courts in particular, ought to be involved in regulating other aspects of the consultation process, is a large question which for reasons of space cannot be considered here. But it could be asked whether an argument might not be made for treating lobby groups as public (and, therefore, in some way and to some extent, publicly accountable) bodies performing public functions.

Secondly, the interest protection view sees the law as primarily concerned with protecting the procedural right of groups to be consulted. It does not see the law as a suitable means of ensuring that the interests of these groups are protected, by reviewing the substance of the decisions made after consultation. Such a function would clearly involve the courts in making decisions which it is the prime function of political bodies to make. In our system it is generally thought that, if the substantive (as opposed to procedural) interests of groups, such as blacks or the disabled, are to be the subject of legal protection, this must be done by means of legislation or perhaps a Bill of Rights. Even this technique is found objectionable by some because it leaves the courts to interpret and apply the legislation. Experience shows that this can involve the courts in making highly contentious political decisions.

On the other hand, it should be noted that, even now, the courts do make decisions which involve (often implicitly) the giving or withholding of support for particular group interests. Perhaps the most famous example is the *Poplar* case[20] in which the decisions of a local authority not to reduce wages despite reductions in the cost of living and to pay men and women at the same rates were castigated by Lord Atkinson as motivated by 'eccentric principles of socialistic philanthropy or by a feminist ambition to secure equality of the sexes'. It has also been argued that, in planning law, the courts consistently favour the interests of private landowners over other interests;[21] that in immigration law the courts show too little regard for the interests of individual immigrants;[22] and that generally courts give effect to 'establishment views' on a wide range of issues.[23] Without commenting on the validity of such arguments, it is worth noting that judicial review is *already*, at the substantive as opposed to the procedural level, a mechanism which to some extent can be used to protect and promote group interests.

A third point to note about the interest protection view of judicial review is this: it might be argued that the cost and complexity of utilizing the judicial process would result in this approach providing wealthy and well-organized interest groups with yet another chance to influence government policy, rather than opening up the governmental process to a wider range of influences. Thus, the interest protection view would not be beneficial, unless it were accompanied by procedural reforms, such as increased legal aid, or rules which facilitate the bringing of class actions by relatively unorganized groups. Fourthly, it might be argued that the courts should not be used as a means of giving those who are disappointed with the political process a

---

[20] *Roberts* v. *Hopwood* [1925] AC 578.
[21] McAuslan, *Ideologies of Planning Law* (Oxford, 1980).
[22] Evans, *Immigration Law* (2nd edn., London, 1983), pp. 417 ff.
[23] Griffith, *The Politics of the Judiciary* (3rd edn., 1985).

'second bite at the cherry'. It would be better to reform the political process, making it responsive to a wider range of interests, than to involve the courts who might, by this involvement, be thought to be putting their independent status in jeopardy.

Fifthly, the common law, as it stands, interprets the right to participate in the administrative and political process almost exclusively in terms of the principles of natural justice, which, as we will see, are designed primarily to ensure individuals a hearing; they are not much use in securing for interest groups a right to participate in the governmental process. Moreover, these rules do not apply to the legislative process, either parliamentary or subordinate, although statutes do sometimes provide for consultation of interested groups before subordinate legislation is made. Another *statutory* mechanism in English law for involving interest groups in the administrative decision-making process is the device of the local public inquiry, which is discussed in Chapter 23. Other examples of statutory involvement of representatives of particular interests in decision-making include lay school governors and members of health authorities.

Perhaps the only feature of English judge-made administrative law which appears to embody a concern to enable interest groups to use the judicial process to control administrative action, are the rules of standing discussed in Chapter 9. It now seems clear that an applicant seeking to challenge the acts of governmental bodies need not show that he has any individual interest in the outcome—it is enough if he shares a genuine interest with other people. Conversely, a body representing interested persons will be allowed to challenge administrative action if the individuals it represents have a sufficient interest in the outcome which would entitle them to bring actions in their own right.

(ii) Protecting individuals

The idea that the courts should play a part in protecting group interests is, as we have noted, a view which reflects a picture of the political process as a mechanism for reconciling and compromising conflicting interests. The classic picture of the British political process, on the other hand, sees politics more in terms of achieving collective goals, of furthering the public interest. Group interests are usually considered as subjective preferences of members of the group as to how society should run, whereas the public interest is seen as objective. It is not just an amalgam of or compromise between interests, but is something different from and superior to them.

This distinction between *the* public interest and private *interests* is implicit in the distinction between public law and private law, and it underlies the currently dominant idea of the role of judicial review (and of the role of the Ombudsman) namely to protect the rights of individuals against unlawful encroachment in the name of the public interest. According to this picture, the activities of government are being controlled in the name of *law*—the rights being protected are legal rights such as property rights. But many of these rights, for example the right to be treated fairly and in accordance with the rules of natural justice, are common law rights 'invented' by the courts. The 'invention' of legal rights by the courts is itself a political (as well as a legal) activity, just as the creation of legal rights by the legislature is a political activity. A legal right comes into existence when a political claim is given legal force by a law-making body.

Because the courts are *primarily* law-applying bodies they must act in the name of legal rights, but we should not allow the language of law to conceal the fact that some of these rights are created by the courts themselves, or to hide the fact that legal rights express and give legal effect to political claims. This can be seen clearly if we ask why we speak of the *rights* of individuals, but of the *interests* of groups. The reason is not that individuals do not have interests, or that groups do not have rights. It is simply that, in our system, law tends to be used to protect the rights of individuals, whereas groups tend to use the political process to secure the enactment of laws, or adoption of policies, which will protect the individual interests of their members or of others whose interests they seek to promote (for example, children).

The 'protection of the individual' view of judicial review is, therefore, a view which asserts that political and governmental power ought to be exercised to further the public interest, but only so far as is consistent with those political claims of individuals which are embodied in individuals' legal rights or legally protected interests. It is, however, also the case that the power to protect individual rights against undue interference in the name of the public interest, entails a power to decide that particular governmental action in the public interest does *not* constitute an undue encroachment on private rights. And, ironically, the most common use of the notion of public interest in administrative law is as a device to resist claims by individuals that their rights have been improperly infringed.

(iii) Protecting the public interest

There is a third view of the function of judicial review which occasionally surfaces in the cases. This might be called the 'public interest' view of administrative law. According to this view, there are certain collective community interests and goals which (almost) everyone would accept because they are very basic to our way of life. These interests may be 'shared' interests such as the interest in clean air, or they may be 'aggregate' interests (that is, interests which each and every individual has) such as an interest in personal liberty. Now, none of these public interests is absolute in the sense that we are prepared to pursue it no matter what the cost. For example, besides an interest in clean air, we also have an interest in economic prosperity; and as well as an interest in personal liberty we have an interest in protecting ourselves from criminal violence. It is the function of the political process, according to this view, to compromise and reconcile these conflicting community interests. The compromise position is then called 'the public interest'.

However, for example, although we all have an interest in economic prosperity, some have a greater interest in it than others. Manufacturers who pollute the air have less interest in clean air and more in economic growth than do others. Again, although we all have an interest in personal liberty, the police have a greater (professional) interest in depriving people of liberty than do others. There is a danger that, in the process of reconciling conflicting public interests, undue weight may be given to one or the other of them because of the political influence of some sectional group which has a special concern with that interest. The public interest view of administrative law would say that, if a governmental body acts contrary to the public interest, then any member of the public should be entitled to challenge that action in a court, because action contrary to the public interest is illegal. In other words, this approach sees the courts as guardians of the public interest against undue encroachment in favour of sectional interests. This view of the judicial role therefore involves the courts in deciding whether the governmental action is in the public interest. This is clearly a political function.

The best example of the public interest approach in action is the series of cases in which Mr Raymond Blackburn attempted to secure more stringent enforcement of gaming and obscenity laws.[24] It is in

---

[24] R. v. *Metropolitan Police Commissioner, ex parte Blackburn* [1968] 2 QB 118; *Same*

these cases that the courts, and especially Lord Denning, have come closest to recognizing what is often called the 'citizen action' by means of which public-minded citizens can challenge government action which they allege is not in the public interest.

(c) Legitimizing the Judicial Role

I am not suggesting that these three views of the role of the courts in administrative law are mutually exclusive of one another. In fact, as we shall discover, all three strands are detectable in various aspects of the present law. Nor am I claiming that these three views provide a framework for analyzing the whole law of judicial review. Most importantly, none of the three views (with the possible exception of the public interest view) directly addresses an issue which figures more or less prominently in many applications for judicial review, namely the proper relationship and division of powers between different governmental bodies (such as central Departments of State and local authorities). Analysis of the application of the rules of judicial review to this issue would, no doubt, suggest a variety of models of the judicial function differing not only according to different views of that function, but also according to different views of the proper function of the particular agencies whose interrelationships were in issue.

The point to stress at the moment is that public law in general, and judicial review in particular, exists in a political environment; and, as has been noted several times, the courts in administering public law perform a variety of political functions. More especially, every time the courts appeal to the idea of the public interest, or to the rights and interests of individuals or groups, they appeal to essentially political notions. And just as political theory is concerned with the legitimacy of the activities of the administration, so too it is concerned with the legitimacy of the role which the courts assume in controlling governmental action.

So how is the political role of the courts to be legitimized? First, a certain negative legitimacy is conferred on judicial decisions by the possibility of legislative reversal. Secondly, while, from one point of view, the constitutionally-protected independence of the judiciary from political control or influence seems to make courts quite unsuited to perform political functions, from another point of view it could be argued that this very independence enables the courts to protect

(No. 3) [1973] QB 241; *R.* v. *Greater London Council, ex parte Blackburn* [1976] 1 WLR 550.

certain interests and principles which are of long-term and abiding importance (such as personal liberty or freedom of information) from undue encroachment for short-term political reasons. In this case, it is exactly because the judiciary is not popularly elected or politically accountable that it can protect the fundamental rights and interests of individuals, groups, and society. But this argument lends legitimacy to the judicial role only to the extent that the individual or group rights and the notion of public interest which the courts adopt, and the way they apply these in particular cases, command wide acceptance in society as a whole. Courts jeopardize their legitimacy if they utilize controversial conceptions of individual or group rights, or of the public interest, since it is for elected and popularly answerable bodies to resolve disputes on such questions.

The demand that the courts should be uncontroversial, however, creates a difficulty. The courts might avoid controversy by appealing to principles which are very abstract (such as 'personal liberty') to which everyone would subscribe. But in practice they are asked to decide what such abstract principles require in concrete situations, and this is typically where controversy arises—people often disagree about the application of mutually agreed principles. The courts, then, are faced with a dilemma. Perhaps the most we can expect of the judges is that they will attempt to be alert to the traditions and present values of society, and to reactions provoked by their past decisions. Of course, it is unlikely that any public law decision will not meet with some objections; but judges must attempt to avoid giving effect, in the name of public interest or individual rights, to arguments with which a significant proportion of the public would disagree.

We should not, however, fall into the trap of thinking that, because judicial decisions can be given some legitimacy by this search for accepted values, judges can make their decisions democratic by referring to the values of the community. Judicial review is *not*, nor is it meant to be, a democratic institution. No matter how conscientious judges are in seeking to reflect community values, the difficulty of ascertaining what those values are and, in particular, the difficulty of ascertaining how they apply to the concrete situations with which the courts are confronted, makes it inevitable that, to some extent, the decisions which judges make will reflect *their* views. And if we dislike the views of our judges then we should either appoint judges with views more to our liking, or remove the powers, which enable judges to give effect to their own views, from the courts, and allocate them to more democratic institutions. To think that judges can resolve all the conflicts with which they are confronted by ascertaining fundamental community values, is self-deception, because such community values as we have are neither detailed nor uncontested enough to solve such a variety of disputes.

A SELECT BIBLIOGRAPHY TO CHAPTER I

This bibliography contains a number of items which readers might find particularly useful. It should be used in conjunction with the footnotes to the chapter.

The Distinction Between Public Law and Private Law

Benn & Gaus (edd.), *Public and Private Law in Social Life* (London, 1983) chapter 2.
C. Harlow (1980) 43 MLR 241.
D. Kennedy (1982) 130 U. of Penn. LR 1349.
A. Linden (1976) 17 Cahiers de Droit 831.
G. Samuel (1983) 46 MLR 558.

Nationalized Industries and Non-Departmental Bodies

R. Baldwin, *Regulating the Airlines* (Oxford, 1985), especially chapter 14.
P. P. Craig, *Administrative Law* (London, 1983), pp. 107–39.
T. Daintith, 'Public and Private Enterprise in the United Kingdom' in *Public and Private Enterprise in Mixed Economies*, ed. Friedmann (1974), p. 206.
Sir A. Knight (1982) 53 Pol. Q. 24.

Constitutional Theory

A. V. Dicey, *Introduction to the Study of the Law of the Constitution* (10th edn., Wade, 1958).
G. Marshall, *Constitutional Conventions* (1984).
—, *Constitutional Theory* (1971), chapters 1, 2, 4, 5.
— & Moodie, *Some Problems of the Constitution* (rev. edn., 1961), chapter 4.

Local Government

T. Byrne, *Local Government in Britain* (2nd edn., 1983).
M. Elliott, *The Role of Law in Central–Local Relations* (SSRC, 1981).
J. Garner, *Administrative Law* (6th edn., 1985), chapters 16, 17.
D. Hill, *Democratic Theory and Local Government* (1974).

Political Theory

G. Alderman, *Pressure Groups and Government in Great Britain* (1984).

A. H. Birch, *Representative and Responsible Government* (1964).

J. A. G. Griffith, *The Politics of the Judiciary* (2nd edn., 1981).

A. H. Hanson & M. Walles, *Governing Britain* (4th edn., 1984).

J. Lively, *Democracy* (1975), especially Part 4.

J. Mackintosh, *The Government and Politics of Britain* (6th edn., Richards, 1984).

C. B. Macpherson, *The Life and Times of Liberal Democracy* (1977).

D. Oliver [1981] PL 151.

J. R. Pennock, *Democratic Political Theory* (1979), especially chapters 5, 7, 8.

J. T. Winkler (1975) 2 Brit. J. of Law & Society 103.

PART II

JUDICIAL CONTROL OF ADMINISTRATIVE ACTION

GROUNDS FOR CHALLENGING
ADMINISTRATIVE ACTION

2

Introduction

THIS section of the book is concerned with what we mean when we say that a public body has acted illegally. On this question English law draws a sharp distinction between public law and private law. There is no necessary link between public law illegality and private law liability. The fact that an authority has acted illegally, for example in refusing to grant a street trader a licence, does not by itself subject the authority to private law liability, for example, to pay damages. The authority can be held liable only if, in addition to establishing public law illegality the claimant can show that the authority has committed some private law wrong such as a tort or breach of contract. A leading case in which illegal action by a public authority made it liable in private law is *Cooper* v. *Wandsworth Board of Works*.[1] In this case workmen employed by the Board acting under instructions demolished a partly completed house without the plaintiff, the builder of the house, first being given a chance to tell his side of the story. The defendant claimed that the plaintiff had not given the required statutory notice of his intention to build. The plaintiff denied this, though he admitted that he had not waited the required seven days from the date of giving the notice before starting the work. It was held that the defendant had acted illegally in the public law sense in not giving the plaintiff a hearing. As a result they had no legal justification for pulling down the house, and this action therefore amounted to the private law wrong of trespass to land. The liability of public authorities in contract and tort will be discussed in greater detail in later chapters.

[1] (1863) 14 CBNS 180.

Just as public law illegality does not entail private law liability, so also private law liability does not necessarily involve public law illegality. For example, a breach of contract by a public authority might not fall under any of the recognized heads of public law illegality. One of the most important consequences of this gulf between public law illegality and private law liability can be seen in the law of remedies. The remedies developed by the courts for use in public law perform three functions: the 'quashing' (that is, the invalidation) of administrative decisions; the prohibition of administrative action; and the ordering of authorities to perform duties. The common law remedy of damages is a private law remedy for private law wrongs. Unless the victim of public law illegality can also show that the authority's action amounts to a private law wrong he will not be entitled, at common law, to monetary compensation.

The public law activities of public bodies are subject to scrutiny and control by the High Court in the exercise of what is called its 'supervisory' jurisdiction. Under this jurisdiction (which is 'inherent', that is, the product of common law rather than statute) the High Court has power to 'review' the activities of public authorities and, in some cases, of private bodies exercising functions of public importance such as licensing.[2] To be contrasted with the supervisory jurisdiction is the court's appellate jurisdiction. The common law never developed mechanisms for appeals as we understand them today, and all appellate powers are statutory.

An understanding of the differences between appeal and review (or supervision) is of great importance. There are two main differences between them. The first relates to the power of the court: in appeal proceedings the court has the power[3] to substitute its decision on the matters in issue for that of the body appealed from. For example, if an appeal court thinks that the victim of a motor accident has been awarded too small a sum of damages for injuries inflicted on him by the defendant's negligence, it can increase the award. In review proceedings, on the other hand, the court's basic power in relation to an illegal decision is to quash it, that is, to hold it to be invalid. If any of the matters in issue have to be decided again, this must be done by the

---

[2] In strict theory the control of these bodies is part of the 'original' private law jurisdiction of the High Court as opposed to its supervisory jurisdiction. The relationship between the two jurisdictions is a matter of considerable complexity and obscurity not suitable for treatment here.

[3] Unless the appeal takes the form of an application for a new trial in cases where the proceedings under review were tried by jury.

original deciding body, not by the supervising court. If the authority was under a duty to make a decision on the matters in issue between the parties, this duty will revive when the decision is quashed and it will then be for the authority to rehear the proceedings. It is also open to the court, in appropriate cases, to issue an order requiring the authority to rehear the case.

Another course open to the High Court, when it quashes the decision of an administrative authority, is to remit the matter to the agency with a direction to reconsider it in accordance with the findings of the High Court.[4] The difference between this and the two previous outcomes is that, under this procedure, the agency does not have to rehear the whole case again. For example, it might be that all the relevant facts have already been ascertained and the findings of the High Court only concern their legal significance. In such a case a complete rehearing, including the taking of evidence and the finding of facts, would be a waste of time and money; so the court can remit the case and direct the authority to reconsider the facts in the light of the law as it has been held to be. This procedure is different from an appeal in only a very formal sense. On the other hand, remission would not be appropriate where the authority is found to have been biased. Then a complete rehearing before a differently constituted body would be needed in order for justice to be seen to be done.

The second main distinction between appeal and review relates to the subject matter of the court's jurisdiction. This distinction can be put briefly by saying that, whereas an appellate court has power to decide whether the decision under appeal was 'right or wrong', a court exercising supervisory powers may only decide whether the decision under review was 'legal' or not. If the decision is illegal it can be quashed; otherwise the court cannot (with one exception) intervene, even if it thinks the decision to be wrong in some respect. The exception is that the High Court has power to quash an administrative decision for 'error of law on the face of the record' even though such errors do not render decisions illegal. We will discuss this exception in detail in the next chapter.

A further complication inherent in the distinction between illegality and wrongness is that in some cases, as we will see, the fact that a decision is wrong in law or fact will render it illegal. Discussion of the notion of illegality is also made difficult by the fact that a number of

---

[4] RSC Ord. 53 r. 9(4); Supreme Court Act 1981 s. 31(5).

different terms are used to convey the idea of illegality. The question of whether a decision was 'legal or not' is sometimes put in terms of whether it was made 'within or without jurisdiction' or whether it is '*intra vires* or *ultra vires*' (that is, literally, 'within or beyond power'). These last terms are widely used as acceptable synonyms for 'legal' and 'illegal' respectively. The concept of jurisdiction is much more difficult, as we will see, and its use is perhaps best avoided since acting without jurisdiction is just one example of acting illegally.

Most administrative powers and duties are created and conferred by statute. The statutory powers and duties of administrative bodies may be broad or narrow, but they are never unlimited. The only body in our system with theoretically unlimited powers is Parliament—in other words, Parliament is supreme or sovereign. Sometimes the statute conferring a power or imposing a duty will state the limits of that power or duty with some precision. But very often these limits are not expressed clearly enough to avoid disputes arising about their exact location. To say that an authority has acted illegally is to say that it has gone beyond the proper limits of its powers or duties.

A crucial question now arises: how is the exact location of these limits to be discovered? One theory, mentioned in the last chapter, says that since Parliament is supreme, the intention of Parliament or of the statute must decide the issue; the question is one of statutory interpretation to which the ordinary rules of statutory interpretation are relevant. Two defects in this approach were noted: the first is that it is now well recognized that very often the courts, when deciding the meaning of statutes, are confronted with two or more alternative meanings between which the court must choose for itself. It is often very difficult, to say the least, to decide the meaning Parliament would have opted for if it had considered the matter. Secondly, some modern decisions seem hard to justify in terms of the traditional principles of statutory interpretation; this suggests that the courts do not see the rules of statutory interpretation as the only factors relevant in this area of the law. Unfortunately our courts have not been at all explicit about what other factors might be relevant, beyond saying that the courts' inherent power of judicial review is of great importance and is not to be whittled away unduly. But perhaps some factors might be suggested as being relevant. The reader can bear these in mind as we consider the cases, and decide on the validity of the suggestions for himself.

FACTORS TO BE CONSIDERED

(1) The degree of expertise and experience possessed by the members of the administrative body. Judges are experts in the law, but not always in the subject matter of the disputes which come before them. This is chiefly because they are required to decide disputes across a wide range of human affairs. On the other hand, the authorities subject to scrutiny by the courts will usually deal frequently with a narrower set of problems. For example, officers who conduct planning inquiries develop considerable expertise in dealing with the difficulties of the job and may develop greater knowledge of *planning* law than is possessed by most judges. Again, supplementary benefits tribunals deal with a very large number of supplementary benefit cases, whereas the High Court deals with very few.

Further, members of administrative bodies such as tribunals are often chosen because of their specialized knowledge of the subject matter of the tribunal's business. For example, members of the Employment Appeals Tribunal (which deals with cases of alleged unfair dismissal) who are either workers' or employers' representatives undoubtedly know more about the realities of the shop floor than do High Court judges. Such knowledge may be important when interpreting and applying legislation where its real (or best) meaning may only be obvious to someone who knows the background against which the statute was drafted. The arguments from expertise and experience will in some cases justify interpreting the powers of the administrative body widely so as to give the expertise and experience of its members the greatest possible scope.

(2) The need for uniformity of results. This factor is of particular importance where there are a number of administrative bodies of original authority, for example, Supplementary Benefits Appeal Tribunals, in different parts of the country. Especially where there is no developed system for reporting and publishing decisions of such bodies, the High Court can play a role in making sure that on issues where uniformity of result is important it can be easily achieved. To treat like cases alike is, of course, a basic requirement of justice, and this gives uniformity a high value in our legal system. If the court thinks that uniformity on a particular issue is desirable, then it will be inclined to interpret the authority's powers in such a way as to enable it to intervene and, in the process, indicate how it thinks the point at issue should be dealt with.

However, this argument from uniformity pulls against the arguments from expertise and experience. We should be wary of turning the argument, 'Uniformity on this point is desirable' into the argument, 'The High Court's view on this point is to be preferred to that of the bodies at the lower level'. There is a danger that the interpretation put on the statute by the High Court will not reflect the expert knowledge of the people 'on the ground'. Yet, this failure is not always to be deplored because one of the functions of the courts (perhaps their main function) is to give effect to general principles of law and justice which ought to be respected by any decision-maker whatever the subject matter of his decision. For example, it may be that *all* decision-makers should observe certain standards of procedural fairness. But it is also important to note that a uniform rule imposed from above leaves less room for the exercise of discretion by administrative bodies. Discretion is central to much administrative decision-making and so the choice of a uniform rule must also be seen in the wider context of the control of discretion. We will examine the control of discretion in greater detail later.

(3) The policy element in the matters in issue. The courts are usually and rightly concerned not to become unnecessarily involved in politically contentious issues.

(4) Although Parliament may have left the exact limits of the authority's powers vague, it may also have indicated that it did not want the courts to exercise powers of judicial review in relation to the authority's activities. Sometimes this is done by including, in the statute defining the powers, a section 'ousting' judicial review. The courts have dealt with such provisions in a complex way which we will consider in a later chapter.

(5) Finally, the courts sometimes take the view that the adversary nature of the judicial process, with its associated procedural rules, is not suited to administrative contexts or to all the types of decisions which administrative bodies are called upon to make. Thus, although the rules of natural justice require administrative bodies to follow broadly judicial procedures, the courts interpret these rules flexibly in deciding whether, because of the procedure followed, a body acted illegally. This complex matter will be the subject of a later chapter.

One final introductory point needs to be made. So far the discussion has mainly concerned administrative *decisions*. But, of course, administrative *action* (and failure to act) can also be illegal. The distinction between acting and deciding to act can be important. If an authority has decided to do an act but has not yet done it then, of course, the applicant will want to challenge the decision to act and to obtain an order instructing the authority not to carry out its decision. If the authority has decided not to perform some duty the applicant will often be satisfied with an order requiring it to act. If the authority has already acted and the act can be easily undone, the applicant can challenge the decision to act and seek an order requiring the authority to undo its action. For example, if an authority has granted planning permission to *A* but building has not yet started, *B* might be able to get the permission revoked. But if the authority's decision has inflicted irreparable damage on the applicant—for example, if it has pulled down his house in pursuance of an invalid demolition order—the remedies of public law are going to be much less satisfactory for him. Public law remedies will enable him to establish the illegality of the order; but, unless he can avail himself of some statutory provision for compensation, he will have to establish an entitlement to damages in private law if he is to have his damage made good by monetary compensation. Public law remedies are not of much use to the citizen who has suffered tangible injury as opposed to one who has an intangible grievance. We discuss in a later chapter whether there ought to be 'public law' rights to compensation.

3

Questions of Law and Questions of Fact

I. THE DISTINCTION BETWEEN LAW AND FACT

ADMINISTRATIVE authorities are often called upon, in the course of exercising their functions, to decide questions of law and fact. Because the rules concerning review of such decisions by the High Court differ according to whether the question at issue is one of law or of fact (crudely put, the courts are more prepared to interfere with the decision of an administrative agency on a question of law than on one of fact), it is necessary to see how the law distinguishes between the two types of question. The distinction is important, not only in the context of judicial review, but also in that of appeals on points of law.[1] There are numerous statutory provisions for appeals on points of *law* from the decisions of administrative bodies to the High Court. The most general of these provisions is section 13 of the Tribunals and Inquiries Act 1971.

There are two main approaches to distinguishing between questions of law and questions of fact. These might be called the analytical approach and the policy approach. According to the analytical approach, a question of fact is a question as to the existence of some phenomenon in the world about us; a legal question is any question about the legal significance of such phenomena. A good example of this approach is *Edwards* v. *Bairstow*.[2] Here the question was whether a joint venture to purchase a spinning plant was 'an adventure in the nature of trade' within the Income Tax Act; on the analytical approach the facts are the details of the joint venture and the law is the meaning of the phrase 'adventure in the nature of trade'. Both Lord Radcliffe and Lord Reid in this case made statements supporting this analysis.

However, this distinction between questions of fact and questions of law is not always strictly observed. In many cases in which the question which the court has to decide is whether particular cases fall within a statutory phrase (as in *Edwards* v. *Bairstow*), different opinions can

---

[1] On the distinction between appeal and review see Chapter 2.
[2] [1956] AC 14; see also *O'Kelly* v. *Trusthouse Forte PLC* [1983] 3 WLR 605.

reasonably be held on the issue. For example, reasonable men can differ about whether a flat is 'furnished', or about whether a house is 'unfit for human habitation', or about whether a particular piece of land is 'part of a park'. In *Edwards* v. *Bairstow* Lord Radcliffe said that any reasonable decision on such an issue would be treated as a decision on a question of 'fact and degree', rather than as a decision on a question of law. Where the form of the proceeding is an appeal on a question of law, as in *Edwards* v. *Bairstow*, the result of adopting this 'fact and degree' classification will be that the court will decline to interfere unless the authority's decision was an unreasonable one, that is one which is so unreasonable that no reasonable decision-maker properly understanding his powers could have reached it. The mere fact that the court might not agree with the decision will not be enough to justify intervention. Another example of the watering down of the law–fact distinction is the principle sometimes used that, when a word in a statute bears its 'ordinary' meaning the application of it to a particular case is a question of fact, not law.[3]

It may be argued that these qualifications can be fitted into the analytical approach just by making the distinction between questions of law and questions of fact more detailed and complex. The distinctive feature of the approach could still be retained, namely that the court first asks whether the issue is one of law or of fact and only when it has answered this question analytically does it know whether it can intervene or not. But this is not really so. Whether or not a question admits of more than one reasonable answer is not capable of being decided analytically; nor is the question of whether a word is being used in its 'ordinary' meaning. To answer these questions the court must make value judgments. This point forms the foundation of the second approach to the law–fact distinction—the policy approach. This says basically that the court first decides, on policy grounds, whether it ought to intervene and then classifies the issue before it as one of law or fact, in order to justify this policy decision in terms of legal categories. The fact that the courts rarely admit that this is what they are doing is not thought to disprove the policy approach because English judges are generally loath to admit that they make policy decisions, for fear of compromising their independence.

In Chapter 2 I suggested a number of factors which might underlie decisions as to the limits of the powers of administrative authorities.

[3] *Brutus* v. *Cozens* [1973] AC 854.

Since the law–fact distinction is usually relevant to whether the court should intervene or not, some of these factors will also be relevant to the policy approach to the law–fact distinction: notably the argument from experience and expertise, the desirability of uniformity, and the desirability of avoiding politically contentious issues. These, it might be thought, are perfectly proper considerations for the courts to take into account. It is sometimes suggested, however, that there is a less acceptable side to the policy approach which allows judges to inject their own political 'ideologies' into the law. Thus one writer suggests that the courts 'have more confidence in' national insurance commissioners than in rent assessment committees, and that perhaps, therefore, they are less prepared to interfere with decisions of the former than those of the latter.[4] Another writer argues that in applying the law–fact distinction in immigration cases the courts would probably be reluctant to overrule the decision of an Immigration Appeal Tribunal.[5] The implication of this is perhaps that the courts are less concerned with (and less prepared to intervene to protect) the rights of immigrants than of other people.

Three points should be made about the policy approach. First, although we have been discussing it in the context of the law–fact distinction, it should be clear by now that it is important whenever the question of whether a court should interfere with the decision of an administrative body arises. So, for example, one writer has suggested that, in dealing with questions of land clearance, the courts have shown themselves more willing to intervene to protect the rights of landowners than to further the public interest or the cause of greater public participation in land-use decisions.[6]

Secondly, the basic difference between what I have referred to as the acceptable and unacceptable sides of the policy approach is that unacceptable policy factors tend to relate to the merits of a particular decision, whereas acceptable policy factors are less related, if at all, to the outcome of the particular case; they are more concerned with the distribution of decision-making power within the structure of government. Of course a decision as to which organ of government should make a particular decision is itself a political decision and can be very contentious—courts are often criticized for intervening or for failing to intervene. But, at the end of the day, someone has to decide

---

[4] de Smith, *Constitutional and Administrative Law* (4th edn.), p. 130.
[5] Griffith, *The Politics of the Judiciary* (2nd edn., 1981), p. 108.
[6] McAuslan, *The Ideologies of Planning Law* (1980), pp. 84 ff.

where power should lie, and so long as the courts can be asked to intervene they will have to decide whether to do so or not. Even a decision not to intervene decides something about where the decision-making power on the points in issue lies, namely that it does not lie with the courts. Since legislation could never exhaustively define the limits of judicial review then, unless we abolish it altogether, the courts will have to make decisions about where decision-making power should lie. This is one reason why it is worthwhile to study the general principles of administrative law. Such study concentrates attention on the aspect of the courts' work which involves making constitutional and political decisions about where power should lie.

The third point to make about the policy approach is this: study of its 'darker side' makes it clear that often, in order to understand a case properly, we must pay close attention to its subject matter: planning, immigration, rent assessment, etc. The study of general principles is not enough in itself, and this should be borne constantly in mind. The question of where the power of decision should lie may often depend in part on the nature of the issues at stake. The constitutional and political principles, on which this book concentrates, present only part of the picture.

A final complication in the law–fact distinction is this: although an error of law can be a wrong answer to a question of law as defined above, the term 'error of law' is often given a wider meaning. It is used to include reaching a factual conclusion on no (or inadequate) evidence, wrongful admission or exclusion of evidence, and a number of forms of abuse of discretion, such as ignoring relevant considerations or taking irrelevant considerations into account. 'Error of law' sometimes seems to be used as a loose synonym of 'illegal action'.

2. QUESTIONS OF LAW

The leading case on the court's power to review decisions on questions of law and to quash them if they are illegal is *Anisminic Ltd.* v. *Foreign Compensation Commission.*[7] Before this case a clear distinction was drawn between errors of law 'going to jurisdiction' and errors of law 'within jurisdiction'. Suppose, for example, as in *Anisminic*, a tribunal denies an applicant compensation for nationalization of his property by a foreign government because the applicant's successor in title is not a

[7] [1969] AC 147.

British national when, as a matter of law, entitlement to compensation does not depend on this issue of nationality. There are two ways of analysing this situation. The pre-*Anisminic* approach would be to ask whether the question of law (i.e. whether the issue of nationality was relevant) went to jurisdiction or not. A question which goes to jurisdiction (sometimes called a 'collateral question') is one on which the existence of the tribunal's jurisdiction (or 'power to act or decide', in this case the power to award compensation) depends. If as a result of answering such a question wrongly a tribunal (or other administrative body) decides that it has jurisdiction (or power to act or decide) which it then goes on to exercise, then it can be ordered not to act, and any act it does or decision it makes in exercise of its functions (in *Anisminic*, awarding compensation) will be illegal. And if it decides wrongly that it has no jurisdiction or power, it can be ordered to exercise the power it legally has. Acts done as a result of a wrong decision on a collateral question of law are said to have been done 'without jurisdiction'.

On the other hand, if the question of law is one 'within jurisdiction', then, subject to an exception which we will consider shortly, the mere fact that the tribunal answers the question incorrectly does not entitle the court to quash the decision. The tribunal has power to answer questions of law within its jurisdiction rightly or wrongly. A wrong answer to a question of law within the tribunal's jurisdiction does not make the tribunal's decision illegal.

Lord Morris, who dissented in *Anisminic*,[8] adopted this traditional approach and held that the Commission's error, in asking whether the applicant's successor was a British national, did not mean that it had no jurisdiction to decide the issue of compensation. The error fell within jurisdiction and so the Commission's decision could not be quashed; it was wrong, rather than illegal.

The main problem with the distinction between the two types of questions of law is that it was very difficult to offer any consistent criterion for drawing it. Rarely do statutes, in conferring functions on administrative authorities, give any guidance as to whether relevant questions of law are preconditions of the power to exercise those functions. The statute in the *Anisminic* case gave no real guidance as to whether the question of nationality was relevant to whether the Commission had power to act at all, or whether it was merely one of

---

[8] Lord Pearson also dissented but on the ground that the Commission had not made any error of law.

the factors which might come up in the process of reaching the decision on compensation. The distinction does not lend itself to being applied analytically.[9] This provides a good reason to suspect that in applying the distinction the courts often adopted a policy approach; that is, they decided whether a question went to jurisdiction or not, according to whether they thought the particular decision *ought* to be quashed or not.

The approach of the majority in *Anisminic* renders the distinction between questions of law which do and those which do not go to jurisdiction to an extent unnecessary, although it is by no means clear to what extent. The traditional way of drawing the distinction has a temporal ring about it. The authority must first decide whether it has power to act at all in the circumstances; 'jurisdictional' questions of law relate to this issue. If it does have this power it can go on and exercise it. 'Non-jurisdictional' questions of law are those which arise in the course of exercising the power. The majority in *Anisminic* rejected this picture and held that the court could intervene and quash a decision for error of law, even though it was an error made in the process of exercising the power rather than an error in deciding whether the power existed. So, even though the question of nationality was one which arose in the course of exercising a power which the Commission had, nevertheless the Commission had to answer the question correctly if its decision was to be legal. Thus an agency can act illegally not only by deciding a question of law wrongly, in such a way as to give itself power which it does not really have, but also by answering a question wrongly and in this way reaching a wrong result on a matter which it has power to decide—in *Anisminic* the question of whether compensation ought to be awarded.

Anisminic, therefore, blurs the distinction between the legality and the correctness of administrative decisions, and in this way blurs the distinction between appeal and review. An authority may have power or jurisdiction to decide and yet act illegally by reaching a wrong decision. The terminology used in this area can be treacherous. The usual word for 'power to decide' is 'jurisdiction'. Thus, a question relevant to whether an authority has power to decide is a jurisdictional question. Questions which arise in the course of exercising that power lie within jurisdiction. Before *Anisminic* to act without jurisdiction was to act illegally; to make a mistake of law within jurisdiction was not to act

---

[9] For a more recent example of this difficulty see *Pearlman* v. *Keepers and Governors of Harrow School* [1979] QB 56.

illegally. But *Anisminic* says that going wrong within jurisdiction may be illegal. This has led to the use of the word 'jurisdictional' in a wide sense to cover all errors of law which entail illegality and for convenience this usage will be followed in this book. It should be remembered, however, that the word covers two sources of illegality, namely acting without power and giving wrong answers to questions of law which arise in the course of exercising power.

It is clear that the *Anisminic* approach has the effect of expanding the limits of judicial review, by subjecting to review a set of questions of law which, under the old approach, would have been beyond review. And yet, at no stage does the House of Lords really confront the issue of whether, in policy terms, this expansion is a good thing. It does not discuss any principles or policies which bear on the 'proper' or desirable scope of judicial review.

Anisminic does not strictly decide that there are no questions of law which administrative agencies have the power to decide rightly or wrongly. Are there any questions of law which fall within jurisdiction, or does any and every error of law result in illegality? There are three views on this question. Some judges and commentators have taken the view that *Anisminic* justifies review of *all* decisions on questions of law. Other judges have said that the distinction between jurisdictional and non-jurisdictional questions of law still exists, but there is very little discussion of how it is to be drawn.

A middle way is that of Lord Diplock in *Re Racal Communications Ltd.*[10] In his Lordship's view, the effect of *Anisminic* is to abolish the distinction so far as the activities of administrative authorities are concerned, but not so far as concerns inferior courts (such as magistrates' courts or County Courts which are also subject to judicial review because they have limited jurisdiction). But this approach has now been rejected by a Divisional Court and, apparently, by Lord Diplock himself.[11] Certainly, it is difficult to find a sound reason for distinguishing between tribunals and inferior courts.

At all events, it is not yet safe to conclude that whenever an administrative agency makes an error of law it acts illegally and its decision may be quashed. There may still be questions of law which the agency can answer wrongly without thereby acting illegally. On the other hand, the willingness of the courts to review decisions on

[10] [1981] AC 374.
[11] *R. v. Greater Manchester Coroner, ex parte Tal* [1984] 3 WLR 643 (D.C.); *O'Reilly* v. *Mackman* [1983] 2 AC 237, 278.

questions of law can certainly be explained in policy terms: the courts are the law experts; uniformity on questions of law is desirable; Parliament has often shown its desire to entrust questions of law to the courts by making provision for appeals on questions of law; and judicial procedure is well designed to facilitate the resolution of disputed questions of law.

3. ERROR OF LAW ON THE FACE OF THE RECORD

Earlier I mentioned that there is an exception to the rule that the High Court has no power to quash a decision affected by error of law within jurisdiction. This exception is that the court may quash decisions affected by errors of law which appear on the face of the record—patent errors of law, as they are sometimes called.[12] This power entitles the court to quash a decision simply because it is legally wrong and even though the authority has not exceeded its jurisdiction in answering the question of law wrongly. This power was first used in modern times in 1952 in *R.* v. *Northumberland Compensation Appeal Tribunal, ex parte Shaw*.[13] The court can quash the decision only if the error can be seen simply by examining the record. Historically the record consisted of the documents by which the proceedings were started; the pleadings, if any; and the agency's decision. It did not include the evidence. It could contain the reasons for the agency's decision if it chose to incorporate them. Further, the parties could, by unanimous agreement, raise issues of law which did not appear on the face of the record by swearing affidavits which disclosed the points of law.

In recent years the scope of the record has been expanded. It has been held that reasons for a decision are part of the record even if they are given orally and are only proved by an affidavit which has not been approved by all the parties.[14] Secondly, section 12 of the Tribunals and Inquiries Act 1971 imposes an obligation on many tribunals to give reasons for their decisions if requested to do so; it also provides for these reasons to form part of the record. Finally, it has been held that the reasons for decision of an agency which is not covered by this provision should, nevertheless, be treated as part of the record by analogy with the statutory provision.[15] Since relevant errors of law most

---

[12] i.e. patent on the face of the record.
[13] [1952] 1 KB 338.
[14] *R.* v. *Chertsey Justices, ex parte Franks* [1962] 1 QB 152.
[15] *R.* v. *Knightsbridge Crown Court, ex parte International Sporting Club (London) Ltd.* [1982] QB 304.

often appear in the reasons for decision, these developments are of considerable importance.

The power to quash for patent error of law is part of the supervisory jurisdiction of the court. However, because it entitles the court to grant a remedy merely because a decision is wrong in law, it shares an important feature of the appellate jurisdiction of the court. The important remaining difference between the two jurisdictions is that the court cannot, when it quashes for patent error of law, substitute its own decision on the law for that of the agency; it can only quash the decision and send the matter back for rehearing by the agency. (We have already noted that this rehearing may not be a full one since the court can exercise its power of remission under RSC Ord. 53 r. 9(4)). So the power to quash for patent error of law should be distinguished from the power to hear appeals on points of law. There are various provisions for such appeals; the most general is contained in section 13 of the Tribunals and Inquiries Act 1971. This power enables the court to substitute its decision on the point of law for that of the tribunal, although it can alternatively remit the matter to the tribunal, or give the tribunal directions. Thus, in practice the power to quash for error of law and the power to hear appeals on points of law are very similar, and the availability of appeals on points of law has somewhat overshadowed the jurisdiction to quash for patent error of law.

As we have seen, the effect of *Anisminic* has been to blur the distinction between non-jurisdictional (or patent) errors of law and jurisdictional (or latent)[16] errors of law. Just as there are three views of the effect of *Anisminic*, so there are three views of its effect on the power to quash for patent error of law. If one takes the view that *Anisminic* has, in practice, abolished the distinction between the two types of error of law, then it follows that there would never be any real need to invoke the power to quash for patent error of law, because all errors of law go to jurisdiction. One advantage of this position for the applicant is that he is not restricted to the record to demonstrate the error—he can make use of any relevant material including the evidence. If one takes Lord Diplock's erstwhile view, then the power to quash for patent error of law will still be useful in respect of inferior courts, but will have no role in challenging the decisions of administrative bodies. If one takes the view that *Anisminic* has only

---

[16] So called because they did not have to appear on the face of the record to justify quashing.

enlarged the category of jurisdictional questions of law and has not eliminated the category of non-jurisdictional questions, then the power to quash for patent error of law will still be important in some cases. In the absence of a right of appeal on a point of law, it may be the only source of a remedy.

Assuming that the distinction between jurisdictional and non-jurisdictional errors of law remains, does it have any practical significance? The answer is a qualified 'yes'. First, as we will see later when we discuss remedies, it appears that the remedy of a declaration is available in relation to jurisdictional errors, but not in relation to non-jurisdictional errors; this may be of practical importance in some cases. Secondly, if the error is non-jurisdictional the applicant is restricted to the record to reveal its existence. Even though the scope of the record is now quite wide, it does not include the evidence unless the parties agree to introduce it by means of affidavits, and this may prove important in some cases.

Finally, it appears that there is a difference between the effect of the remedy of quashing in so far as it concerns jurisdictional errors on the one hand and non-jurisdictional errors on the other. When a decision is quashed because of jurisdictional error it is quashed *ab initio*;[17] in other words, it is treated as if it never existed, as a 'nullity'. It cannot provide legal justification for any act done in pursuance of it; if such action amounts to a private law wrong, the injured party will be entitled to damages. On the other hand, if the decision is quashed because of non-jurisdictional error, the decision is only invalidated from the date of the order to quash. This means that, up until that date, it is legally effective and can provide legal justification for acts done under it. So, in an action in tort, for example, the agency which did such acts may be able to plead statutory authorization in answer to a claim for compensation for damage resulting from the acts.

This distinction between the remedies for the different types of error of law is sometimes expressed by saying that decisions affected by jurisdictional error are void, whereas those affected by non-jurisdictional error are merely voidable. As we will see later, when we discuss remedies in more detail, this terminology is apt to be misleading, and it might be better to describe the difference by saying that, whereas quashing for jurisdictional error has retrospective effect, quashing for non-jurisdictional error has only prospective effect. The important

---

[17] Literally 'from the start'.

point to bear in mind at this stage is that the distinction affects the availability of private law damages for acts done in pursuance of the agency's decision prior to the date of its being quashed. This is the chief importance of the rule that decisions affected by patent error of law are not illegal.

It is worth pausing briefly to note the way in which policy arguments can enter the courts' treatment of patent errors of law. In *R.* v. *Preston Supplementary Benefits Appeal Tribunal, ex parte Moore*[18] a number of points of law arose relating to eligibility for certain benefits under the supplementary benefits scheme. Lord Denning, MR stated a reasonableness doctrine similar to that which we have come across in the context of the law–fact distinction, when he said that the courts should intervene to correct patent errors of law only when 'the decision of the tribunal is unreasonable in the sense that no tribunal acquainted with the ordinary use of language could reach that decision'. The main reason given for this restraint was that Parliament had intended that the scheme should not become weighed down with legal technicality. Uniformity of result was important but it did not follow that the view which should prevail was that of the court: 'Individual cases of particular application must be left to the tribunals'.

In *R.* v. *National Insurance Commissioner, ex parte Michael*[19] the challenged decision concerned whether the applicant, when injured, was acting in the course of his employment. Lord Denning, MR thought that the court should intervene only when some general principle was at stake and not when the case was 'isolated or special or rare'. Roskill, LJ noted that there was no right of appeal on points of law from decisions of the Commissioners to the High Court; thus Parliament had expressed its intention that normally decisions of the Commissioners on points of law should prevail, and so the court should only intervene where there was 'a clear error of law appearing on the face of the decision . . . a gross error of law'.

You may by now have detected a certain inconsistency in the approach of the courts to errors of law. On the one hand, the distinction between jurisdictional and non-jurisdictional errors of law assumes that all questions of law have one right answer. On the other hand, in dealing with the law–fact distinction and in deciding whether to grant a remedy for patent error of law, we have noted a willingness

[18] [1975] 1 WLR 624.
[19] [1977] 1 WLR 109.

to acknowledge that many questions, which could be called questions of law, admit of more than one acceptable answer, and that reasonable men could disagree about which answer was the best. The latter view of the nature of questions of law is clearly the more realistic. It is now widely accepted that in 'hard cases' the courts often have to choose between competing answers to questions of law, not on the basis that one is right and the others wrong, but because for policy reasons one is better or more acceptable than the others. Judges of the Court of Appeal and Law Lords who dissent on questions of law are not thought irrational because they dissent. In fact the views of dissenters often receive considerable approval. Further, as we have seen, many questions about the legal significance of facts are questions of degree—whether a flat is furnished; whether an alteration to a house is a structural improvement; whether a commercial deal is an adventure in the nature of trade. There can be no 'right' answer in the normal sense to such questions. The 'right' answer is simply that answer which appeals to the body with the last word on the question.

Why, then, do courts ever adopt the less realistic view that questions of law always have one right answer? Part of the reason is, no doubt, that English judges have traditionally seen their role as finding out what the law actually *is*, rather than as saying what it reasonably ought to be. But there is also a constitutional reason for treating questions of law as having only one right answer. If an administrative authority can be said to have answered a question of law wrongly, then it is clearly the court's duty to say what the right answer is. But, if it is accepted that the answer which the authority gave is only one of a set of possible answers, then the court may only be justified in intervening if the answer given is unreasonable in a rather extreme sense. Further, in applications for judicial review, if the court accepts that a question of law could reasonably be answered in more than one way, it is only justified in saying that the answer given is unreasonable; it must leave it to the authority to decide between the reasonable answers.[20] In other words, the 'right answer' thesis justifies more judicial intervention than the 'reasonableness' doctrine, which gives administrative authorities more freedom in choosing answers to questions of law—more freedom, that is, to *make* law. In practical terms, under the right answer thesis, the reviewing court's view of the law will prevail, whereas,

---

[20] If the proceeding is not judicial review but an appeal on a point of law the court must decide the question of law. Classifying an issue as one of fact is a way around this.

under the reasonableness doctrine, the administrative authority's view of the law is much more likely to prevail.

It is sometimes suggested that the courts should abandon the jurisdictional theory of review of questions of law and instead subject all questions of law decided by administrative agencies to review, according to the standard of reasonableness. This change would do away with the need to draw a distinction between jurisdictional and non-jurisdictional questions of law which has always been recognized as difficult to draw consistently. The suggested change would also have the effect of subjecting to review some questions of law not at present so subject, that is, errors of law within jurisdiction but not patent on the face of the record. But its more important effect would probably be to reduce the overall level of judicial control of the administration, as the courts would not interfere just because they disagreed with a decision on a point of law, but only if it was unreasonable.

4. QUESTIONS OF FACT

The distinction between jurisdictional and non-jurisdictional questions of law is paralleled by a distinction between jurisdictional and non-jurisdictional questions of fact. The classic exposition of this latter distinction is found in *R.* v. *Nat Bell Liquors Ltd.*[21] Put crudely, questions of fact are questions about what happened, or about what is the case. Facts are established by evidence, and if an agency's findings of fact (that is, its decisions about what happened or about what is the case) are not adequately supported by the evidence, then the agency has made an error of fact. The Privy Council in *Nat Bell* made it perfectly clear that the court could not quash the decision of an agency, which the agency had power to make, simply because it was unsupported by the evidence. It could interfere if the agency had made an error of fact on which its jurisdiction depended but not if it made an error of fact in exercising a jurisdiction which it undoubtedly had. Thus, in *White & Collins* v. *Minister of Health*[22] a local authority had power to acquire land compulsorily but not if it was part of a park. The power to make a compulsory acquisition order was held to depend on the question of fact, as to whether the land in question was part of a park. On the other hand, in *Dowty Boulton Paul Ltd.* v. *Wolverhampton*

[21] [1922] 2 AC 128; see also *R.* v. *Fulham, Hammersmith, and Kensington Rent Tribunal, ex parte Zerek* [1951] 2 KB 1.
[22] [1939] 2 KB 838.

Corporation (No. 2)[23] a local authority had leased an airfield to the plaintiff; the authority sought to exercise a power to reacquire the airfield for development on the ground that it was no longer required for use as an airfield. The Court of Appeal held that the question whether the land was still required as an airfield was a question of degree and comparative need, and was for the authority to make.

It has also been held by a majority of the Court of Appeal that a decision may not be quashed merely because fresh evidence has been discovered since the hearing.[24] Both the power to overturn decisions unsupported by evidence and the power to consider fresh evidence are possessed by appeal courts, but not by the High Court exercising its supervisory jurisdiction.

The courts have for a very long time recognized the difficulties of the fact-finding process. Appeal courts are unwilling to interfere with findings of fact by courts of first instance unless they are convinced that the findings are wrong. Very often direct evidence of what happened will be lacking or inadequate, and so inferences will have to be drawn about what actually happened; in other words, circumstantial evidence will often be important. Assessing evidence, both direct and circumstantial, often depends a great deal on seeing the witness giving the evidence in person in order to assess his credibility; this an appeal court never does and so it is at a disadvantage which leads to caution in reversing the findings of the court which actually saw the witnesses.

It is probably for similar reasons that courts exercising powers of judicial review of administrative action are just as unwilling to review questions of fact. Whereas the distinction between jurisdictional and non-jurisdictional questions of law has broken down to a considerable extent, the distinction between jurisdictional and non-jurisdictional questions of fact has not been blurred anything like as much. The courts are still very willing to hold questions of fact to fall within jurisdiction, as a way of justifying non-intervention. Even when the question of fact is classified as jurisdictional, there is evidence that the courts are sometimes reluctant to intervene where there are real disputes as to the facts. This is partly because the procedure of judicial review (which we will consider in a later chapter) is not suited to resolving disputes of fact.[25]

---

[23] [1976] Ch. 13.
[24] *R. v. West Sussex Quarter Sessions, ex parte Albert and Maud Johnson Trust Ltd.* [1974] QB 24.
[25] See, e.g. *IRC v. Rossminster Ltd.* [1980] AC 952, 1025–6 *per* Lord Scarman.

Further, the courts have been willing to recognize that questions of fact often do not admit of one correct answer and that more than one interpretation of the evidence might be equally reasonable. An important case in this context is *Zamir* v. *Home Secretary*[26] in which the question of fact at issue was whether an immigrant's entry certificate had been obtained by fraud. In the first instance, this question had to be answered by an immigration officer at the point of entry into Britain. Lord Wilberforce stated the distinction between jurisdictional and non-jurisdictional questions of fact in the following terms: in some cases 'the exercise of power, or jurisdiction, depends on the precedent establishment of an objective fact. In such a case it is for the court to decide whether that precedent requirement has been satisfied'. In other cases, however, of which this was an example, all the High Court can do is 'to see whether there was evidence on which the immigration officer, acting reasonably, could decide as he did'.

This approach is important for a number of reasons. First, it acknowledges that the issue with which the theory of jurisdiction is essentially concerned is that of who should decide particular questions of fact. Secondly, it recognizes that the issue of substance is not whether the finding of fact is correct but whether it is reasonable. Where the question of fact is a precondition of jurisdiction, the court's task is not well described as finding the correct answer, but as choosing the answer which seems to it most reasonable. Thirdly, Lord Wilberforce explicitly states the reasoning which led him to the result he adopted: the immigration officer has to take into account a large variety of factors of varying and contestable weight; when the court reviews his decision it is limited as to the amount of material it can consider—the procedure of judicial review is not well suited to resolving questions of fact. Again, in the case of *Dowty Boulton Paul* mentioned earlier Russell, LJ was influenced by the fact that the local authority was in a much better position to know about land use needs in its area than was the court. His mention of comparative needs may also show that he thought that there were political issues involved, which the local authority, as a democratically elected body, ought to decide.

It is now clear that the actual application in *Zamir* of the principles laid down by Lord Wilberforce was wrong. In *R.* v. *Home Secretary, ex parte Khawaja*[27] it was held that where, as in *Zamir*, the applicant for

---

[26] [1980] AC 930.
[27] [1984] AC 74.

judicial review is challenging an order that he be personally detained, then the court must decide for itself the factual issues on which the validity of the order depends. Personal liberty is too important an issue to be left to the decision of immigration officers, subject only to the requirement of reasonableness. In effect the House decided that giving correct answers to all questions of fact relevant to personal liberty is a condition precedent to the validity of any detention order. But Lord Wilberforce's general approach still seems valid. Of course, as *Khawaja* shows, the crucial and difficult question is into which category any particular question of fact should be placed.

Despite a general unwillingness to review decisions on questions of fact, it is not the case that the court will never intervene and quash a decision for error of fact, unless the error goes to jurisdiction. In the first place, it is a well established rule that an agency which has reached a conclusion of fact which is wholly unsupported by evidence, either literally or to all intents and purposes, has erred in law and therefore its decision can be quashed. Secondly, if an agency wrongly admits or refuses to admit evidence, it errs in law. Thirdly, as Lord Wilberforce said in *Zamir*, the court will interfere if the agency reaches an unreasonable conclusion on the facts. Lord Denning has made similar statements in *Ashbridge Investments Ltd.* v. *Minister of Housing and Local Government*[28] and *Coleen Properties Ltd.* v. *Minister of Housing and Local Government*.[29] If these statements mean that the court can intervene whenever the agency reaches a decision which the court considers unreasonable, this approach would seem to run counter to *Nat Bell*. On the other hand, in administrative law the word 'unreasonable' is usually interpreted more narrowly to mean 'so unreasonable that no reasonable authority properly understanding its powers could reach such a decision'. This interpretation would mean that only cases of serious error would justify court intervention, and it may just amount to a rephrasing of the rule that it is an error of law to make findings of fact wholly unsupported by evidence. In any case, the word 'unreasonable', however understood, is vague and gives the court considerable scope for intervening or not, as it thinks fit in the light of relevant policy considerations.

Finally, in *Secretary of State for Education and Science* v. *Metropolitan Borough of Tameside*[30] Lord Wilberforce seems to have suggested that lesser factual errors, such as misunderstanding the evidence, or taking

---

[28] [1965] 1 WLR 1320.
[29] [1971] 1 WLR 433.　　　[30] [1977] AC 1014.

account of irrelevant facts, or ignoring relevant facts, might give cause for interference even when the evaluation of the facts is clearly within the jurisdiction of the authority. It is sometimes suggested that the courts are moving towards what is called a 'substantial evidence' rule. This rule would replace the theory of jurisdictional fact and would provide that all decisions of fact by administrative authorities would be liable to be upset if they were not supported by substantial evidence. The proponents of this rule contemplate that it would lead to more judicial intervention; but this would depend very much on how the rule was applied. It seems clear from *Khawaja* that what would qualify as 'substantial evidence' in one context and on one issue, might not be sufficient on some other issue. The greater the evidence required, the less leeway for 'error' would administrators have.

4

Control of the Exercise of Discretionary Powers

I. THE RELATIONSHIP BETWEEN JURISDICTION AND DISCRETION

A DISCRETIONARY power is a power to act or to decide which leaves to the power-holder a certain degree of choice as to what he will do or as to what decision he will reach. A discretionary power allows the power-holder to choose between a number of options. Discretions can be contrasted with duties: these give the duty-bearer no choice as to what he will do. They can also be contrasted with the power to decide a jurisdictional question of law or fact because such a decision will be valid only if it is in accordance with the supervising court's view of what the correct answer should be. An administrative agency has to decide jurisdictional questions 'rightly'. On the other hand, the power to decide non-jurisdictional questions of fact and, to some extent, non-jurisdictional questions of law is in essence a discretionary power because, provided the decision reached is not unreasonable, the supervising court will not intervene and hold the decision invalid simply on the ground that *it* would have decided the question differently. However, powers to decide questions of fact or law are usually not labelled as discretionary powers. The term 'discretionary power' is usually applied to powers to act or decide to act.

In terms of the theory of jurisdiction the question of whether a discretionary power (or a power to decide a non-jurisdictional question of fact or law) has been validly exercised will arise only once any jurisdictional question has been decided in the authority's favour. Suppose, for example, that a rent assessment committee has power to fix a fair rent of premises (a discretionary power) but only if the premises are furnished (a jurisdictional question). The question of whether the decision as to what a fair rent would be is valid or not, will only arise if the premises in question were furnished.

The theory of jurisdiction which we discussed in the last chapter concerns preconditions to the exercise of power which turn on matters of fact or questions of law. But sometimes the debate about whether an agency has a particular power will not turn on questions of law or fact which the agency itself must decide in the first instance but more simply on whether, as a matter of interpretation of the relevant legislation, Parliament gave it that power. For example, in *Bromley LBC v. Greater London Council*[1] as interpreted in *R. v. London Transport Executive, ex parte Greater London Council*[2] there were two questions: (a) did the GLC have the power to subsidize the LTE at all, and (b) was the subsidy plan it settled on valid? Such questions of statutory interpretation are always for the court although, of course, the agency will in the first instance have to adopt a particular interpretation of the statute as a working rule specifying the scope of its powers.

2. DISCRETIONS AND RULES

Discretion lies at the heart of administrative activity. Should a developer be granted planning permission? Should any conditions be attached to the grant of a cinema licence, and if so what conditions? Should a stall-holder at a fair be deprived of his licence? Should a taxi-driver be deprived of the right to ply his trade at Heathrow? Should some industrial assistance payment be made to a company? What should the price of electricity be? Questions such as these face administrative authorities daily. The antithesis of granting an administrative authority a discretion is to make a rule telling the authority what it must do in certain specified circumstances.

The legislative choice between making a statutory rule and conferring a statutory discretion is very important for the legal control of administrative activity. Rules create duties which authorities must perform; discretions confer choice. Both rules and discretions have their advantages and disadvantages. Rules make for certainty and uniformity of result; they may also make the administrative process more efficient, in the sense that if there are no choices to be made, less time need be spent on each case. Rules create rights and entitlements for citizens dealing with the administration. This is often thought particularly important in the area of social welfare—many think that citizens should receive the basic necessities of life from the state as a

[1] [1983] 1 AC 768.
[2] [1983] QB 484.

matter of entitlement, not as a matter of gift or charity. On the other hand, rules are inflexible and rigid: they do not provide for the special details of particular cases to be taken into account. Rules must be complied with to the letter. Also, they may lead to impersonal administration which has little concern for the citizen as an individual.

Discretion, by contrast, is flexible; it allows the merits of individual cases to be taken into account. Discretion is concerned with the spirit, not the letter. It is also useful in new areas of government activity as it enables administrators to deal with new and perhaps unforeseen circumstances as they arise. But it does put the citizen much more at the mercy of the administrator, especially if the latter is not required to tell the citizen the reason why he exercised his discretion in the way he did. Discretion also opens the way for inconsistent decisions, and demands a much higher level of care and attention on the part of the administrator exercising it; discretions are expensive of time and money. In political terms, the conferral of an administrative discretion may be used as a technique for off-loading onto administrators difficult and politically contentious policy choices as to the way a governmental programme ought to be carried out, and as to the objectives of the programme. In this way, political debate and opposition may be avoided. But if, as a result, the aims and purposes of the programme are never stated clearly, judicial control of the exercise of the relevant discretion may become very difficult, and itself a source of political controversy. When judges and Civil Servants are thus forced to make contentious political choices, the legitimacy of their decisions may be threatened.

3. CONTROLLING DISCRETION

The most important constitutional idea relevant to the control of discretion is that of the rule of law. One aspect of Dicey's exposition of the idea was that discretionary powers should always be subject to control by what he called the 'ordinary courts', by which he meant the High Court. Dicey was unduly suspicious of discretionary power which he identified with arbitrary government and also with extensive state intervention in social life of which he disapproved. However, the idea that discretionary power should always be subject to legal control is still central to administrative law. English law recognizes very few discretions which are not subject to some degree of legal control, although there are some. The Attorney-General's discretions to enter a *nolle prosequi* in criminal proceedings and to lend his name to relator proceedings[3] are unreviewable in the courts, as is the police discretion whether to prosecute or not. The courts have shown themselves willing to hold the exercise of emergency powers in wartime to be unreviewable, probably on the basis that courts are not suitable bodies to review the exercise of such powers.[4] In one case the Court of Appeal held unreviewable, except in very extreme circumstances, decisions by a local council to refer tenancy agreements to a rent tribunal to have rents under those agreements fixed, because the tenants would have ample opportunity to put their case to the tribunal.[5]

But, on the whole, administrative discretions are subject to control, sometimes by way of an appeal to a tribunal or Minister, but very often, too, by way of judicial review by the High Court. The concern of the High Court when it reviews the exercise of discretionary powers is only to ensure that the power-holder has not acted illegally (we will see what illegality means in this context in a moment) whereas a tribunal or Minister who hears an appeal will be chiefly concerned to ensure that the decision, even though not illegal, was the *right* decision and a sound exercise of the decision-maker's power of choice.

There is at least one way in which Dicey's approach to the control of discretion was deficient. Both judicial review and appeals take place after the discretion has been exercised and they are concerned with whether the discretion was legally and properly exercised in the circumstances of the particular case. But this type of *ex post facto* control is only one, and perhaps not the most important, way of controlling administrative power. Certainly, given the tiny number of cases which come before the High Court, judicial review seems unimportant, although the cases which do come before the High Court usually have an impact far beyond the particular case. At least as important as judicial review and appeals are techniques for controlling discretion before it is exercised. One writer[6] has divided prospective controls into two types: confining and structuring discretion.

Confining discretion involves setting the limits of discretion as

---

[3] We will discuss this procedure later when we consider applications for injunctions against public bodies.

[4] This now seems to be the criterion for judging the reviewability of the exercise of so-called 'prerogative powers': *CCSU* v. *Minister for the Civil Service* [1984] 3 WLR 1174.

[5] *R.* v. *Barnet and Camden Rent Tribunal* discussed further on in this chapter, in the section headed '(iv) Irrelevant considerations'.

[6] Davis, *Discretionary Justice: A Preliminary Inquiry* (Urbana, 1977).

clearly as possible, by the laying down of rules. This really amounts to determining the amount of discretion a decision-maker will have. Structuring discretion involves controlling the way in which the choice is made by the administrator between alternative courses of action which lie within the limits of his discretion. This can be done in two ways: first, by establishing guiding (but not binding) principles as to how discretion ought to be exercised in particular cases; and secondly, by laying down procedural rules which the administrator must observe in exercising his discretion.

It is worth discussing briefly each of these techniques. Let us look first at a recent example of the structuring of discretion. An important part of the supplementary benefits system used to be that claimants for benefits could, in certain circumstances, be given discretionary extra payments to cover extraordinary needs. The exercise of the discretionary power to make extra payments was under the control of the Supplementary Benefits Commission which, over the years, developed a long and detailed code of practice governing the award of discretionary benefits. In Davis' terminology, this code 'structured' the discretion, because it was not legally binding; if it had been, it would have confined the discretion. According to Professor David Donnison,[7] a former Chairman of the Commission, in some offices extra rules of thumb were applied to cut down the number of cases which had to be considered for discretionary payments. Neither the code nor the informal accretions to it were ever published.

Professor Donnison thought that the discretionary system and the code suffered from a number of serious defects: it was often degrading for applicants to have to ask for help; it was inefficient because the payments involved were usually small; because the code was not published claimants did not know where they stood; the system generated a very large number of appeals; it required experienced staff to operate it well and it often caused staff to become harassed. Donnison was of the view that much of the discretion needed to be taken out of the system. Discretion to deal with hardship created by urgent and unforeseeable needs should be clearly defined and limited. Payments to meet extraordinary needs should be clearly defined and should be a matter of rule-based entitlement, not discretionary charity. When social situations arise which the scheme has never had to deal with before, there is a need for some discretion at first, but it should be

[7] *The Politics of Poverty* (1982), pp. 91–2.

quickly limited by legislation and judicial review.[8] Donnison considers that discretion is often positively harmful. In a few exceptional cases it is positively beneficial, but experienced staff and careful planning are needed to deal with these cases.

In due course much of the discretionary element was purged from the supplementary benefits system and was replaced by legally binding regulations.[9] Perhaps predictably, these regulations have come in for criticism[10]—they are said to be difficult to understand and unduly complex; it is also said that they do not expel discretion from the system but just relocate it in the rule-makers and thereby weaken external control of its exercise.[11]

In theory, in English law, rigid rules which *confine* discretion must be contained in legislation made either by Parliament or a delegate of Parliament, such as a Minister. On the other hand, principles and codes of practice which give flexible guidance to administrators and *structure* their discretions in a way which nevertheless allows the circumstances of particular cases to be taken into account may be laid down in documents which do not have the force of law—the Supplementary Benefits code mentioned above and the Immigration Rules[12] are examples—and may also be developed by the administrator himself as he goes along.

Discretion can be structured by guidelines in a number of ways: for example, the guideline may lay down a general purpose or policy which the administrator is to aim at in exercising his discretion; or it may list factors to be taken into account in exercising the discretion—for example, in deciding whether to deport a member of the family of a deportee, immigration authorities consider all relevant factors including length of residence, family ties, the ability to subsist without recourse to public funds, and compassionate circumstances.[13] Or, finally, the power given to the administrator may, instead of conferring on him an unfettered right to act 'as he sees fit', require him, for example, to act 'reasonably'—this gives him a degree of freedom because people can fairly disagree about what is reasonable, but it rules out certain results as unacceptable.

---

[8] cf. Davis op. cit. p. 108.   [9] Social Security Act 1980.

[10] Harlow (1981) 44 MLR 546.

[11] See further on this point Chapters 7 and 24 below.

[12] See Evans, *Immigration Law* (2nd edn., 1983), pp. 400–407.

[13] Evans op. cit. p. 346. For a sophisticated discussion of the use of guidelines by the Civil Aviation Authority see R. Baldwin, *Regulating the Airlines* (1985), especially chapter 11.

The law, as we will see, is prepared to allow administrators to use non-binding guidelines to structure their discretion, provided they are not used rigidly so as to exclude what is of the essence of discretion, namely a readiness to deal with each case on its merits. The importance of informal guidelines is difficult to overestimate because there is a tendency on the part of all decision-makers to attempt to structure their discretionary powers; and because such guidelines have no legal force there is very little legal control over their formulation or their application. A striking illustration of this last point is provided by recent research into the control of water pollution.[14] The powers of water authorities to control pollution are very broadly phrased in the legislation, and the way these powers are exercised is left almost entirely to pollution control officers and their superiors in the authorities. Although a scheme of strict liability criminal offences is established by statute for the control of pollution, the criminal law is *very* infrequently used, and both the setting of levels of acceptable pollution and the enforcement of those levels is done almost entirely by consensus, negotiation, and cooperation between the controllers and the controlled. Indeed, there is a very strong feeling amongst the controllers that the criminal law should only ever be used against a polluter who has in some sense been at fault, despite the fact that the statutory offences are offences of strict liability. It appears that the way the pollution controllers have structured their powers is very well suited to achieving the statutory ends as efficiently and as completely as possible. The striking thing is that the law apparently plays an insignificant role in regulating the way the controllers' powers are exercised.

4. JUDICIAL REVIEW OF DISCRETIONARY POWERS

In terms of Davis' terminology, some of the rules of judicial review of discretionary powers confine discretion, others structure it. In the next chapter we will consider rules of procedure which the courts require administrative authorities to observe in making decisions and exercising discretions. These rules structure discretion. Most of the other rules confine discretion; they define when the authority can be said to be acting within the limits of its discretion or, as it is put, 'within power', or '*intra vires*', or 'legally'; and when it can be said to have stepped

[14] See Richardson, Ogus, & Burrows, *Policing Pollution* (1983), and Hawkins, *Environment and Enforcement* (1984).

outside the limits of its discretion or, as it can be put, when it has acted '*ultra vires*', or 'illegally'.

A distinction is sometimes made between abusing a discretionary power and exceeding it. In one sense, to take an irrelevant consideration into account or to use a discretion for an improper purpose is to abuse it, while to make an unreasonable decision is to exceed the limits of the discretion. But when we are considering judicial review this distinction is not of much importance, because abusing and exceeding a discretion have the same legal result—they make the decision or action taken illegal or *ultra vires*.

It might be suggested that three basic concerns underlie the rules governing the control of discretions. Some of the rules are concerned with the *substance* of the authority's decision: was it unreasonable; did it faithfully pursue the aims of the legislation conferring the power? Other rules are concerned with the *procedure* by which discretionary powers are exercised: the rules of natural justice, the rule against self-created rules of policy. Thirdly, some rules are concerned with the *legitimacy* of the decision-making process: does the decision have the stamp of legitimate authority? The rule against delegation is an example of this type of rule. With these three aims in mind let us examine the chief grounds on which exercises of discretion can be held invalid.

(a) Discretions must not be Fettered

A discretion is by its very nature a power to choose. However acceptable in substance a decision or action may be, if it is not the outcome of an exercise of free choice by the decision-maker then it is not acceptable as a *discretionary* decision. Even the fact that the decision-maker would have reached exactly the same decision if he had freely exercised the choice does not make the decision *intra vires*, if he did not choose it freely. Three varieties of fettering are usually identified.

(i) Acting under dictation

In *R.* v. *Stepney Corporation*[15] a local authority had a duty to pay a redundant clerk compensation for the loss of his part-time job. Instead of calculating the compensation themselves, taking into account the considerations laid down in the statute, they asked the Treasury how

---

[15] [1902] 1 KB 317.

they calculated compensation for the loss of a part-time office and then applied that formula. The authority was ordered to exercise its discretion to calculate the compensation, applying the statutory criteria. It is worth noting that under the statute the applicant was entitled to appeal to the Treasury if he was dissatisfied with the council's decision on compensation. But this did not mean that the council need not decide the matter in exercise of its *own* discretion first; an appeal is not a substitute for a first instance decision.

In *H. Lavender & Son Ltd.* v. *Minister of Housing and Local Government*[16] the Minister refused the applicant permission to develop land as a quarry just because the Ministry of Agriculture objected. Willis, J said that it was acceptable for the Minister to hear the views of the Ministry of Agriculture and even to adopt the policy of always paying careful attention to those views. What he must not do is to allow the Ministry of Agriculture in effect to make the planning decision for him, by always and automatically yielding to its objections. It is worth noting that the refusal of planning permission was quashed even though the judge thought it unlikely that the applicant would be able to establish that the refusal was unreasonable as a matter of substance.

It can be seen that there are three strands of reasoning in these decisions: not only must the agency not allow itself to be dictated to; also it must not adopt rigid criteria for the exercise of its discretion; and it must not allow someone else to make its decision for it. So the cases reveal a mix of concerns about procedure and legitimacy.

(ii) Self-created rules of policy

This head of *ultra vires* is concerned with the extent to which the courts are prepared to allow administrators to structure their discretion with non-binding guidelines and standards. In *Lavender* (above) Willis, J said that the Minister was 'entitled to have a policy . . . he can and no doubt should reject any recommendation which runs counter to his policy'. However, this statement is rather too simple.

In *British Oxygen Co. Ltd.* v. *Minister of Technology*[17] the Board of Trade refused the applicant an investment grant to pay for a large number of gas containers, because it had a policy of not awarding grants for the purchase of items individually costing less than £25,

---

[16] [1970] 1 WLR 1231.
[17] [1971] AC 610; see also *R.* v. *Port of London Authority, ex parte Kynoch Ltd.* [1919] 1 KB 176.

however many such items were bought at once. Here the containers cost on average £20 each, but BOC had spent more than £4 million on them over a period of three years. The House of Lords held that the decision not to make a grant was *intra vires*. Lord Reid said that, where an authority has to deal with a large number of similar applications, there can be no objection to its forming a policy for dealing with them, provided that authority is willing to listen to 'anyone with something new to say' and to alter or waive its policy in appropriate cases. Viscount Dilhorne thought that it would be 'somewhat pointless and a waste of time' for the Board of Trade not to have a policy, but that representations could be made to the Board that the policy should be changed.

The obvious advantage of policies is that they save time, and promote certainty and uniformity. But the policy can only be proper if it is relevant to the discretion granted, and if it deals similarly with cases which are truly similar. So a policy can be held improper if it is based on irrelevant matters or ignores relevant ones; or if it treats similarly cases which are different in some relevant way. And since, by definition, policies are not binding rules and since they structure discretion rather than confine it, they must not be applied without regard to the individual case. If the applicant raises some relevant matter which the authority did not take into account in forming its policy, it must listen and be prepared not to apply its policy to the case, if it turns out to be irrelevant to that case. Viscount Dilhorne's approach seems to remove this element of individuality from the operation of policies and to turn them into rules. Rules can be changed, but unless and until this happens, they must be applied.

On the other hand, if a policy is going to be of any use in structuring discretion, it must apply unless some good reason can be shown why it should not apply. There must be a bias in favour of a policy.[18] Policies are a compromise between discretion and rules, which help the decision-maker by saving time and energy, but which can also help the citizen by giving him guidance as to how to present his case and its likely outcome—provided of course that the policies are published, which is not often the case. Important also to the proper operation of policies are the rules entitling applicants to be heard before decisions affecting them are made. They have to be able to put their side of the case.

[18] For a more detailed consideration see Galligan [1976] PL 332.

The law, then, is in theory prepared to hold the application of a policy to have been unlawful if insufficient account has been taken of the facts of the particular case which render the policy inappropriate to it. But, because such guidelines have no legal force, a citizen cannot normally complain just because some policy guideline which would have operated for his benefit, if it had been properly applied, has not been applied to his case. There are, however, cases in which a governmental authority may be held to have created a legitimate expectation of being treated in a particular way, as a result of establishing a known (lawful) policy guideline, or of consistently following a particular (lawful) course of conduct, or of giving a (lawful) undertaking or assurance which leads citizens dealing with it reasonably to believe that they will be treated in that way. The authority may then be held to have acted unfairly (and hence illegally) if it departs from its policy, or acts contrary to its usual practice or undertaking—at any rate if it does not give the applicant an opportunity to be heard and to give reasons why he ought to be treated in the way he expected.

Thus, in one case a local authority undertook that it would not increase the number of taxi licences issued by it until certain legislation was passed. The Court of Appeal held that the authority ought to have given the taxi-owners' association a hearing before going back on its assurance.[19] In another case, the Hong Kong immigration authorities were held to have acted illegally in going back on an explicit assurance that illegal immigrants would be given a hearing before being deported.[20] Again, the Home Office was held to have acted unfairly in laying down conditions for the issue of entry certificates to immigrant children whom UK residents wished to adopt and then adding further conditions without notice.[21] In the GCHQ case, the fact that for many years union officials had been consulted before changes in working conditions were made was held, prima facie, to have generated a legitimate expectation of consultation.[22] The expectation was, however, defeated in that case by the demands of national security.

On the other hand since legitimate expectations relate to the exercise of discretionary powers, not every change of policy or practice,

[19] *R.* v. *Liverpool Corporation, ex parte Liverpool Taxi Fleet Operators' Association* [1972] 2 QB 299.
[20] *Attorney-General of Hong Kong* v. *Ng Yuen Shui* [1983] 2 AC 629.
[21] *R.* v. *Home Secretary, ex parte Khan* [1984] 1 WLR 1337; cf. *HTV* v. *Price Commission* [1976] ICR 170.
[22] *CCSU* v. *Minister for the Civil Service* [1984] 3 WLR 1174.

or withdrawal of undertaking will be illegal, but only those which can be described as an 'abuse of power'[23] or 'unreasonable'.[24] The very nature of a discretionary power requires that its holder be given considerable freedom in deciding what to do in exercise of it, and this includes a power, in suitable circumstances, of changing direction and replacing existing policies with new ones.[25] Provided there is some good reason for the change of direction it will not be held to be unfair or illegal, at least so long as the applicant is given a chance to say why the authority should not change direction.

An important feature of all these cases is that, viewed in isolation, the original policy guideline, or course of conduct, or assurance, was perfectly valid; and so also was the new guideline, or action, or decision. But the cases show that, put side by side, two decisions perfectly lawful in themselves can create unfairness if the authority making them can give no good reason for changing its mind, having created a legitimate expectation that it would act in a particular way. Sometimes the unfairness might be held to reside in the change of mind; in other cases fairness just requires that the applicant be given a hearing before the authority decides whether to take a new course.

It emerges clearly from these cases that the idea of having (and giving) good reasons for decisions is of central importance in judging the validity of the use of and departure from policy guidelines. All discretionary powers are given for particular *purposes*, and authorities must be able and prepared to give reasons for their decisions which explain how their decisions further (or, at least, do not frustrate) those purposes. But the idea of unfairness not only implies the procedural point that decisions must be reasoned, but also the point that the court will decide whether any reason given for a decision is *properly* related to the purposes for which the power was given—an authority could not repel the charge of unfairness by giving a totally spurious or irrelevant reason, or by giving an applicant a hearing and then ignoring the reasons he put forward as to why he should be treated in the way he expected. By requiring reasoned and rational action the courts exercise control over the substance of decision-making.

We can see, therefore, that although administrative policies and guidelines do not have direct legal force, their use is, to some extent, *regulated* by law.

---

[23] *R. v. IRC, ex parte Preston* [1985] 2 WLR 836.
[24] See p. 81 below.
[25] *In re Findlay* [1984] 3 WLR 1159, 1173.

(iii) Contracts and undertakings

Clearly, if an authority is given a discretion it cannot normally be right for it to undertake in advance, and without considering the merits of individual cases, to bind itself to exercise the discretion in a particular way, or not to exercise it at all.

In *Stringer* v. *Minister of Housing and Local Government*[26] a local authority agreed with Manchester University that it would discourage development in a particular area so as to protect Jodrell Bank telescope from interference. In pursuance of this agreement it rejected a development application. Cooke, J held that this refusal was *ultra vires* because in honouring the agreement the authority had ignored considerations which the statute said were relevant. Four points are worth noting about this decision. First, it was held to be irrelevant whether the agreement between the authority and the university was legally binding or not; the important point was the effect it had had on the consideration by the council of the application. Secondly, the fact that the authority's refusal of permission on the basis of the agreement was held illegal did not mean that protection of the telescope was not a relevant consideration, on the basis of which, and without reference to the agreement, the Minister could uphold the refusal of permission on appeal. Thirdly, the agreement in this case related expressly and directly to the way a particular discretion would be exercised in the future. The relevance of this point will be taken up in a moment.

Fourthly, in *Stringer* the attack by the applicant (who was not a party to the agreement) was on the exercise of the discretion. But sometimes, in cases such as this, the attack might be on the contract itself by one of the parties to it. For example, a successor of the original contracting authority might want to get out of the contract, as happened in *Ayr Harbour Trustees* v. *Oswald*[27] where the Trustees wanted to be free of a covenant, given by their predecessors, not to build on Oswald's land. A mirror image of such a case is *William Cory & Son Ltd.* v. *London Corporation.*[28] Cory contracted with the Corporation to remove garbage in its barges; later the Corporation passed new health regulations making it more expensive for Cory to perform its contract. Cory argued that a term ought to be implied into the contract, to the effect that the Corporation would not exercise its power to make by-laws in such a way that the contract became more

[26] [1970] 1 WLR 1281.
[27] (1883) 8 App. Cas. 323.　　[28] [1951] 2 KB 476.

expensive for Cory to perform. The Court of Appeal held that since such a clause, if put expressly into the contract, would be void as a fetter on the Council's power to make health regulations, it could not be implied into the contract so as to protect Cory. In fact, in one case it was held that a term should be implied into a lease to the effect that, in making the lease, the Crown (the lessor) was not undertaking not to exercise its power to requisition the premises, should they be needed in case of war emergency.[29]

It is clear, however, that not all contracts which in some way limit the exercise of statutory discretionary powers are for that reason void as fetters on the discretion. The difficult task is to identify those which are void. In the first place, it might be useful to draw a distinction between contracts which are specifically intended to regulate the exercise of a discretion, as in *Stringer* (above), and those which aim not to limit an authority's action but, on the contrary, to exercise one of its powers. At first sight it might be thought that contracts of the first type are more likely to be void, and in some cases they are indeed void. For example, in the *Ayr Harbour* case (above) the covenant not to build on Oswald's land was held to be a void fetter on the powers of the Trustees to build.

But contrast *Birkdale District Electric Supply Co. Ltd.* v. *Southport Corporation*.[30] In this case the company agreed not to raise the price of electricity produced by it above the price charged by the Corporation for electricity supplied by it. When the company, disregarding the agreement, tried to raise its prices and the Corporation attempted to stop it doing so, the company argued that the agreement was a void fetter on its power to fix prices. The House of Lords rejected this argument on the ground that the agreement did not run counter to the intention of the legislature in setting up the company. It was not intended that it should make a profit, and there was no reason to think that any of the statutory functions of the company had been or would be adversely affected by compliance with the agreement.

So it would appear that the question of incompatibility of a contract with a discretionary power is a question of statutory interpretation— has the contract already, or is it reasonably likely in the future, seriously to limit the authority in the exercise of its statutory powers, or the performance of its statutory functions? Ultimately the court has to make a choice: what is more important in this case, the interest of the

---

[29] *Commissioners of Crown Lands* v. *Page* [1960] 2 QB 274.
[30] [1926] AC 355.

citizen who is the other party to the contract and the principle that contracts should be kept, or the public interest in the exercise of the statutory power? There can be no general answer to such a question; it all depends on the facts of the particular case. And although the terms of the statute provide the basic material for answering this question, we have several times noted how much choice the terms of statutes often leave to the courts in interpreting them. Seen in this light the question gives the court a heavy responsibility to make policy choices between public and private interests. No analytical formula will solve the problem; the court must make a value judgment.

Two cases will serve to illustrate the type of case in which the contract is intended primarily as an exercise of discretion rather than a limitation of it. In *Stourcliffe Estates Co. Ltd.* v. *Bournemouth Corporation*[31] the Corporation bought some land for a public park and covenanted to build on it only a band-stand or such like structure. On its face the contract was designed to acquire land for a park, which the council had power to do. When the council sought to exercise a statutory power to build public conveniences, by putting them in the park, the plaintiff was awarded an injunction to restrain the building. The court rejected the argument that the covenant was a void fetter. In *Dowty Boulton Paul Ltd.* v. *Wolverhampton Corporation*[32] the Corporation conveyed to the plaintiff for ninety-nine years certain land for use as an aerodrome. Some years later, when use of the aerodrome had somewhat dropped off, the council sought to exercise a power to reacquire the land for development, on the ground that it was no longer required for use as an airfield. Pennycuick, VC held that the company was entitled to keep the airfield and that the contract was not a void fetter.

The crucial difference between the contract in these two cases and that in *Stringer*, for example, is that the former two were made as part of a genuine exercise of a statutory power other than the one which the contract adversely affected. In *Stourcliffe* the council was validly exercising a power to acquire land; in *Dowty* the council was exercising a power to dispose of land. Each contract was an unexceptionable way of exercising the power in question. In both cases it was pointed out that to hold the contract void would be to put an unreasonable restriction on the power of the authority to enter into contracts relating to land. It might have been different if the statutory power to build

[31] [1910] 2 Ch. 12.
[32] [1971] 1 WLR 204.

conveniences or to reacquire had related only to the specific piece of
land involved, because then it might have been said that the contract
was a specific attempt to fetter that power. But since the powers related
to land generally, to hold such contracts to be void fetters on the
powers would be to put an excessive limitation on the contract-making
power. When two powers impinge on each other in this way some
compromise adjustment has to be found. Should the contract-making
power prevail to the benefit of the citizen, or should the public interest
in the exercise of the conflicting power be protected?

So in all these cases, at the end of the day, the court is called upon to
balance public and private interests. This, it might be thought, is not a
suitable job for an unelected and unrepresentative body like the High
Court. Certainly it requires the court to say more than that the
authority has acted unreasonably in entering into the contract. It
requires it to choose the outcome which the public interest demands.

(b) The Rule against Delegation: 'delegatus non potest delegare'

The rule against delegation is closely related to the rule against acting
under dictation. They are both designed to ensure that when a specific
person or body is given a discretion, the discretion is exercised by that
person or body, and not by someone else. The rule applies primarily to
discretionary powers because part of the point of conferring a
discretion on a particular person is to obtain the decision which
that person thinks best. The rule does not impose an absolute
prohibition on delegation; it usually operates as a principle of statutory
interpretation to the effect that a statute will only be interpreted as
permitting delegation of discretionary powers if express words to that
effect are used, or the power to delegate is very clearly implied in the
statute.

In *Barnard* v. *National Dock Labour Board*[33] the Board had power to
suspend workers who breached a disciplinary code. It passed a
resolution which effectively gave the power to suspend to the London
port manager. A worker suspended by the manager successfully
challenged his suspension. It is worth noting that Denning, LJ held
that not only had the Board no power to delegate the suspending
function, but also that it had no power to ratify a suspension by the port
manager since 'the effect of ratification is . . . equal to a prior
command'. It would have been permissible for the Board to receive a

[33] [1953] 2 QB 18.

recommendation from its subordinate and then to decide, in exercise of its discretion, whether to accept the recommendation or not. But it was not entitled simply to rubber-stamp what someone else had decided. This makes clear the similarity between this rule and that against acting under dictation.

There is an important qualification to the non-delegation rule which rests on the principle of ministerial responsibility. In *Carltona Ltd.* v. *Commissioner of Works*[34] an official in the Ministry of Works and Planning, in purported exercise of emergency powers, wrote a letter to Carltona requisitioning premises which it occupied. Carltona challenged the requisitioning, but the Court of Appeal held that within departments of state quite a large degree of delegation of functions is both permissible and necessary, since it would be physically impossible for the Minister to exercise personally all the discretionary powers which are vested in him in his official capacity as Minister. The Minister is responsible to Parliament if things go wrong or if he delegates an important decision to too junior an official; and so there is not the same need for the courts to enforce the principle of non-delegation in this case as there is in the case of administrative bodies which are not under the direct control of Ministers and so do not fall under the umbrella of parliamentary accountability. And where account has to be made to Parliament, it would be wrong for the courts to step in and usurp the political process. It has been suggested that part of the reason for this decision was the traditional reluctance of the courts to review the exercise of emergency powers in wartime. But there is at least one case in which the *Carltona* principle has been applied in peacetime.[35]

The main difficulty with the *Carltona* decision is that it relies on a rather outdated view of the effectiveness of ministerial responsibility as a vehicle of political accountability. However, the decision does seem justifiable by the pragmatic argument that one man is incapable of personally exercising all the functions conferred on Ministers of State. The problem of accountability is a separate one which rules about delegation are not sufficient to cope with.

As we have noted, the power to delegate can be given by statute, either expressly or by implication. Perhaps the most important example

[34] [1943] 2 All ER 560; Lanham (1984) 100 LQR 587.
[35] *R. v. Skinner* [1968] 2 QB 700; but there are some situations in which, by statute, specific authorization is needed before a Civil Servant can make a binding decision, e.g. Immigration Act 1971 s. 4(1) and Schedule 2.

of an express statutory power to delegate is contained in section 101 of the Local Government Act 1972. This allows local authorities to delegate the discharge of any of their functions to a committee, sub-committee, officer, or other local authority. A statute may also specify formalities which have to be observed in delegating a function. And so there are two ways in which the non-delegation principle may be breached: an authority may purport to delegate a function which it has no power to delegate, or it may fail to observe some formality required to be observed if a function is to be lawfully delegated. In either case the decision of the 'delegate' will be unlawful.

Delegation is a public law notion. It is related to agency, which is basically a private law concept, but the relationship between the two is rather obscure. Since the non-delegation principle is basically one of statutory interpretation, it is often said that the term 'delegation' only properly applies to transfers of power authorized expressly or impliedly by statute. On this view it is sometimes said that the *Carltona* case is not concerned with delegation because the internal organization of departments of state is not regulated by statute, but by non-statutory rules of law, or merely by administrative practice. This would make the relationship between Minister and official more like that of principal and agent, rather than of delegator and delegate. Often a person is made an agent of another by a contract between them defining what the agent is empowered to do on behalf of the principal. But the powers of an agent are not limited to those he is actually given by the contract. They may extend to powers which the principal has put the agent in a position to represent to third parties that he has. Thus, whereas the limits of delegation are in theory defined by statute (i.e., by the legislature), the limits of agency and of the *Carltona* principle are defined ultimately by the common law (i.e., by the courts) which can extend the limits of the agency as defined in the contract between the parties and can determine when the *Carltona* principle is applicable. For example, it has been held that the *Carltona* principle does not apply as between a commissioner of police and a superintendent.[36] The force of saying that matters of internal organization are not strictly matters of delegation is presumably that this gives the courts more power to say who can decide and do what within government agencies.

This distinction between agency and delegation can be very important. Suppose an official does an act (such as granting planning

---

[36] *Nelms* v. *Roe* [1969] 3 All ER 1379.

permission) the doing of which his employing authority has no power to delegate to him, or has not properly delegated to him. But suppose, too, that the authority has put him in a position to make it appear to a citizen that he does have authority to do the act, for example by always rubber-stamping what the official does. According to the public law principle of non-delegation, the act is illegal. But if the principles of agency were applied a court might well hold the authority bound by what the official had done. We will look at this problem more later when we discuss estoppel.[37]

(c) Unreasonableness

(i) Introduction

Unreasonable decisions are illegal. The term 'unreasonable' is, of course, very vague; its function is, in part, to give the High Court, when reviewing administrative decisions, a degree of discretion in deciding whether administrative bodies have acted illegally. The notion of unreasonableness is the main tool used by the courts to exercise control over the *substance* of administrative decisions. Whether an administrative action is unreasonable depends ultimately on the court's interpretation of the provisions of the statute conferring the discretion and all the circumstances of its exercise. So the court is itself involved in making the same sort of assessment of the aims and purposes for which the discretion was conferred and of the circumstances of individual cases, as the administrative authority must make. However, it is not for the court to say how the discretion ought to have been exercised. If it were, this would effectively transfer the power from the authority to the court. Its only job is to ensure that the authority has not acted unreasonably and in doing this job the courts have traditionally shown considerable restraint (in theory at least). This restraint is expressed in the rather special meaning which has been given to the word 'unreasonable'. In *Associated Provincial Picture Houses Ltd.* v. *Wednesbury Corporation*[38] Lord Greene, MR said that if an authority's decision was 'so unreasonable that no reasonable authority could ever have come to it, then the courts can interfere'. The court does not decide what the reasonable authority *would* do, but only what *no* reasonable authority *could* do. So the idea of unreasonableness only sets a limit on the exercise of discretions; it does not structure their exercise.

---

[37] Ch. 18 below.
[38] [1948] 1 KB 223.

In a moment we will look at a number of categories into which the doctrine of unreasonableness is often divided. There is sometimes discussion as to whether these categories are each separate heads of illegality or whether they are just illustrations of unreasonable conduct, unreasonableness being the only ground of challenge. The importance of the distinction can be seen by an example. Suppose a body in reaching a decision has ignored some relevant consideration (this is a recognized head of *ultra vires*). Is its decision for that reason illegal, or is it illegal only if it can also be described as unreasonable?[39] This question cannot really be answered in the abstract because so much depends on the facts of particular cases. What we can say, perhaps, is this: the courts generally consider it right to exercise restraint when reviewing discretionary decisions of administrative bodies. They are not willing to interfere simply because the court or some other authority would have reached a different decision from that arrived at by the authority. The court must be able to say that the decision lies so clearly outside the limits of the authority's powers that no sensible person could consider it a proper exercise of the discretion. On the other hand, the fact that a court could not fit a case into one of the recognized heads of unreasonableness would probably not prevent it invalidating the decision if it felt it could be described as unreasonable, although a court will usually want to find and state some specific reason why it thinks the decision bad.

Perhaps the main reason for the restraint exercised by the courts in this area is that the judges fear that, if they go too far into the merits of discretionary decisions, they will open themselves to criticism for making 'political' decisions, and thus compromise their independence. It is for Parliament to exercise political control over the administration and for the courts to ensure that the *legal* limits of administrative power are observed. Even so, opinions can differ about where 'sensible people' would place the outer limits of reasonable discretion, and an appeal to reasonable opinion may only be a device for legitimizing one's own opinions. The courts may open themselves to criticism even when they try to exercise restraint as they see it. But this is a danger from which there is no escape. When we give the courts power to decide that certain decisions are unreasonable we give them power to make value judgments on matters which may be politically very contentious. It is unrealistic to expect that a court will be able to give an apolitical or

---

[39] There is an inconclusive discussion of this point in *Pickwell* v. *Camden LBC* [1983] QB 962.

value free answer to a disputed political question, as no such answer exists.

Unreasonableness, as we have noted, depends very much on the facts of particular cases and on the statutory provision conferring the discretion which falls to be applied in the case. So the cases at best provide illustrations of the general principles, and it may be that to get any real guidance one would have to group together cases on the same subject matter, or even on the same statutory provision. At least the context should always be borne in mind.

(ii) Unreasonableness as a particular ground of challenge

The term 'unreasonable' is sometimes more particularly used in relation to statutes which confer powers, for example, on a Minister to act if he has 'reason to believe' or 'is satisfied' that something is the case; or to take such steps as he 'thinks fit'. It is such cases that we will consider in this section.

Such phrases immediately raise the question whether the action is to be judged according to the authority's own sense of reasonable belief (or satisfaction or fitness) or by some more objective standard. We might think that the notion of unreasonableness as defined in *Wednesbury* could only be applied objectively and that there is hardly any point in applying a subjective test because very rarely will an authority act in a way which it does not honestly (if mistakenly) believe to be reasonable. But in a few cases a subjective approach has been adopted. The most famous is *Liversidge* v. *Anderson*[40] which was an action for false imprisonment. The Home Secretary had power to detain any person whom he had reasonable cause to believe to be of hostile origins or associations. A majority of the House of Lords held that the Home Secretary's action in detaining the complainant would be justified, provided he had acted honestly believing that there was reason to think that the detainee was hostile.

A somewhat similar case is *McEldowney* v. *Forde*[41]. This case involved a challenge to a regulation (which proscribed republican clubs and like organizations in Northern Ireland) made under a power 'to make regulations . . . for the preservation of peace and the maintenance of order'. A majority of the House of Lords held that the power gave the Minister a very wide discretion which would only be interfered with if it could be shown that the Minister had not acted honestly, or if the regulation bore no relation to the purposes for which the power had

---

[40] [1942] AC 206.   [41] [1971] AC 632.

been given. But these cases are exceptional and are probably to be explained by the fact that both concerned the preservation of peace and security.

The leading authority for the proposition that even subjective statutory language ought to be given an objective interpretation is *Padfield* v. *Minister of Agriculture, Fisheries, and Food.*[42] In that case the Minister had power to refer to an investigation committee complaints about decisions of the Milk Marketing Board fixing milk prices. It was held that the Minister was under a duty to give proper consideration to the question whether to refer the complaint and that any such decision had to be based on good reasons. Moreover, if the Minister gave no reason for a refusal to refer, the court would consider for itself whether there were good reasons.

Another important case is *Secretary of State for Education and Science* v. *Metropolitan Borough of Tameside.*[43] Here the Minister had power to give directions to a local authority as to the performance of its statutory functions, if he was satisfied that the local authority was acting or was proposing to act unreasonably. The issue at stake was the highly contentious one of the 'comprehensivization' of schools: a Conservative local authority decided to reverse a scheme, worked out by its Labour predecessor and approved by the Secretary of State, for the abolition of selective schools in its area. It was made clear in this case that the test to be applied in judging the Minister's satisfaction was an objective, not a subjective, one: was the opinion which the Minister had formed of what the local authority had done or was about to do one which a reasonable person could entertain? In this case much turned on evidence concerning the amount of disruption to the school system which the proposed reversion to the selective entry criteria would cause.

Licensing cases of various sorts provide many examples of the use of the concept of unreasonableness. The *Wednesbury* case itself involved licensing. The local authority had the power to attach to a licence to operate a cinema on Sundays 'such conditions as the authority think fit to impose'. The authority granted a licence subject to the condition that no children under the age of 15 were to be admitted, whether or not accompanied by an adult. In the event the Court of Appeal held that the condition was not unreasonable.

Planning and land-use legislation often contains similar provisions

[42] [1968] 2 WLR 924.
[43] [1977] AC 1014.

empowering authorities to attach such conditions as they see fit to the grant of planning or land-use permission. Five of the many cases on such provisions will provide us with a useful case-study.[44] In *Pyx Granite Co. Ltd.* v. *Ministry of Housing and Local Government*[45] Lord Denning made it clear that although the phrase in the legislation was 'such conditions as they think fit', the conditions imposed had to relate fairly and reasonably to the permitted development of the land and must not be imposed for some ulterior motive; and that it was for the court to police this restriction. In *Fawcett Properties Ltd.* v. *Buckingham CC*[46] the council gave permission for the erection of two cottages on the condition that they were to be reserved for farm workers and not to be let to city-dwellers. This condition was held to be a fair and reasonable, if imperfect, way of giving effect to the valid policy of preserving the green belt. In *R.* v. *Hillingdon LBC ex parte Royco Homes Ltd.*[47] the Divisional Court struck down conditions attached to the grant of permission to build flats. The reason given was that the conditions in effect required the developer to fulfil, at its own expense, a significant part of the duty of the local authority, as housing authority, to provide public housing.

The next two cases concerned the grant of a licence to run a caravan site. The relevant legislation stated a number of matters which the authority could regulate by attaching conditions to the site licence— they related chiefly to the state and layout of the site. In *Chertsey UDC* v. *Mixnam's Properties Ltd.*[48] the authority sought, by conditions imposed, to regulate relations between the site owner and the caravan owners on matters such as security of tenure. The House of Lords struck down the conditions as being insufficiently related to the purposes for which the statute intended conditions to be made, namely, regulating the state of the site. In another case[49] it was held that, in deciding what conditions could be imposed about the use of the site, general considerations of the effect of the site on the surrounding community could be taken into account. For example, if too many caravans were allowed on the site, this might overload local educational and other facilities, and this would affect the caravan owners as much as other local inhabitants. On the other hand, in

---

[44] For a more detailed consideration of these cases see McAuslan, *The Ideologies of Planning Law* (1980), pp. 162 ff.

[45] [1958] 1 QB 554.

[46] [1961] AC 636.

[47] [1974] QB 720.

[48] [1965] AC 735.

[49] *Esdell Caravan Parks Ltd.* v. *Hemel Hempstead RDC* [1965] 3 All ER 737.

granting a site licence, as opposed to planning permission, preservation of the green belt was not a relevant consideration.

The basic issue raised by all of these cases is whether it is permissible to use conditions to achieve certain specific ends. So the preservation of the green belt is a permissible end in some cases but not in others; protection of the amenities of the community around the caravan site is permissible but regulating relations between the site owner and the caravan owners is not; the provision of housing for persons on a local authority housing list is not a permissible use of planning conditions. The value of looking at these cases is that they show how the judgment of unreasonableness is essentially a value judgment. The legislation in question did not in any of these cases dictate the result or even give a clear indication as to what it should be. It all depends on what those making the decisions think planning and land-use control is for.

Should judges have power to give effect to personal values in this way? We might say that the fact that, in theory, they only intervene in cases of extreme unreasonableness helps legitimize their decisions. The trouble with this argument is that whether one thinks a decision is extremely unreasonable, or even unreasonable at all, depends on what one thinks the legislation is designed to achieve. It is in deciding this question of statutory purpose that the most important and far-reaching value judgments are made by the courts. We might say that this is acceptable so long as Parliament can reverse judicial decisions. But in practice what the courts say is often the last word, and indeed, if every court decision was reconsidered by Parliament there would be no point in having courts. So the question remains: why are we prepared to allow judges who are neither representative nor responsible to make such political value judgments?

(iii) *Improper purposes*

In a sense, the cases we have just considered concerned whether the authority had pursued some improper purpose in imposing conditions. However, in those cases the question of the intention or motive which the authority entertained when it made the decision did not really arise. The only question which arose was the retrospective one of whether the action taken was illegal or not. But sometimes the subjective purpose or motive of the authority is relevant.

The word 'improper' does not necessarily imply dishonesty or corruption, although actual dishonesty or fraud will, of course, invalidate an administrative decision. But the word does indicate that the authority consciously pursued a purpose identifiably different from the statutory purpose. For example, in *Sydney Municipal Council* v. *Campbell*[50] the Council had a power to acquire land compulsorily in order to improve or remodel areas of the city. In this instance the only reason for acquisition was to enable the Council to reap an expected increase in the value of land resulting from the building of a highway by the Council. So the acquisition was illegal. Again, in *Congreve* v. *Home Office*[51] the applicant had bought a new TV licence before his current one had run out because he (correctly) anticipated an increase of the annual fee from £12 to £18. The Home Secretary decided to exercise his discretionary power to revoke licences and revoked the licence of the applicant and of other 'overlappers' after only eight of the twelve months covered by the licence had expired, because this was all that had been paid for. The Court of Appeal held that this revenue-protecting device was an improper use of the power of revocation.

Very often an authority will have more than one purpose in mind when it acts. For example, in *Westminster Corporation* v. *London & North Western Railway*[52] the Council, in exercise of a power to build lavatories, erected conveniences under Parliament Street to which access was provided from both sides of the road by subways. It was argued that the Council had no power to build a subway, but the House of Lords held that the primary aim of the Council had been to build conveniences and that there was no evidence that the building of lavatories was a mere pretext for building a subway. The most that could be said was that the Council had realized that the public might use the subway as a means of crossing the street. The proper question is what was the dominant motive or purpose. So, in *R.* v. *Brixton Prison Governor, ex parte Soblen*[53] an order for the deportation of Soblen to the United States was not invalidated, even though it would deliver Soblen into the hands of the United States Government which sought his extradition for a non-extraditable offence. The court was satisfied that the Minister's prime motive was deportation of an unwelcome alien. The fact that the Minister was happy thereby to be able to help the US Government did not render the order illegal.

So we can see that in these cases the debate is not usually about what the intentions of Parliament were in conferring the discretion (as was the position in the 'unreasonableness' cases) but rather about

[50] [1925] AC 338. [51] [1976] 1 QB 629.
[52] [1905] AC 426. [53] [1963] 2 QB 302.

whether the authority shared Parliament's undoubted purpose. These
cases are therefore well described as being about abuse, rather than
excess of discretion.

(iv) Irrelevant considerations

It is an error either to take account of irrelevant considerations
or to ignore relevant ones. This principle is closely related to other
heads of review. In *Wednesbury* it was held that it was proper for the
authority to take into account 'the physical and moral health of
children' in attaching conditions to a cinema licence. The idea of
irrelevant considerations also extends beyond the area of discretionary
powers. *Anisminic Ltd.* v. *Foreign Compensation Commission*[54] which we
considered in Chapter 3 was a case in which a decision was held illegal
because the Commission had asked itself the wrong question of law, by
treating as relevant the nationality of the applicant's successor.

Sometimes statutes list relevant considerations. We have already
looked at two cases about the granting of caravan site licences under a
provision which stated a number of matters on which conditions could
be made. Very often, however, the statute conferring a power does not
lay down what considerations are relevant to its exercise. Then it is up
to the court to lay down criteria of relevance by extracting what implied
guidance it can from the legislation. Sometimes the courts have held
that when a statute states no relevant considerations the intention is
that this head of review should not apply. In *R.* v. *Barnet and Camden
Rent Tribunal, ex parte Frey Investments Ltd.*[55] it was held that a decision
by a local council to refer a tenancy agreement to a local rent tribunal
was not subject to challenge on the ground that some material matter
had not been considered by the referring council. The basis of the
court's decision was that the decision to refer did not by itself
prejudice the landlords, as all issues relevant to the proper rent would
be considered by the tribunal.

The classic example of a case where a decision was struck down for
taking irrelevant considerations into account is *Roberts* v. *Hopwood*.[56] A
decision was made by the Poplar Borough Council (under a power to
pay its employees such salaries and wages as it thought fit) to pay its
employees uniform wage increases considerably greater than the rate
of inflation, and unrelated to the sex of the employee and to the nature
of the work done. In a famous statement Lord Atkinson said that the
Council had allowed itself 'to be guided by some eccentric principles

[54] [1969] 2 AC 147.   [55] [1972] 2 QB 342.   [56] [1925] AC 578.

of socialistic philanthropy or by a feminist ambition to secure equality of the sexes in the matter of wages in the world of labour', rather than by ascertainment of what was fair and reasonable remuneration for services rendered. The importance of this case is not only as an illustration of reasoning in terms of irrelevant considerations, improper purposes, and unreasonableness; it also shows how relative to changing political and social views these terms are. Very many discretionary powers can be used to achieve different ends favoured by groups with divergent political views. Very often the legislation does not rule out all but one of such ends and so the courts must choose between them. Thus, once again the courts are involved in politics.

(d) Fiduciary Duties

Roberts v. *Hopwood* also rests on the idea that, since a local authority is dealing with funds contributed by ratepayers, it owes a duty (called a 'fiduciary' duty) to those ratepayers to consider their interests as well as those of the intended beneficiaries of any spending programme, before deciding how to spend the rates. The classic example of the fiduciary duty reasoning is *Prescott* v. *Birmingham Corporation*.[57] Birmingham Council had power to charge such fares as it thought fit on its public transport. It introduced a scheme of free travel for old people which was invalidated by the court, on the ground that the Council was in effect making a gift to one section of the public at the expense of the ratepayers. The effect of this decision was subsequently negated by statute but the principle on which it rests remains.

The important point about the principle is this. Central government does not owe a fiduciary duty to the body of taxpayers. Political parties campaign at elections on the basis of certain policies and if elected into government they put those policies more or less into effect, raising and using taxes for that purpose. In modern political practice the idea of the electoral mandate is used to legitimize spending, subject of course to parliamentary approval in the form of Finance and Appropriation Acts. But it seems that the idea of the electoral mandate is not perceived as having the same legitimizing force at the local level. Local government election campaigns turn at least in part on schemes for local spending programmes—for example the GLC's 'Fares Fair' scheme for reduced fares on London Transport[58] was a major issue in

---

[57] [1955] 1 Ch. 210.
[58] See *Bromley LBC* v. *Greater London Council* [1983] 1 AC 768; *R.* v. *London Transport Executive, ex parte Greater London Council* [1983] QB 484.

the elections which preceded the introduction of the scheme. Nevertheless, local authorities are required to pay continuing attention to the interests of ratepayers in moulding their policies, and may even be required, in fulfilment of their fiduciary duty, to give up some policy which they were apparently elected to put into effect.

We discussed in Chapter 1 the way in which English law subordinates local government to central policy, by subjecting it to the doctrine of *ultra vires*. Here we have a concrete example of the way in which the law can prevent the formation and implementation of local policies. But the fiduciary duty is probably based on an additional consideration. Whereas most taxpayers can vote in central government elections, paying rates to a local authority and being entitled to vote for it do not by any means always go together. Many ratepayers are commercial concerns which cannot vote. The individuals who comprise those concerns often live in a different local authority area, where they in turn pay domestic rates and can vote. So commercial concerns often do not have a voice in local government elections, while spending decisions often affect them. This is not, however, a conclusive argument because it is also true that companies pay taxes to central government and yet have no vote as to how those taxes will be spent. On the other hand, those who own and run such companies do have a vote. Also, the process of consultation and lobbying is very highly developed at the central level so that, although central government is under no formal fiduciary duty to taxpayers, the realities of political life ensure that the government consults interested parties. It may be that, in practice, the pressures put on local government by interested parties are not as great as those at the central level.

The fiduciary duty of local authorities to their ratepayers is reinforced by the rule of standing—that ratepayers as such have standing to challenge local authority spending decisions whereas taxpayers apparently have no right to challenge central government spending decisions.

5

Natural Justice

So far in this part we have discussed grounds of invalidity of administrative decisions which relate to the substance of the decision —is it based on an error of law, is it unreasonable, and so on. In this chapter we will consider grounds of invalidity which relate to the procedure which the administrator follows in reaching his decision. In some cases, most notably in relation to the decisions of statutory tribunals and public inquiries, there will be statutory procedural rules governing the decision-maker's activities. As we will see later, the decision-maker is not always under an obligation to observe such statutory rules because failure to comply with certain rules does not render a decision invalid. If failure to comply with a particular statutory rule renders a decision invalid, that rule is called a 'mandatory' rule of procedure. If failure to comply does not have that effect, the rule is called a 'directory' rule.

Administrative decision-makers are also subject to a set of common law procedural rules which are known collectively as the rules of natural justice. The rules of natural justice embody two main principles: 'the rule against bias', that a man must not be judge in his own cause (*nemo iudex in sua causa*); and that a person must be given a fair hearing (*audi alteram partem*).

The term 'natural justice' might be thought to suggest that these rules have some objective validity and that in these rules the law is simply giving effect to certain self-evident moral truths about how decisions ought to be made. There is a certain amount of truth in this. Most people would agree that there is good reason to be suspicious of a decision for or against a party made by a person who has an interest, financial or otherwise, in the outcome of the case. It is not necessarily the case, of course, that an interested decision-maker will, because of his interest, make an unfair decision. He may succeed in standing back from the situation and making the decision purely on the merits of the case. But the point of this rule is not just that justice (or fairness) should be done but that it should also be seen to have been done. What matters is not whether the decision-maker *is* biased but whether he could reasonably *appear* to be biased. On the other hand, the appearance of justice does not guarantee that justice will be done, any more than the appearance of bias necessarily leads to a biased decision. But while the appearance of impartiality carries no guarantee with it, it does increase the chance of a fair decision.

The rule against bias is designed mainly to foster and maintain confidence in decision-making processes, and it is basic to our idea of fair decision-making. It is only in very special circumstances (where, for example, a party has willingly waived his right to an impartial decision-maker, or where *all* suitable decision-makers might appear to be biased) that observance of the rule can be dispensed with.

The rule requiring a fair hearing might be thought to be equally basic. It seems clear that no decision unfavourable to anyone ought to be made without that person being given a fair chance to put forward his case. But in various ways, especially in recent years, the courts have indicated that they accord to the fair hearing rule somewhat less importance than we might at first be inclined to attribute to it. Indeed, statements can be found in the cases which suggest that the demands of natural justice can be satisfied without giving a hearing at all, provided only that the rule against bias is not breached. Less dramatically, it has always been said (but perhaps more now than previously) that the requirements of a fair hearing are not fixed in advance but must be moulded to the circumstances of the particular case.

A great many things might be demanded in the name of a fair hearing—notification of the date, time, and place of the hearing, notification in detail of the case to be met, adequate time to prepare one's case in answer, access to all material relevant to one's case, the right to present one's case orally or in writing or both, the right to examine and cross-examine witnesses (including one's opponent), the right to be represented (perhaps by a qualified lawyer), the right to have one's case decided solely on the basis of material which has been available to (and so answerable by) the parties, the right to a reasoned decision which takes proper account of the evidence and answers one's case. The courts have never been prepared to concede all these things as a matter of automatic right in every case; indeed, there is considerable doubt whether legal representation and (even more) a reasoned decision are requirements of natural justice in *any* case.

Why have the courts found the fair hearing rule more problematic than the rule against bias? A number of reasons may be suggested, and they take us to the very centre of the basic theory of natural justice. The first and perhaps most obvious reason why the courts have not been prepared to accord all the rights enumerated above in every case is that hearings are expensive of both time and money. So, for example, it was held in *Re H. K.*,[1] one of the leading modern cases on natural justice, that an airport immigration officer—given the circumstances in which he did his job, and the fact that he was required to make an on-the-spot decision whether to allow a person to enter the country—could not be required to conduct a full scale inquiry, in the nature of a trial, as a preliminary to deciding whether a person in front of him who was claiming a right to enter the UK was over sixteen years of age. All that could be required was that the officer should tell the immigrant that he suspected that he was over sixteen years of age and give the immigrant a chance to dispel his suspicion.

In general terms, the cases show that the right to a hearing is not an absolute one, but one which can be traded off against the demands of administrative efficiency and the avoidance of undue expense. Again, it is clear from modern cases[2] that the elaborateness of the hearing to which a person is entitled depends in no small measure on what is at stake for him: the importance of the interest he is seeking to protect and the seriousness of the consequences for him of an adverse decision.

2. THEORETICAL CONSIDERATIONS

(a) *The Rules of Natural Justice and the Adversary System*

A second source of difficulty, in relation to the right to a fair hearing, is the fact that the rules of natural justice are, in essence, a skeletal version of the elaborate rules of judicial procedure to be found in their fullest form in the Rules of the Supreme Court. English judicial procedure takes the form it does because our courts operate under what is called the 'adversary system' (which is usually contrasted with an 'inquisitorial system' prevalent on the Continent). The basic idea underlying the adversary system is that the truth is best discovered by allowing parties who allege conflicting versions of what happened (or of what the law is) to each present, in its strongest possible form, his

---

[1] [1967] 2 QB 617.   [2] e.g. *McInnes* v. *Onslow-Fane* [1978] 1 WLR 1520.

own version of the truth, and leave it to an impartial third party to decide which version more nearly approximates to the truth. An inquisitorial system depends much more on the third party making his own investigations and, by questioning each of the parties and other relevant persons, deciding for himself where the truth lies.

It will be appreciated that, while impartiality is equally important in both systems, the rules of procedure, which determine how the case is to be presented and decided, are rather different, according to whether a combative or a non-combative mode of discovering the truth is adopted. In particular, under the adversarial model the decision-maker contributes very little to the fact-finding process whereas under an inquisitorial system his input is much greater. Procedural rules will reflect this difference. Furthermore, whereas the adversary system always tends to operate in a rather formal and technical way (partly because people in conflict usually want to stand on their rights), inquisitorial methods of fact-finding can be (although they are not always) much more informal. The fact-finder can foster a spirit of co-operation in the search for truth which is inimical to the adversary system. The activities of the Ombudsman[3] provide a good example of non-combative inquisitorial fact-finding methods.

The adversary model embodied in the rules of natural justice has other important features. It involves authoritative imposition by a third party of a solution to the dispute. This feature it shares with certain other decision-making mechanisms, notably legislation, non-legislative (administrative) orders (sometimes called 'managerial direction'), and arbitration. By contrast, there are forms of dispute settlement which involve the parties reaching a solution by mutual agreement. Sometimes impartial third parties may be called upon to assist. In mediation the third party is essentially a facilitator. His role is to help the parties see each other's point of view and to emphasize points of agreement; but it is not for him to suggest or promote particular solutions to the conflict. In conciliation, too, the third party is a facilitator, but in addition he may promote agreement by suggesting a solution and pointing out its advantages. All of these alternatives to the adversarial model have been used in the English administrative process[4] and it is not difficult to see the attractions of each which would encourage their use in certain circumstances.

The adversary model has some obvious disadvantages. It tends

[3] See Chapter 21 below.
[4] See G. Ganz, *Administrative Procedures* (London, 1974).

to accentuate difference and disagreement, rather than to seek out points of agreement and encourage the parties to reach a willing accommodation on their points of disagreement. The adversary system is geared to dealing in black and white terms with rights and obligations. Even when parties settle their differences without resort to litigation, they tend to do so within an adversary framework, except that the decision of an authoritative third party is replaced by a decision largely moulded according to the relative bargaining strengths of the parties. The adversary system also promotes formality; this not only makes the system expensive and time-consuming, but it also tends to intimidate ordinary people who have only occasional contact with the law and legal processes.

The important point to note in this context is that the adversary model embodied in the rules of natural justice is not the only possible model of decision-making, and this perhaps goes some of the way to explaining an unwillingness on the part of the courts to require all administrative decisions to be made in accordance with these rules. In some cases it might be thought more appropriate to utilize inquisitorial or investigative methods of fact-finding, or non-adversary methods of conflict resolution.

(b) Fair Procedure and Natural Justice

All the models of decision-making which have been mentioned can be abused. Rules of fair procedure, different for each model and expressing the proper mode of operation of that model, could be developed, just as the rules of natural justice have been developed for the adversary model. For example, the conciliation model is very sensitive to the relative strengths of the parties and great care is needed to ensure that any agreement reached is truly voluntary on both sides. This may require strong and active participation by the conciliator. Such rules of fair procedure could be enforced by the courts. Perhaps wisely, however, the courts, when asked to intervene in cases in which it has seemed to the judges that the adversarial model of decision-making is inappropriate, have simply declined to apply the rules of natural justice, either completely or in some of their aspects, and have not attempted to construct a set of procedural rules more appropriate to the case.

It should be noted, however, that in deciding whether and when not to require compliance with rules of natural justice, the courts are making decisions about the sort of circumstances in which such rules are appropriate, and that such questions, when raised in Parliament in various contexts, have often proved contentious.[5] There is no simple answer to the question of which procedure is relevant in which circumstances or to which decisions. There is no necessary relationship between particular models of procedure and particular types of question. It is up to us to decide which questions ought to be decided according to one procedure or another. For example, the guilt of an alleged murderer could be decided by the toss of a coin, or by trial by ordeal, or by a closed court in the absence of the accused, or by the most scrupulously conducted criminal trial. A more or less convincing justification could be given in support of most of these methods. Again, a variety of procedures could be contrived for deciding whether a particular stretch of motorway should be built—ministerial fiat, wide public consultation, legislation, technical studies of traffic flows, and so on. What is crucial in the choosing of a procedure is that those affected by the decision should as far as possible feel confidence in, and willingly accept the validity and authority of the outcome of, whatever procedure is adopted. What we need to ask is which procedure seems to us most fair and suitable for deciding particular questions.

(c) The Duty to Act Judicially

The attempt of the courts to decide the proper ambit of the rules of natural justice was contained in the (now much criticized) notion of the duty to act judicially. According to this approach, a decision-maker ought to comply with the rules of natural justice (and so conduct his activities in a more or less adversarial fashion) if he is under a duty to act judicially. This concept is, unfortunately, a very vague one. In the first place, the notion of judicial duty, and the related concepts of judicial function and judicial power, play a part in a number of very diverse areas of the law: contempt of court;[6] absolute privilege in the law of defamation; immunity from liability in tort;[7] the availability of the prerogative remedies,[8] as well as in the law of natural justice. It seems that the notion of judicial function used in these different areas is not the same.

Secondly, even in the context of natural justice, there are at least three meanings which could be given to the statement that an agency is

---

[5] See e.g. G. Ganz [1972] PL 215, 216–19.
[6] *A.-G.* v. *BBC* [1981] AC 303.   [7] *Sirros* v. *Moore* [1975] QB 118.
[8] See Chapter 8 below.

under a duty to act judicially. First, it might refer to a duty to follow a certain procedure conceived of as being judicial or appropriate to a court. This seems to have been the sense adopted by the Privy Council in *Nakkuda Ali* v. *Jayaratne*[9] when, in deciding whether the rules of natural justice were applicable, it looked to the legislation under consideration for some indication, express or implied, that the Controller of Textiles was required to give notice of his intention to revoke the applicant's licence; or to hold an inquiry before revoking it; or that the applicant had a right of appeal from his decision. The obvious difficulty with this meaning, as a test of whether the rules of natural justice must be complied with, is that the duty to act judicially in this sense is essentially synonymous with the duty to observe the rules of natural justice. So the 'test' is a circular one.

A second possible meaning of the duty to act judicially is that the decision-maker, although not necessarily exercising judicial functions in the sense to be discussed below, must bring to bear on the performance of his functions 'a judicial mind—that is, a mind to determine what is fair and just in respect of the matters under consideration'.[10] This meaning hardly makes sense as a test for deciding when particular rules of *procedure* have to be complied with but, as we will see in due course, there are indications in recent cases that in some situations the requirement of natural justice might be satisfied by this non-procedural idea of fairness.

Thirdly, and most importantly, the notion of the duty to act judicially might arise out of the fact that the agency performs functions usually associated with a court or judge. 'Judicial function' in this sense refers to a situation in which there is a dispute between two parties (often referred to in Latin as *lis inter partes*) as to their respective rights and obligations, which is resolved by adjudicating upon disputes of fact and applying to the facts as found rules of law determined to exist by the court; the decision of the court will bind the parties for the future and the court will often have power to enforce its decision. In other words, the traditional view is that the adversary system of procedure as embodied in the rules of natural justice is best suited to resolving disputes of fact and law as they relate to rights and obligations. A good example of the use of this sense of judicial function is found in *R.* v. *Criminal Injuries Compensation Board, ex parte Lain*[11] (although this was

---

[9] [1951] AC 66, 78–9.
[10] *Royal Aquarium etc. Society* v. *Parkinson* [1892] 1 QB 431, 452 *per* Lopes, LJ.
[11] [1967] 2 QB 864, 882F (Lord Parker, CJ); 887B–C (Diplock, LJ); 890F (Ashworth, J).

not a case on natural justice, but one in which the relevant question
was whether the decisions of the Board as to awards of compensation
ought to be subject to judicial review). It was argued that since
applicants for compensation had no strict legal right to an award, even
if the Board decided that one should be made, the decision of the
Board ought not to be subjected to judicial review because it was not
judicial in nature. But two of the judges were impressed, *inter alia*, by
the fact that questions of entitlement to and calculation of compensation
were to be decided by the Board, basically in accordance with common
law rules of entitlement to damages in tort cases. The Board had to
decide questions of fact and law, and so its function was judicial in
nature, and a suitable subject for judicial scrutiny.

This sort of approach was adopted in 1932 by the Committee on
Ministers' Powers (the Donoughmore Committee).[12] The Committee
recommended that a distinction ought to be observed between judicial
functions (which involve the finding of facts and the application of law
to facts) and what it called 'quasi-judicial' functions (which involve the
use of discretion by administrators in applying public policy rather than
law). The former should ideally be committed to courts or other bodies
following judicial procedures, while the latter should be left to
administrators. The approach came under very heavy fire[13] partly on
the ground that it failed to recognize that the judicial function very
often involves the exercise of discretion both in finding facts and in
determining law, and that such exercises of discretion often depend on
matters of public policy. For example, in novel tort cases such as
Donoghue v. *Stevenson*[14] or *Hedley Byrne* v. *Heller*[15] the court, in
imposing a new liability, was exercising a certain amount of discretion
on the basis of arguments of policy, even though it was constrained in
what it could do by precedents and rules.

It seems, therefore, that there is no clear-cut distinction between
rules and principles on the one hand, and policy and discretion on the
other, which would enable us to decide when a court rather than an
administrator should decide a question, and the extent to which
adversary procedures are appropriate. What we have to decide is which
policy questions we are prepared to leave to courts and other bodies
following adversary procedures, and which we want decided by some
other method. The main shortcoming of adversary procedures for

[12] Cmnd 4060.
[13] e.g. W. A. Robson, *Justice and Administrative Law*, (London, 1951).
[14] [1932] AC 562.   [15] [1964] AC 465.

deciding many policy questions is that the adversary system concentrates on the interests of the parties before the court, whereas policy questions often concern a much larger class of persons who have no say in the judicial process. Procedures, such as class actions, which enable the representation of large interest groups in litigation and which are quite highly developed in the United States, have not taken off in this country. This is partly because they lead to changes in the role of the judge and the judicial process: they tend to turn judges into administrators by requiring them to construct, and police the implementation of, 'remedies' or remedial schemes which will deal with the grievances of very many people.

Another shortcoming of the adversary system is that the decision-maker has to choose between the outcomes contended for by the litigants: he cannot consider and investigate other and possibly better alternative outcomes. Methods of consultation and investigation are more suited to examining multiple policy alternatives than is the adversary trial. In general, the more controversial and wider in impact the policy issues in a case are, the less appropriate is it that judges should decide them by adversarial procedures.

Given this idea of judicial function and the limitations of the judicial process, it can be argued that one of the basic ideas underlying the legal concept of the duty to act judicially as a device for limiting the scope of judicial review and the applicability of judicial procedures is the recognition that, since adversary procedures are of limited usefulness, and since a court would not be a suitable body to decide certain types of issues, it is also inappropriate that a court should have a supervisory power to review a decision on such an issue by a decision-maker following a different and more suitable procedure.

It is, incidentally, worth noting that the notions of right and obligation, which are the centre of attention in formalized adversary procedures, are of less relevance in the context of conciliation, for example, because the whole point of this procedure is that participants should not insist on their strict legal rights. Again, consultation of an interest group is usually aimed at compromise, at satisfying as many of the demands of that group as possible, consonant with satisfying a suitable number of the demands of others without necessarily recognizing that any group has a *right* to satisfaction of any particular set of their demands. This may be part of the explanation of why courts have sometimes been seen as unsuitable bodies to exercise detailed control over the award of discretionary social security payments—

supplementary benefits were not seen as rights in a strict sense, but more as state charitable provision for individual needs.

(d) Polycentricity and Natural Justice

The best known non-judicial attempt to identify the sort of question for which the judicial adversary process is most appropriate is that of the American jurist Lon Fuller. Fuller, in a famous article written in 1957 but not published widely until 1978,[16] put forward the idea that judicial procedure was not suitable for dealing with what he called 'polycentric' disputes, that is disputes requiring account to be taken of a large number of interlocking and interacting interests and considerations. Fuller gave several examples of polycentric problems: how to divide between two art galleries 'in equal shares' a collection of paintings left by will; the task of establishing levels of wages and prices in a centrally controlled economy; how to decide what positions the members of a football team will play in.

The essential feature of the judicial process which makes it unsuitable to deal with polycentric problems is its bipolar and adversary nature. It is designed for one party to put forward a proposition which the other party denies or opposes. For example, the plaintiff asserts that he owns Blackacre and the defendant denies it; or the plaintiff asserts that he is entitled to compensation from the defendant and the latter denies it. None of Fuller's examples lends itself to being dealt with in this all-or-nothing way. For example, one of the galleries might want the Picasso if it also gets the Cézanne but not the Turner; but it would not insist on the Picasso if it got the Turner; but would want both if it did not get the Cézanne. The other gallery might have an equally complex set of preferences, and the greater the number of works involved, the more complex the preference sets might become. Again, the workers in an industry might claim a wage increase of £X, and their employers might resist it and offer £Y; but the interests of another part of the economy might be affected in such a way by either proposal that neither is acceptable. A classic example of this sort of difficulty in English law is *Launchbury* v. *Morgans*[17] in which the House of Lords declined to extend the vicarious liability of the owner of a car for negligence of its driver, because it lacked information about the impact this would have on the insurance industry.

[16] (1978) 92 Harvard LR 353.
[17] [1973] AC 127.

Finally, it might be impossible to decide whether John should play in a particular position on the football field without knowing where other players are going to be: the permutations are numerous and interdependent. In all these cases some form of consultation of all interested parties and groups, and mutually acceptable or advantageous adjustment of the competing possibilities in as wide a context as possible is desirable.

A good example in the administrative law context of a polycentric problem is provided by a motorway inquiry.[18] The ramifications of the decision whether to build a motorway or not are enormous. At stake are not only the interests of potential motorway users and of persons whose land might be compulsorily acquired to provide a path for the motorway; also involved are the inhabitants of villages and towns which will be relieved of through-traffic by the motorway; British Rail may have an interest in inhibiting the development of alternative means for the transport of goods; improved transport and communications facilities provided by the motorway may benefit some businesses at the expense of others; and motorways have, of course, serious environmental effects which lovers of the countryside and people who live near the proposed route will be anxious to avoid. Not only would accommodation and compromise between these various interests be desirable, but also it may be that the best solution would be some alternative to a motorway, or some alternative route not already considered. The complexity of the issues involved makes the model of bipolar adversary presentation of fixed positions by parties in conflict seem inappropriate to the sound resolution of the issues involved. And since the adversary model of dispute settlement is inappropriate, so too is a standard of the validity of particular decisions on such issues which rests on the rules of natural justice.

It is important to realize, however, that problems do not present themselves pre-labelled as polycentric or not. It depends on how they are viewed. Many problems which we are prepared to treat as bipolar have ramifications which could be taken into account if they were thought to be as important as the impact of the decision on the two contestants. For example, the decision in *Paris* v. *Stepney BC*,[19] in which it was decided that the employer of a one-eyed motor mechanic

---

[18] e.g. *Bushell* v. *Environment Secretary* [1981] AC 75; see also *Ridge* v. *Baldwin* [1964] AC 40, 72, 76 *per* Lord Reid. See also Baldwin, *Regulating the Airlines* (1985), chapters 10, 11.

[19] [1951] AC 367.

had a special duty of care to provide him with goggles to protect his good eye, may have had the perhaps unexpected and certainly undesired consequence of making it harder for disabled workmen to get jobs in which they need special protection. The wider interests of disabled people could not easily have been taken into account in that case but they were undoubtedly *relevant*. Conversely, we could decide the question of whether a motorway should be built solely by considering whether landowners, whose property is to be acquired, will be properly compensated; but to do so would be to ignore a large number of other important interests. Very many court decisions have an impact far beyond the interests of the litigants, if only because the doctrine of precedent makes them relevant to the affairs of others. The bipolar adversary process often involves paying little attention to these wider interests. Furthermore, polycentricity is a matter of degree. How many of the ramifications of a particular decision ought to be explicitly taken into account by the decision-maker?

If confronted with a problem which it conceives as polycentric, a court might reformulate it in a bipolar form, although obviously at the risk of producing an unsatisfactory decision; or it could decline, as in *Launchbury* v. *Morgans*, to decide the issue (a disadvantage of this approach is that there may be no other satisfactory alternative forum); or the court could depart from strict adjudicative procedures and adopt procedures more appropriate to a polycentric question. In the context of judicial review English courts have either forced the issue into a judicial mould by requiring the administrator to observe natural justice, or relaxed the requirements of natural justice without prescribing any alternative procedure. In a moment we will examine the sorts of case in which the courts have seen fit to relax the requirements of natural justice.

(e) Summary

It should be clear from this discussion that the legal concept of the duty to act judicially and the theoretical notion of polycentricity both embody the same basic idea: that some matters do not lend themselves to adjudicatory treatment because they involve issues and interests more numerous, complex, and diverse than could be properly considered in the context of an ordinary judicial trial 'fairly' conducted.

3. THE RULES OF NATURAL JUSTICE

The detailed rules which we must now consider are directed to two questions: whether the rules of natural justice apply to the situation at all; and if so, what procedural steps do those rules dictate in this case?

(a) *Cases in which the Rules of Natural Justice are Inapplicable*

(i) *The rule against bias*

The rule against bias is only very rarely excluded. It may be excluded by statute (see further below); and a party can waive his right to have a tribunal which appears to be unbiased. The acceptance of a tribunal which could reasonably be suspected of bias would probably only bind a person if he had a free choice and if the tribunal was not *in fact* biased. In some cases necessity may justify disregard of the rule if all the available qualified decision-makers could reasonably be suspected of bias. This would not mean, however, that if it could be shown that the decision-maker had in fact acted with partiality, his decision would not be invalidated.

A difficult situation can arise in this area where a department of state has the responsibility of initiating a particular proposal and where the Minister also has the final power of deciding whether the proposal will be adopted. This happened in *Franklin* v. *Minister of Town and Country Planning*[20] in relation to the proposal for the establishment of a new town. The Minister had made certain public statements which, it was argued, indicated that he was determined that the particular proposal should go ahead regardless of objections. It was held that, since the Minister was not performing a judicial function, and provided he complied with the statutory procedure for processing such proposals, his adoption of the proposal could not be challenged on the ground of bias. The relevant question was not whether the Minister *appeared* to be biased against the objectors, but whether he had *in fact* genuinely considered their objections. There was no evidence that he had not done this.

The reasoning that natural justice only applies to judicial functions might not be adopted today, but the case raises an important issue about what we mean by 'bias'. Clearly, a person who has a financial interest in a case, or is closely related to one of the parties, could reasonably be suspected of bias. The rule against bias will also disqualify a person from acting as judge if he is acting or has acted as

[20] [1948] AC 87.

accuser. But the concept of bias becomes more difficult to apply when dealing with beliefs and ideas. A judge is not disqualified just because he holds views (even strong views: for example, that all rapists deserve to be castrated) which, if given free rein, could prejudice a litigant. All decision-makers have views of their own which may be relevant to the outcome of the case, and they must be credited to some extent with the ability to act impartially despite their views. Indeed, in some circumstances a certain interest in the outcome might be a good thing. Thus it has been held that a challenge on the ground of bias will not succeed merely because the majority of the members of a professional disciplinary body are members of the profession.[21] Their knowledge of the profession and its ways might be important in ensuring that they make a correct assessment of the gravity of the alleged offence against the rules or mores of the profession.

In *Franklin* the Minister's enthusiasm for the new town had a large political component, and rightly so. Having initiated the project, he could not reasonably be expected to *appear* neutral as to whether it went ahead or not. All that could be required was that he would give proper consideration to the objections.[22]

(*ii*) *Audi alteram partem*

(*a*) *Delegated legislation*   It has been held that failure to comply with the rules of natural justice in the course of making delegated legislation does not invalidate the legislation.[23] The reasons for this are fairly obvious: delegated legislation tends to affect large numbers of people, and if all had a right to be heard the system would grind to a halt for lack of time and money. Furthermore, the process of delegated legislating is seen as part of the political rather than of the judicial system. Political modes of consultation and political modes of control are considered more appropriate since delegated legislation very often deals with contentious polycentric issues. Judicial techniques of decision-making are not always superior to political ones. The procedures for and controls on the making of delegated legislation are considered later.

(*b*) *Exclusion by statute*   When will a statutory scheme of procedure

---

[21] *Re S. (A Barrister)* [1981] QB 683.
[22] *R.* v. *Amber Valley DC, ex parte Jackson* [1985] 1 WLR 298, 307.
[23] *Bates* v. *Lord Hailsham* [1972] 1 WLR 1373. The rules do not, of course, apply to the parliamentary process. Delegated legislation is discussed in Chapter 7.

oust the common law rules of natural justice? As a practical matter, it is worth noting that the enactment of a set of procedural rules which parties feel to be fair can go a long way to reducing the volume of complaints on the ground of procedure. The relative dearth of cases concerning tribunal procedure is probably a tribute to the sound drafting of procedural rules.

Statutes sometimes specifically allow a person to act as a decision-maker despite his having some interest in the outcome. A specific ouster of the fair hearing rule is less common. Here the question is whether the statutory scheme was intended to be exhaustive of the procedural rights of the applicant. The statute might explicitly provide that the statutory code is to apply to the exclusion of rules of natural justice. But this is very rare. In the absence of such express provision, the more detailed the statutory scheme the more likely it is that the rules of natural justice will not operate. On the other hand, it has been recognized for over a hundred years that the common law can 'make good the omission of the legislature',[24] and if the statutory scheme provides the applicant with less procedural protection than the common law, the rules of natural justice can be used to fill the gap. In the end, whether the procedural safeguards provided by the statutory scheme are considered adequate or not, will depend on whether and to what extent the model of judicialized procedure is thought appropriate to the sort of decision in question.[25]

(*c*) *Exclusion by contract* The rules of natural justice can apply to the activities of 'domestic tribunals' such as trade unions or private licensing bodies whose powers are derived solely from a contract between the body and its members rather than from a statute. If such a body exercises powers of discipline or expulsion against one of its members or refuses an applicant a licence to engage in some activity controlled by it, then, provided something of sufficient value, such as the applicant's ability to exercise his chosen trade or profession, is at stake, the courts will imply into the contract a term requiring compliance with the rules of natural justice in the exercise of such powers. But what if such a contract purports to exclude the rules of natural justice? Although the law is not clear on the point, there are

---

[24] *Cooper* v. *Wandsworth Board of Works* (1863) 14 CBNS 180.
[25] See e.g. *Local Government Board* v. *Arlidge* [1915] AC 120; *R.* v. *Commission for Racial Equality, ex parte Cottrell & Rothon* [1980] 1 WLR 1580; *Selvarajan* v. *Race Relations Board* [1967] 1 WLR 1686.

indications, at least where a person's livelihood is at stake, that such a provision could be held invalid on grounds of public policy.[26] The relevance of public policy (as opposed to contractual agreement) in this context arises from the fact that there is technically no contract between an applicant for a licence and the licensing body until a licence is granted; nevertheless the courts have been prepared to exercise control over licensing activities of private bodies which control entry to a trade or profession, even in the absence of a contract.[27] By extension, there may well be general limits, imposed by public policy, on the ability of a domestic body to exclude the operation of the rules of natural justice by contractual provision.

(*d*) *Master and servant*   As a matter of simple contract law, a servant can be dismissed without being given a hearing.[28] One reason for this appears to be that a servant owes duties only to his master, not to the public at large, and so there is no relevant public interest which would justify an application of the requirements of natural justice which are seen as part of public law in a broad sense. Thus, an employee (sometimes called an 'officer') who does have responsibilities towards the public as well as towards his employer (for example, a police officer) cannot be removed from office without a fair hearing. It is by no means easy to decide in some cases whether the public's interest in a particular trade or profession is strong enough to justify treating a practitioner of that trade or profession as a public officer. In a recent case it was held that a senior psychiatric nurse in an NHS hospital was not an officer in the relevant sense.[29]

The idea that mere servants are not entitled to the protection of the rules of natural justice because they owe no duties to the public, is somewhat difficult to reconcile with the cases discussed in the previous section which suggest that, at least where a body has some sort of monopoly power over employment in a particular trade or profession, it must comply with the rules of natural justice, regardless of any particular public interest in the exact nature of the applicant's job. The public interest in such cases seems to be a wider one of preventing abuse of monopolistic powers which affect a person's 'right to work'.

[26] See *Edwards* v. *SOGAT* [1971] Ch. 354.
[27] *Nagle* v. *Fielden* [1966] 2 QB 633; not a natural justice case but relied on in relation to natural justice in *McInnes* v. *Onslow-Fane* [1978] 1 WLR 1520.
[28] *Ridge* v. *Baldwin* [1964] AC 40.
[29] *R.* v. *East Berkshire Health Authority, ex parte Walsh* [1985] QB 152; but see *Stevenson* v. *URTU* [1977] ICR 893, 902 *per* Buckley, LJ.

Especially at times when unemployment is high and dismissal from one job may sentence the dismissed employee to long-term unemployment, it seems hard to justify allowing any employer to dismiss an employee without giving him a chance to put his side of the case.

A stronger explanation of the rule is that the law is unwilling, for good practical reasons, to enforce a contract of service by requiring an employer to go on employing a servant he does not want. To hold a dismissal invalid for breach of natural justice amounts to an order for reinstatement. The trouble with this explanation is that it proves too much: even if the dismissed person is an officer, there may be good reasons not to require the employer to take him back on which will lead a court to decline to order reinstatement.[30] Sometimes this difficulty does not arise because the applicant's interest is not in reinstatement but, for example, in preserving pension rights dependent on his not having been validly dismissed,[31] or in clearing his reputation.

At all events, the line between dismissals of purely private concern and those of sufficiently public concern that a hearing is appropriate is a very hazy one. Further, it seems clear that, although at common law the dismissal of a servant cannot be challenged for failure to comply with the rules of natural justice, such a failure can make a dismissal 'unfair' under statutory provisions concerning unfair dismissal.[32] Since the court has power under the legislation either to award compensation for unfair dismissal or to order reinstatement, there seems little to justify adherence by the common law to its traditional distinction between servants and officers.[33] More generally, although the rules of natural justice have usually been seen as part of public law, it may be that the principles which underlie them are so basic that the courts will be prepared to apply them to many cases where a decision by one private citizen affects another, if the interest of the latter in the decision is sufficiently great.

(*e*) *Technical decisions* Courts are unlikely to hold breach of the rules of natural justice to be an available ground for challenging decisions of a technical nature, such as whether a student ought to be admitted to an educational institution or to a course, or whether he should be awarded a scholarship, or whether a student's examination

[30] See e.g. *Chief Constable of North Wales* v. *Evans* [1982] 1 WLR 1155.
[31] e.g. *Ridge* v. *Baldwin* [1964] AC 40.
[32] Employment Protection (Consolidation) Act 1978 (as amended).
[33] See *R.* v. *BBC, ex parte Lavelle* [1983] 1 WLR 23, 31–6.

script has been given the right mark, or whether a patient in a National Health hospital should be treated in a particular expensive way. Such an approach cannot be justified on the ground that courts do not adjudicate on technical matters, because very many cases in the courts involve conflicts of expert testimony which the court must resolve. But it is arguable, nevertheless, that judicial adversary techniques are not well suited to the decision of certain technical issues.[34] In the case of students a court would probably say that questions of academic merit are not suitable ones to be reviewed in litigation so that, for example, an applicant for a place at a university could not challenge, on the ground of breach of natural justice, a decision not to interview him because his examination marks were very poor. On the other hand, it is clear that if an institution decided, for example, to expel a student on *non-academic* grounds, such as misbehaviour, the rules of natural justice would apply.[35]

A further relevant consideration, in the case of medical treatment, is that judicial techniques might not be thought particularly appropriate for the making of what have been called 'tragic choices', that is, choices about the allocation of scarce resources between highly desirable human goals such as health and education;[36] although whether such choices should be made on technical (as opposed to political) grounds may also be contentious. It is probably felt, too, that professional men ought to be accorded a high degree of autonomy in making professional and technical judgments; and, given the choice, the courts prefer to stay out of highly technical areas. Besides, if all of life's choices became judicialized, ordinary life would grind to a halt and an unhealthy spirit of litigious antagonism would be encouraged.

(*f*) *Preliminary decisions*   A decision will not generally be invalidated for failure to give a hearing if the decision is merely preliminary to a later decision for which a hearing must be given; 'preliminary' in the sense that no issue will be conclusively settled by the earlier hearing in such a way as to prevent its being raised at the later hearing. This principle has been applied, for example, in relation to a decision as to whether there was evidence sufficient to justify issuing a late assessment in respect of wilful non-payment of tax;[37] and to a decision

---

[34] *Bushell* v. *Environment Secretary* [1981] AC 75.

[35] e.g. *Glynn* v. *Keele University* [1971] 1 WLR 487.

[36] G. Calabresi & P. Bobbitt, *Tragic Choices* (New York, 1978).

[37] *Pearlberg* v. *Varty* [1972] 1 WLR 534; but contrast *Wiseman* v. *Borneman* [1971] AC 297.

to appoint inspectors to investigate the affairs of a company.[38] A related rule is that, in cases of emergency, an officer may be removed from office without a hearing, pending investigations;[39] but he cannot, of course, be finally removed from his office without being heard. There is good sense in the general position—it avoids unnecessry duplication of hearings and undue interference with speedy administration.

On the other hand, even preliminary recommendations may influence later decisions, especially if the individual has to argue against the recommendation at the later stage. This fact argues in favour of some procedural protections even in relation to preliminary decisions.

(b) *The Requirements of Natural Justice*

(i) *The rule against bias*

If a person can show that a decision has actually been affected by bias on the part of the decision-maker he is, of course, entitled to have that decision quashed. But if he relies on an apperance of bias, what must he show? The cases contain two different formulae: that there must be a 'reasonable suspicion' of bias, and that there must be 'real likelihood' of bias.[40] There has been much discussion as to whether there is any significant difference between these two tests. Two points only need to be made. First, both tests are objective in the sense that the relevant question is how the outside observer would view the situation, given knowledge of the facts bearing on the question of bias.[41] Secondly, the test of reasonable suspicion sounds easier to satisfy than the test of real likelihood, but neither test gives by itself any indication of how easy or difficult it is to satisfy. The outcome depends on a judgment by the court on the facts of the particular case. If the court feels the decision ought to be quashed for bias, it will choose terminology which enables it to reach that result; similarly if it thinks the opposite.[42]

(ii) *Fair hearing*

As we have noted, a great many procedural steps can be demanded in the name of a fair hearing. It is not appropriate in a book of this size

[38] *Norwest Holst Ltd.* v. *Department of Trade* [1978] Ch. 201.
[39] *Lewis* v. *Heffer* [1978] 1 WLR 1061.
[40] *Metropolitan Properties Co. (FGC) Ltd.* v. *Lannon* [1969] 1 QB 577.
[41] *Steeples* v. *Derbyshire CC* [1985] 1 WLR 256.
[42] One judge thinks that 'reasonable suspicion' applies to judicial decisions and 'real likelihood' to administrative decisions: *Steeples* v. *Derbyshire CC* [1985] 1 WLR 256, 287.

to consider in detail each of these steps. Instead, we will consider the general approach of the courts to the question of what steps are required to satisfy the obligation to give a fair hearing.

(a) *The nature of the applicant's interest*   In *Ridge* v. *Baldwin*[43] Lord Reid said that any body having the power to make decisions affecting rights was under a duty to give a fair hearing. Unfortunately, the term 'rights' is a vague one. Clearly, it covers property rights;[44] but it does not necessarily include contractual rights because, as we have seen, a mere servant (holding no office) is not entitled at common law to a hearing before being dismissed, even if his employer is a public body. On the other hand, it appears that public policy may impose an obligation to observe the rules of natural justice even in the absence of a contract between the applicant and the decision-maker, if the applicant's livelihood is at stake.[45] The 'right to work' is a right in the relevant sense for the purposes of Lord Reid's formula, even though it is not enforceable against any particular individual but is in the nature of a 'fundamental human right'. In Australia the High Court has been prepared to impose on a racecourse control body an obligation to give a hearing before issuing a warning-off notice prohibiting a person from entering racecourses owned by third parties.[46] Clearly, punters have no enforceable right to make a contract of entry with the owner of a racecourse, so what the court seems to be protecting in this instance is the freedom to enter into contracts and freedom of movement, both of which are so basic to human flourishing that no body should be entitled to deprive someone of them without giving him a chance to be heard.

In *McInnes* v. *Onslow-Fane*[47] Megarry, VC drew a distinction between three types of case according to the nature of the interest at stake. In what his Lordship called the 'forfeiture cases' the applicant is deprived of some right or position which he already holds; where, for example, a person is expelled from a society or an office. In such cases the applicant is entitled to the full panoply of procedural protection afforded by the rules of natural justice. In 'legitimate expectation cases' the applicant seeks the renewal or confirmation of some licence, or

[43] [1964] AC 40.
[44] See e.g. *Cooper* v. *Wandsworth Board of Works* (1863) 14 CBNS 180.
[45] *McInnes* v. *Onslow-Fane* [1978] 1 WLR 1520.
[46] *Heatley* v. *Tasmanian Racing and Gaming Commission* (1976–7) 137 CLR 487; *Forbes* v. *NSW Trotting Club* (1979–80) CLR 242.
[47] n. 45 above.

membership, or office which he already holds; in such cases, apparently, the applicant would be entitled to be told, before being refused renewal or confirmation, why his application had failed so that he could say something in his defence. Thirdly, in 'application cases' the applicant merely seeks a licence, membership, or office which he has not previously held. Here the decision-maker's only obligation is to act 'fairly'. It must reach its decision honestly and without bias or caprice (that is, without abusing its decision-making power), but provided it does so, it is under no duty to tell the applicant even the gist of the reasons for its refusal of his application, or to give him a chance to address it unless, perhaps, the refusal of the licence would cast a slur on the applicant's character (as in the *Gaming Board* case below).

This exposition raises difficulties of fundamental importance. First, the distinction between expulsion, expectation, and application cases seems to run counter to ideas such as the right to work. In each of these types of case a man's livelihood may be at stake. The same objection can be levelled at the concept of a privilege. In *R. v. Gaming Board for Great Britain, ex parte Benaim & Khaida*[48] the applicants sought to challenge the refusal of a certificate necessary to support an application for a licence to run a gaming establishment. Lord Denning said that since the applicants were seeking a privilege rather than to enforce a right, the Board had no duty to give them detailed reasons for the refusal of the certificate, but need only tell them their impressions and give them a chance to disabuse the Board if the impression was wrong. Yet the grant of the certificate was essential to the applicants' ability to earn their living by running a lawful casino. There were hints in this case of a certain antipathy on the part of the court to the merits and substance of the applicants' case, but it is, to say the least, unsatisfactory that a desire that the applicants should not succeed should lead to a denial of procedural safeguards. Perhaps a better justification for Lord Denning's approach was a desire to protect confidential sources of information, the identity of which might have been revealed if reasons had been given.

It is, however, undesirable that the law concerning procedure should contain within it concepts which will pull in opposite directions and which can be appealed to as the court sees fit to produce a result which accords with its view of the merits. It would be better to tailor the right to procedural protection according to the effects on the applicant of

[48] [1970] 2 QB 417.

denial of his application, whether his interest be technically a right, or a legitimate expectation, or a 'mere privilege'. If a man's livelihood or reputation are at stake then he deserves a proper hearing.

A second unfortunate aspect of Megarry, VC's approach in *McInnes* resides in its use of the concept of legitimate expectation. This concept has become increasingly popular with judges, but its use is infected with a crucial ambiguity. Sometimes the term is used to refer to an interest (for example, in having a licence renewed) which is less than a right but more substantial than the hope of a first-time applicant. A legitimate expectation in this sense is an interest which is protected by the applicant's right to be told the gist of the case against him, and to be given a chance to meet that case before a decision is made which adversely affects his interest. Legitimate expectations can arise in a number of ways: an agency may give an undertaking,[49] or adopt a policy guideline,[50] or follow a course of conduct,[51] which leads a person dealing with the agency to expect that he will be treated in a particular way. Or again, if the award of some benefit is in part dependent on good behaviour, then an applicant for that benefit may have a legitimate expectation of receiving it, provided he is well behaved, which expectation would entitle him to be heard before he was denied the benefit on the ground of misbehaviour.[52] In Megarry, VC's exposition a legitimate expectation seems to require and deserve less procedural protection than certain higher interests, but in other more recent cases no conclusion has been drawn from the fact that the applicant's interest is a legitimate expectation about the degree of procedural protection due.

In one sense, then, a 'legitimate expectation' is an interest deserving of procedural protection of some sort. But the term has also been used differently to refer to whether the plaintiff can legitimately expect a hearing, in the sense that he deserves a hearing, or that a hearing would do him any good. A clear illustration of this ambiguity is found in Lord Denning's judgment in *Cinnamond* v. *British Airports Authority*[53] where the authority sought to prohibit taxi-drivers, who had been prosecuted on numerous occasions for loitering and touting for

---

[49] *R.* v. *Liverpool Corporation* [1972] 2 QB 299; *A.-G. of Hong Kong* v. *Ng Yuen Shin* [1983] 2 AC 629.

[50] *R.* v. *Home Secretary, ex parte Khan* [1984] 1 WLR 1337.

[51] *CCSU* v. *Minister for the Civil Service* [1984] 3 WLR 1174.

[52] *O'Reilly* v. *Mackman* [1983] 2 AC 237; Megarry, VC's renewal category fits here.

[53] [1980] 1 WLR 582; cf. *A.-G. of Hong Kong* v. *Ng Yuen Shin* [1983] 2 AC 629, 636–7; see also *Glynn* v. *Keele University* [1971] 1 WLR 487.

business on airport property, from entering the airport. The drivers claimed that they ought to have been given a hearing before being excluded. Clearly something of considerable importance was at stake for them (in fact, in terms of Megarry, VC's classification, the case looks like a forfeiture case, not a legitimate expectation case), but his Lordship held that because of their repeated misconduct, and because of the fact that they must have known that this was why they were being banned, and since a hearing would have done them no good, they had no legitimate expectation of being heard. This is an objectionable use of the concept of legitimate expectation, because it enables the court, in the name of procedural fairness, to judge the merits of the case.

The confusion of procedural and substantive fairness is even more obvious in the third aspect of Megarry, VC's reasoning. His Lordship held that a decision-maker could act fairly without giving a hearing. This may be true, but it assumes that the only function of procedure is to produce results which are *in fact* fair; it ignores the importance of the *appearance* of justice and of creating a situation where those who are in fact treated fairly feel that they have been treated fairly and where this appears to be the case. The point of having rules of natural justice and requirements of procedure, in addition to heads of review based on abuse of decision-making discretion (which are designed to invalidate unfair or unreasonable decisions), is that procedural fairness has importance, regardless of the merits of the case. If a decision is held to have been unfair, it does not much matter whether the unfairness is in the procedure or the decision itself. But if the decision is held to have been fair, it is crucial to know whether this refers to procedure or substance, because a decision may be fair in substance, but unfair in procedure and so invalid.

In cases in which it is held that the rules of natural justice do not apply it is often said that the only duty is to reach a bona fide honest decision, that is, not consciously to abuse power.[54] The classic position is that a court exercising supervisory jurisdiction should not, when presented with a challenge on procedural grounds, concern itself with the merits of the case. This principle was recently reaffirmed by the House of Lords in *Chief Constable of North Wales* v. *Evans*,[55] but it is unfortunately not clear that the courts will be prepared to exercise this restraint in cases where they are not in sympathy with the applicant.

[54] e.g. *Norwest Holst Ltd.* v. *Department of Trade* [1978] Ch. 201, 230 *per* Geoffrey Lane, LJ.
[55] [1982] 1 WLR 1155.

It might be thought that there is a lot to be said for avoiding the time and expense involved in a hearing, where it seems clear that the hearing will not affect the outcome. Furthermore, it might be argued that if a decision is clearly good in substance and so could not successfully be challenged as unreasonable, or vitiated by error of fact, an applicant should not be able to improve an unmeritorious case by seeking to have the decision quashed on procedural grounds. But there are two important objections to such arguments. The first is that they assume that the applicant will have nothing to say in his favour. Yet it cannot be concluded, from the fact that there are certain things which he could not say, that there is nothing he could say in his favour, even if only in mitigation of penalty. Secondly, by pronouncing on the merits, the courts are taking for themselves a power of decision which has been entrusted to another body, either by statute or contract.

The temptation to pronounce on the merits of a case can take subtle forms. In *Calvin* v. *Carr*[56] the Privy Council was confronted with the question of when an appeal, properly conducted in accordance with the rules of natural justice, will make good a defect in procedure at the original hearing. The case concerned a contract and the question was whether, as a matter of interpretation of the contract, the applicant was entitled to have two proper hearings, or whether he must be taken to have agreed to accept the result of a proper hearing on appeal, despite an earlier improper one. The Privy Council said that this depended on 'whether, at the end of the day, there has been a fair result, reached by fair methods, such as the parties may fairly be taken to have accepted when they joined the association'. In other words, whether a proper hearing mends an improper one depends, in part, on whether the appeal produces what the court considers to be a substantially fair result.

This objection to the confusion of procedural and substantive fairness is not confined to procedure in the sense of natural justice. Procedure is important in its own right no matter what procedural model is used.

(*b*) *Natural justice and fairness*   It will be noticed that the words 'fairness' and 'fair hearing' have been used frequently in discussing the above cases. In fact, the term 'fairness' is now used much more frequently than the term 'natural justice'. The earliest modern

<hr>

[56] [1980] AC 574.

discussion of the duty to act fairly is in *Re H. K.*,[57] and in that case, as in the much earlier case of *Local Government Board* v. *Arlidge*,[58] the phrase seems to have been used to indicate a duty to act in a way which in some sense fell short of the traditional concept of natural justice. In the *Gaming Board*[59] case, too, Lord Denning was at pains to stress that the Board had to act fairly even if not in accordance with traditional notions of natural justice.

A great deal of ink has been spilt in an attempt to elucidate the relationship between fairness and natural justice. Sometimes they appear to be equated, as when natural justice is described as 'fair play in action'.[60] On the other hand, there are dicta which suggest that natural justice is the standard of procedure appropriate to judicial functions, while fairness is a lesser standard applicable to the performance of non-judicial functions;[61] or that there is a continuum from natural justice to fairness, and from judicial to administrative functions.[62] Cases such as *Re H. K.* and *Gaming Board*, cited above, certainly support the idea that fairness describes a lesser set of *procedural* requirements than natural justice does. There are two ways of interpreting this fact. One is that the notion of fairness has encouraged courts to exercise some degree of control over procedure in cases where they would not formerly have done so (e.g. immigration officers, Gaming Board, Companies Act inspectors[63]).

The other interpretation is that the idea of fairness has enabled courts to evade the full implications of Lord Reid's dictum in *Ridge* v. *Baldwin* (that anyone having the power to make decisions affecting rights must comply with the requirements of natural justice), by holding that some lesser 'rights' deserve lesser procedural protection. This second, cynical interpretation of the development of the concept of fairness is supported by those cases in which it has been said that a decision can be fair even if not preceded by a hearing, and that in some circumstances undeserving applicants are not treated unfairly even if

[57] [1967] 2 QB 617. For early use see *Board of Education* v. *Rice* [1917] AC 179 which is the origin of the seductive statement 'the duty to act fairly . . . lies upon everyone who decides anything'.
[58] [1915] AC 120, 133 *per* Viscount Haldane, LC.
[59] n. 48 above.
[60] *Wiseman* v. *Borneman* [1971] AC 297, 309 *per* Lord Morris.
[61] *Pearlberg* v. *Varty* [1972] 1 WLR 534, 547 *per* Lord Pearson; cf. *B. Johnson & Co. (Builders) Ltd.* v. *Minister of Health* [1947] 2 All ER 395, 398–401 *per* Lord Greene, MR.
[62] *McInnes* v. *Onslow-Fane* [1978] 1 WLR 1520.
[63] *Re Pergamon Press* [1971] Ch. 388; *Maxwell* v. *DTI* [1974] QB 523.

they are not given a hearing[64] (although the first emergence of these ideas predates the modern introduction of the notion of fairness). These cases give to fairness a substantive connotation which is at variance with the traditional concept of natural justice.

Some modern writers suggest that fairness is merely a more flexible concept than natural justice. It has always been recognized that the requirements of natural justice vary according to the facts, but cases have traditionally been divided into *classes* or *types* according to their facts (e.g. according to the type of function being performed, or the type of interest at stake). Fairness, on the other hand, is seen, on this view, as more closely dependent on the detailed facts of particular cases. Categorization is frowned upon as mechanical. The result of this emphasis on detailed facts seems to be that fairness comprehends lower procedural standards than the traditional notion of natural justice. This has generally had the result that the requirement of a hearing has been given a truncated meaning, or has been subordinated to the idea of substantive fairness. But it is just possible that the notion of fairness could be used to provide procedural protections not usually seen as part of the requirements of natural justice, notably a right to legal representation and the obligation to give reasons for a decision.

It does not matter much in theory whether fairness is seen as synonymous with, or an extension of, or different from, the traditional concept of natural justice, because in practice the courts now seem to feel free to develop in the name of fairness a new charter of procedural (and to some extent substantive) rights, without being constrained by the classic forms of natural justice. This is not in itself a bad thing. But the new approach does foster uncertainty because fairness is then treated as a concept which can only be given concrete content by considering the facts of individual cases; and the introduction of substantive ideas into the concept of fairness does threaten to alter the balance of decision-making power between the courts and administrative bodies, by giving the courts an excessive degree of control over the merits of administrative decisions.

(*c*) *The circumstances of the decision*   Another factor usually taken to be relevant in deciding exactly what the demands of natural justice (or fairness) are, in particular cases, is the factual background against which the administrator's decision falls to be made. For example, in

[64] e.g. *Glynn* v. *Keele University* [1971] 1 WLR 487; *Cinnamond* v. *British Airports Authority* [1980] 1 WLR 582.

R. v. *Home Secretary, ex parte Hosenball*[65] the applicant challenged the
validity of a deportation order made against him. The court held that,
since the information relevant to the making of the order was highly
sensitive from the point of view of national security, the normal
requirement of disclosure of the case against the applicant did not
apply. Nevertheless, Lord Denning was prepared to say that the
authorities must act fairly, clearly indicating that deportation without a
hearing can be fair.

In some cases the need to act quickly as a matter of emergency may
justify dispensing with any sort of hearing. For example, in *Lewis*
v. *Heffer*[66] it was held that the National Executive Council of the
Labour Party did not have to comply with the rules of natural justice in
deciding temporarily to suspend the officers of the constituency
Labour Party, as a matter of urgency, pending an investigation of the
affairs of the branch. In *Re H. K.* the court was clearly influenced by
the impracticability of requiring an airport immigration officer to
mount a full hearing, in the physical surroundings of an airport and
given the volume of entrants to be processed.

(iii) Legal representation

Many people who are affected by administrative decisions do not
have the training or ability to put their case in its most convincing form.
This is true whether the 'hearing' is oral, or in the form of written
submissions. In theory it would not seem difficult, in cases where the
adversary model of procedure is appropriate, to justify a right to
representation as part of a person's right to have his side of the story
fairly heard. It does not follow from this that there should always be a
right to be represented by a lawyer. The presence of lawyers tends to
make proceedings more formal, long-winded, and legalistic, and in
some cases, such as those concerned with social security benefits for
disadvantaged groups, this may be undesirable. Indeed, there is
evidence to suggest that non-legal representatives, such as social
workers, have higher success rates on behalf of clients appearing
before social security tribunals than do lawyers. A right to *legal*
representation has also been denied to a prisoner appearing before a
Board of Prison Visitors Disciplinary Committee charged with a
breach of prison discipline, on the ground that this would interfere

---

[65] [1977] 1 WLR 766.
[66] [1978] 3 All ER 354.

with the smooth and speedy administration of discipline within the closed environment of a prison.[67]

A right to representation is less easily justified in cases in which the decision-maker takes a more active role in the proceedings, although even here it may not be appropriate for the decision-maker to do as much to facilitate the presentation of the applicant's case as a representative would. But even if representation is not appropriate in every procedural model, it is certainly appropriate in the adversary model (at least in serious cases), and so should be one of the requirements of natural justice.

The trend in the cases dealing with legal representation appears to be to deny that fairness imposes an *obligation* on any decision-maker, whether a domestic body the jurisdiction of which derives from contract, or a statutory body the procedure of which is regulated by statute or by regulations, to allow the applicant to be represented, whether by a legally qualified person or not.[68] Whether to allow representation or not is a matter within the discretion of the body (but the discretion must be exercised reasonably). It seems that a provision in a contract, purporting to exclude entirely any right to legal representation, would not be held to be contrary to public policy,[69] nor could regulations which excluded such a right be held for that reason to be unreasonable and *ultra vires*.[70]

On the basis of the argument in earlier paragraphs, the existence of a right to representation (whether legal or otherwise) should depend on whether the proceeding under review is adversarial in nature or, if it is not, whether it is nevertheless one in which the applicant would be disadvantaged by not being represented. Whether *legal* representation should be allowed should depend on the degree of legal technicality of the matter in dispute.

It might be thought unnecessary to insist on establishing certain *rights* to representation, when it is clear that by virtue of the general principle that a decision-making body is master of its own procedure (subject to contract and statute), it has a discretion to allow

---

[67] *Fraser* v. *Mudge* [1975] 1 WLR 1132; but it has been held that Boards of Visitors have a *discretion* to allow representation by a lawyer or some other person: *R.* v. *Home Secretary, ex parte Tarrant* [1984] 2 WLR 613.

[68] But even if there is no right to representation based on natural justice there may be one based on principles of agency: Alder [1972] PL 278.

[69] See *Pett* v. *Greyhound Racing Association Ltd.* [1968] 2 All ER 545; [1969] 2 All ER 221; *Enderby Town FC* v. *FA Ltd.* [1971] Ch. 591; *Maynard* v. *Osmond* [1977] QB 240.

[70] *Maynard* v. *Osmond*, see n. 69 above.

representation. But the whole point of the rules of natural justice is that they constitute a framework of procedural rights which limit the discretion of decision-makers to control their own procedure.

Finally, it should be noted that, while a right to representation can be very important, it is by itself of little value if, for lack of funds or of legal aid, the applicant cannot afford to be represented.

(*iv*) *Duty to give reasons*

Here we are concerned not with informing an applicant of the case he has to answer but with the giving of reasons for the decision once it has been made. It can be argued that if the right to be heard is to have any real meaning, then it must entail a duty on the part of the decision-maker to take account of the applicant's arguments in reaching his decision; to address and either to accept or reject in a reasoned way the points he makes. Furthermore, unless a party is given reasons for the decision, he is deprived of a proper chance to challenge the decision if he thinks it is wrong. For example, it is only if reasons are given that a party can know whether a decision-maker took account of some irrelevant consideration.

The strength of this argument depends to some extent on whether the matter in issue is one of which it is thought that the 'rights' of the parties ought to be determinative. The more polycentric a matter is conceived of as being, the less crucial to the final outcome are the rights of individuals. So if a person's rights determine the outcome, as in adjudication, he should also have a right to a reasoned decision saying why he has lost, in order that he can determine whether his rights did in fact determine the outcome. But if individual rights are not determinative in this way, the most that a party can legitimately expect from being heard is that he might influence the mind of the decision-maker. In such a case a right to reasons would serve little purpose, because even if the decision-maker ignored what the applicant said, he would have no legal cause for complaint. In other words, if judicialized procedure in the form of the rules of natural justice is appropriate in a particular case, because the rights of a party are in issue, then there is a strong case for recognizing a right to reasons.

According to the present law, if a body is under a statutory duty to give reasons for its decisions[71] then those reasons must satisfy a

---

[71] See e.g. Tribunals and Inquiries Act 1971 s. 12.

minimum standard of clarity and explanatory force, and must deal with all the substantial points which have been raised. But if there is no statutory duty, the common law does not impose a duty. It may be possible to infer from a failure to give reasons that the decision-maker had no legally satisfactory or relevant reason for his decision, or did not consider the matter properly; this would amount to an abuse of his decision-making power. And if he gives reasons from which it can be inferred that he has, for example, ignored some relevant consideration, this, too, would justify quashing the decision for abuse of power. But failure to give reasons, or the giving of inadequate reasons, is not, at common law, by itself a breach of duty for which a remedy can be given.[72] It should be, if the natural justice model of procedure is relevant.

4. CLASSIFICATION OF FUNCTIONS AND NATURAL JUSTICE

The concept of a duty to act judicially played, as we have seen, an important part in the law of natural justice at one stage. There are many cases in which the duty to comply with the requirements of natural justice was in some sense made dependent on the administrator's function being classified as judicial or quasi-judicial, as opposed to administrative. This technique of relating the obligation to observe procedural rules to the classification of functions fell into disfavour, because it was felt that there were many situations in which citizens deserved procedural protection, even though the function being performed was classified as administrative. So, in *Ridge* v. *Baldwin* Lord Reid tied natural justice chiefly to the nature of the applicant's interest, rather than the nature of the administrator's function.

On the other hand, we have seen that there is a core of good sense in the idea that judicial procedures are not equally suitable for the making of all decisions. We have also noted an increasing tendency since *Ridge* v. *Baldwin* to qualify and modify Lord Reid's uncompromising approach, by creating a sort of hierarchy of interests. It is certainly true that the distinction between judicial and administrative functions is no longer central to the law of natural justice, but not to the extent that judges have accepted the proposition that the whole administrative process ought to be judicialized. The distinction between judicial and

---

[72] See particularly *Crake* v. *Supplementary Benefits Commission* [1982] 1 All ER 498.

administrative functions is a crude form of categorization, but the idea
of types of decision-making function, with accompanying appropriate
procedural models, is not an absurd one and perhaps deserves greater
judicial attention and elaboration.

5. THE EFFECT OF A BREACH OF NATURAL JUSTICE

A breach of natural justice may, as we have seen, have no adverse legal
effect on an administrative decision. This may be because the
applicant has waived compliance with the requirement, or has
contractually agreed to abide by a fair result despite procedural
inadequacies; or because the court decides that the breach has caused
no substantial injustice to the applicant. If a breach of natural justice is
held to have had no adverse legal effect, the decision will remain
perfectly valid and legally effective. If the breach is held to have
rendered the decision invalid, it now seems accepted that the decision
will be void rather than voidable, in the senses in which these terms are
explained below.[73]

6. STATUTORY PROCEDURAL REQUIREMENTS

Just as a breach of natural justice does not necessarily render a
decision invalid, so failure to comply with statutory procedural
requirements does not render a decision invalid if the requirement is
'directory' rather than 'mandatory'. The nature of a particular
provision is ultimately a matter of statutory interpretation, and since
the statute will usually not state the nature of the requirement, the
court will normally have to make the decision on all the facts of the
case including the terms of the statute, the seriousness of the
procedural defect and the seriousness of its effects on the applicant
and the public, and, possibly, the merits of the case. In general, it
seems that the courts will consider it in their discretion to choose the
classification which achieves justice in all the circumstances of the
case.[74] This position produces considerable uncertainty and allows
courts to pronounce on the merits of a case in the name of procedural
review, in a way similar to that noted in the context of natural justice.

[73] This is so even if the breach was caused solely by the fault of the respondent or the
applicant or even the applicant's advisers: *R.* v. *Diggines, ex parte Rahmani* [1985] 2
WLR 611.
[74] *London & Clydeside Estates Ltd.* v. *Aberdeen DC* [1980] 1 WLR 182, 189–90 *per*
Lord Hailsham.

7. NATURAL JUSTICE AND MODELS OF ADMINISTRATIVE LAW

The rules of natural justice reflect the 'protection of the individual' view of administrative law. The rules are designed to guarantee to each individual who comes into contact with the administration a right to fair treatment. Modern departures from and dilution of natural justice tend to be informed much more by the 'public interest' view of administrative law, under which the role of judicial review is to ensure that governmental bodies act in the public interest. In some respects this is a good development as it may lead to a recognition that, in relation to decisions to which individual rights are not crucial, the individual needs and deserves less protection. It also prevents the judicialization of the whole administrative process. There are, however, dangers in this. Judicialized procedure tends to be slow and expensive, and there is a danger that the interests of individuals will be sacrificed to the public interest, in the form of the need for economy and efficiency. We need to be sure that there are good arguments for thinking that some alternative to judicialized procedure will actually be fairer and produce better decisions, before we abandon judicial procedure. In some respects the development of the public interest view is to be deplored; it has in some cases led to the denial of individual procedural rights in situations acknowledged to fit into the adversary model, on the basis that no substantial injustice or illegality has been done. It is good to recognize that different procedural models can be fair, but bad to move from this to the idea that procedural unfairness can be cured by substantive fairness.

As we have seen in this chapter, the rules of natural justice are concerned primarily with the *ex post facto* settlement of disputes between individuals and administrative bodies. They do not apply to the legislative process, and they have not been used as the basis for securing group participation in the governmental process. It may be that there are good grounds for this approach: the expertise and constitutional position of the courts may well justify concentration on protecting the rights of the individual. However, an important result is that the judicial process is irrelevant to important areas of administrative activity, and offers no procedural framework for many interactions between individuals (and groups) and the administration. As we will see in Chapter 24, *ex post facto* dispute settlement is only one technique for regulating administrative activity, and we have already noted at various points that other techniques, such as rule-making, are largely outside the purview of the courts. Furthermore, governments use a variety of means of regulating social and economic life (such as contracts, informal agreements, and encouragement of self-regulation)[75] which are not only largely beyond the scope of judicial review, but also are often beyond public gaze.

The common law rules of natural justice must, therefore, be seen as limited in at least three important ways: they are primarily concerned with the protection of *individuals*; they are based on an *adjudicative* model of dispute settlement; and they have little or nothing to say about interactions between citizens (and groups) and the administration which are concerned with providing a framework for future conduct and relations, and with *avoiding* (as opposed to *resolving*) disputes.

[75] See p. 255 below; Winkler (1975) 2 Brit. J. of Law & Society 103; Page (1982) 9 J. of Law & Society 225.

6

Breach of Duty

1. POWERS AND DUTIES

ALL administrative functions fall into one of two categories: powers
and duties. The word 'power' is used in two senses. First, to say that a
body has a power to do X means simply that it is entitled to do it. In this
sense there is nothing wrong with saying that a body has both the
power and a duty to do X because, of course, if a body by law must do
X, then it is legally entitled to do X. The approach of English law to the
question of what governmental bodies are entitled to do is rather
complex. Bodies which owe their existence to statute (such as local
authorities) are basically legally entitled to do only those things which
by statute they are empowered or required to do. However, some of
the things which they have statutory power to do (e.g. to make
contracts) carry with them certain common law powers. So, while a
statute may lay down the sort of subject matter which local authorities
may contract about, it is less likely to make detailed provision about the
contents of contracts or methods of contracting. In these respects the
activities of the authority are subject to the common law rules of
contract law. Furthermore, governmental officers, notably Ministers of
State, who do not owe their legal existence to statute possess, in
addition to their statutory powers, a large amount of common law
'prerogative' power, that is, power which central government possesses
simply by virtue of being central government. These common law
powers are, of course, subject to statutory limitation and also to
common law limitations, such as that no governmental body or officer
is entitled to enter the premises of a private citizen unless he or it has
some specific legal power to do so.

On the other hand, in respect of their common law powers,
governmental bodies enjoy the benefit of the general principle that
everything is permitted by law unless it is specifically prohibited. So,
for example, public authorities enjoy freedom to make such contracts
as they choose, with whomever they choose, subject only to statutory
limitation and such restrictions as the common law imposes upon free-

dom of contract. Again, in *Malone* v. *Metropolitan Police Commissioner*[1] it was held that, since there was no law against telephone tapping and it did not amount to any common law wrong, it was not unlawful for the police to engage in it.

The second meaning of the word 'power' is the one we have been concerned with in the preceding chapters of this book, namely 'discretion'. In this sense of the word, a body cannot have both a power and a duty in respect of the same action. A duty is something black and white: once we know what it is that a body has the duty to do and what it actually did, we can say either that the authority has performed its duty or that it has not. Furthermore, it is not for the duty-bearer to decide what his duty requires of him. Some other (superior) body, such as the legislature or a court, will decide exactly what the body has to do and then it must do it. Discretionary powers are quite different. They give the power-holder a choice. That choice is not, as we have seen, unlimited. In fact it is limited in accordance with the doctrine of *ultra vires*. But, within the limits laid down by that doctrine, it is for the power-holder to decide what he will do. Failure to act in a particular way will not be an abuse of power, unless the decision not to act in that way is beyond the limits of the discretion given to the body. The discretion given to a power-holder may relate to one or more aspects of his activity. It may be a choice as to whether he will do X or not, or as to whether he will do X, Y, or Z, or as to how or when he will do X.

Many statutory administrative functions involve an amalgam of duties and discretionary powers. For example, the Independent Broadcasting Authority has the statutory function of ensuring that programmes shown by it comply with certain standards as to balance, quality, and decency. This function is made up of a duty to do what is necessary to inform its mind about the programme, and a discretionary power to decide whether the programme complies with the statutory standards. The decision on the latter point could be challenged only if *ultra vires*.[2] On the former point the court would decide whether the IBA had taken the necessary steps. .

Administrative functions can also consist of an amalgam of statutory and common law components. First, a body under a statutory duty to do X will also often be under a common law duty of care in the doing of X. Secondly, as we will see later, a statutory discretionary power to do X may carry with it a common law duty of care, both in deciding whether

[1] [1979] Ch. 344.
[2] *A.-G., ex rel. McWhirter* v. *Independent Broadcasting Authority* [1973] QB 629.

to do *X* and in doing *X*. Finally, every statutory, public law discretionary power carries with it a common law duty to give proper consideration whether and how to exercise the discretion. This is a public law duty, enforceable by an application for the public law remedy of mandamus.

2. JUDICIAL REMEDIES FOR BREACH OF DUTY

If a public authority breaches a statutory duty it acts unlawfully. Breach of statutory duty can take the form either of non-feasance (i.e. failure to perform the duty) or misfeasance (i.e. bad performance). In certain circumstances[3] a person who suffers damage as a result of a breach of statutory duty by a public authority can bring an action in tort for damages. But public authorities can also be attacked for non-feasance by being required to perform their duty. The remedy for this purpose is mandamus (or an injunction in lieu) under RSC Ord. 53.[4] It is not clear whether this prophylactic remedy is available in respect of *any* failure by a statutory authority to perform a statutory duty. It may be that it only applies to duties which public authorities do not share with private citizens. For example, it is unlikely that a private plaintiff could seek mandamus to enforce duties contained in industrial safety regulations against a public authority, since if the defendant were a private citizen the only remedy would be for damages once injury had been inflicted. Probably mandamus is available as a remedy only in respect of *public* duties, that is, duties which are not shared with private citizens. If this were not so a plaintiff could, by seeking mandamus, evade the restrictive rule that an action for damages will lie only if the duty is owed to the plaintiff individually because all the applicant for mandamus needs to show is that he has a 'sufficient interest' in the performance of the duty.[5]

3. THE CONTENT OF THE DUTY

As was said above, the logic of the distinction between duties and powers dictates that someone other than the duty-bearer himself must decide what the content of his duty is. Sometimes the legislature does this when it imposes the duty, by couching the duty in very clear, concrete, and specific terms. But often, by contrast, a statutory duty

---

[3] See p. 212 below.
[4] See pp. 167 *et sqq.* below.   [5] See p. 159 below.

will be couched in quite vague terms and it will be necessary for some body other than the duty-bearer to decide what the vague language requires the duty-bearer to do in concrete situations. For example, if a local authority has a duty to cause streets in its area to be 'sufficiently lit', how many lights does this require it to install?[6] Or, if it has a duty to maintain the highway, does this require it to clear snow and ice from every road and path in its area?[7] The question in such cases will be whether the duty requires the authority to do what the plaintiff alleges it ought to do. Courts are not always happy about deciding what vaguely worded public duties require of public bodies. The reason for this is related to the way the courts view their role in judicial review. Often the question of what a public authority ought to have done in performance of its duties will be politically contentious, and the court would prefer not to have to pronounce on the issue.

In a tort action for breach of statutory duty, once the court has decided that such an action will lie, it has to decide whether the authority has breached its duty or not. So one of the factors which courts no doubt take into account, in deciding whether such an action lies, is whether the court thinks itself the right body to decide what the authority ought to have done. Some duties are of such a political nature that the courts would not entertain any action (whether in tort or not) in respect of them; they are meant to be enforced, if at all, only by the political process. An example would be the duty of the Minister of Health under the National Health Service Act 1946 to promote the establishment of a comprehensive health service.

4. MINISTERIAL DEFAULT POWERS

Sometimes the statute imposing the duty also confers on the appropriate Minister what are called 'statutory default powers', that is, powers to give directions to the defaulting authority as to what it must do in pursuance of its duty. In some cases[8] courts hold that such default powers provide the only remedy for someone aggrieved by an authority's action or lack of it. This is probably because the court perceives the issue at stake to be an essentially political one unsuitable for judicial resolution. But if the alleged breach of duty raises no

---

[6] *Carpenter* v. *Finsbury BC* [1920] 2 KB 195.

[7] *Haydon* v. *Kent CC* [1978] QB 343.

[8] e.g. *Watt* v. *Kesteven CC* [1955] 1 QB 408; *Cumings* v. *Birkenhead Corporation* [1972] Ch. 12; *Pasmore* v. *Oswaldtwistle UDC* [1898] AC 387.

difficult political questions then a court might be prepared to entertain an action in tort for breach of statutory duty[9] or an application for judicial review[10], despite the availability of recourse to ministerial default powers.

The exercise of ministerial default powers is itself subject to judicial review.[11] This is so even if the issue at stake (for example, the comprehensivization of schools) is one which the court might consider non-justiciable if it fell for consideration in an application for mandamus. This seems curious until it is remembered that, in a challenge to the exercise of the default powers, the court's consideration of the issue would be constrained by the doctrine of *ultra vires*—it would not have to decide whether the authority ought to do what the Minister directed it to do and what it had refused to do, but only whether the Minister's direction on the issue was *intra vires*, that is, not unreasonable in the strict public law sense.

In a recent case the Court of Appeal has taken a more subtle approach to the question of whether the presence of ministerial default powers rules out an action in tort for breach of statutory duty or an application for judicial review. Where the duty is a broadly framed one (for example, the duty of local authorities under section 8 of the Education Act 1944 to provide sufficient schools) it can be interpreted as a duty coupled with a power. Local authorities are under a duty to provide a minimum of educational facilities and the courts will decide what this minimum is. But beyond that minimum they will leave it to the authority to decide what to provide, especially if the decision raises difficult political issues. For example, in *Meade* v. *Haringey LBC*[12] the issue was whether the council had breached its duty by closing its schools during a strike of ancillary workers. The court said that the decision whether to close the schools was within the area of discretion left to the authority. Thus on ordinary principles the court would intervene only if the council had acted *ultra vires* in deciding to close the schools. If it had not then the parents' only remedy was to ask the Minister to exercise his default powers.

This technique of dividing duties up into a mandatory and a discretionary element, although strictly illogical (how can a duty be discretionary?), is a useful device to enable courts to keep out of

---

[9] e.g. *Reffell* v. *Surrey CC* [1964] 1 WLR 358.
[10] e.g. *Bradbury* v. *Enfield LBC* [1967] 1 WLR 1311.
[11] e.g. *Education Secretary* v. *Tameside MBC* [1977] AC 1014.
[12] [1979] 1 WLR 637.

contentious areas; and it has received indirect support from the House of Lords in a different context in *Cocks* v. *Thanet DC*[13] in which it was held that the duty of local authorities to house the unintentionally homeless was made up of a power to decide whether a person was intentionally homeless, which could only be challenged in accordance with the principles of the public law doctrine of *ultra vires*, coupled with a duty to provide housing once the applicant had been held to be entitled to it, which could be enforced by an action for breach of statutory duty, or an application for mandamus, or an injunction.

5. CONCLUSION

In summary, therefore, we can say that while a failure by a governmental body to perform its public duties is an unlawful act, such a breach of duty will not necessarily give rise to the right to be awarded a judicial remedy. If the duty is vaguely worded and the court, in order to decide its content, would have to decide delicate political questions, or questions better left to the duty-bearer and the political process, then it may decline to intervene at all or only do so if the authority interprets its duty unreasonably.

[13] [1983] 2 AC 286.

7

Delegated Legislation

I. INTRODUCTION

THE word 'legislation' can refer both to the activity of legislating and to the product of that activity. All legislation has the force of law and most legislation consists of general rules of conduct. Legislation made by Parliament is called 'primary' legislation. Delegated (or 'subordinate', or 'secondary') legislation is legislation made by bodies other than Parliament (Ministers, local authorities, nationalized industries, and private bodies, such as the Law Society) in exercise of statutory powers to legislate granted by Parliament. Sometimes, in addition to a power to legislate, a delegate is also given a power to delegate his power to legislate to some other person or body. Legislation made by this other person or body is usually called 'sub-delegated' legislation.

The volume of subordinate legislation is very considerably greater than that of primary legislation, and subordinate legislation probably touches the day-to-day life of the ordinary citizen much more than primary legislation. The main reason why there is so much subordinate legislation is clear: Parliament has insufficient time to pass all the legislation required to regulate in detail the multifarious activities of modern government and to implement government policy. Further, the more detailed legislative provisions are, the more likely is it that they will need to be changed quite frequently to meet changing conditions. This is particularly so when the legislation deals with activities not previously the subject of legislative regulation. Frequent changes to deal with unforeseen circumstances are more easily effected by subordinate legislation, because the process of making it is less complex and time-consuming than that for making primary legislation. The main function of parliamentary legislation is to establish a policy framework; the main role of delegated legislation is to work out the detailed application of these policies.

In practice, however, this distinction between broad policy and detailed application is not always maintained. The powers of delegated legislators are sometimes cast in very wide terms which give the legislator considerable scope for dealing with matters of policy. Also, delegates often have power to amend or repeal provisions in Acts of Parliament. One of the advantages for the government in leaving questions of policy to be dealt with in delegated legislation is that, in this way, it can prevent possibly contentious decisions being subjected to much discussion in Parliament, and increase the speed and ease with which the legislation is passed.

Delegated legislation goes by a variety of names: Orders-in-Council, rules, regulations, orders, by-laws, and so on. But these differences of nomenclature are not of legal significance. The only important distinction between different types of subordinate legislation resides in whether they are 'statutory instruments' or not, within the terms of the Statutory Instruments Act 1946. We will examine this Act in due course.

2. JUDICIAL REVIEW OF DELEGATED LEGISLATION

In theory all legislative power (with a few minor exceptions) resides in Parliament, and so any legislative power exercised by other persons or bodies is subordinate to that of Parliament, and is delegated to that person or body by Parliament. In this sense all local authority legislation is subordinate, even though local authorities are popularly elected, because they owe their existence and their powers to Acts of Parliament. For present purposes, the most important difference between parliamentary and subordinate legislation is that the latter is subject to judicial review, while the former is not. Parliament is in theory omnicompetent: it can pass whatever legislation it chooses, on whatever topic it chooses. On the other hand, the legislative powers of subordinate legislators are limited and defined by the statute which confers them. These statutory limits on subordinate legislative powers can be enforced by the courts by means of judicial review. Just as in the case of attempts to oust judicial review of administrative action, the courts have set their face against attempts by Parliament to protect delegated legislation from judicial scrutiny. In 1931 the House of Lords held that a provision in the enabling Act (that is, the Act conferring the subordinate legislative power) to the effect that delegated legislation made under it was to have effect as if it was enacted in the Act (i.e. by Parliament) did not prevent the court considering whether the delegated legislation was within the statutory powers and, if it was not, declaring it invalid.[1] Parliament no longer attempts to oust judicial review in this way.

In addition to ensuring that subordinate legislators observe statutory limits on their powers, the courts also subject subordinate legislation to scrutiny on a number of other grounds.

(a) Basic Constitutional Principles

In the first place, there are two heads of review which embody fundamental constitutional principles. Delegated legislation will be invalid if it purports to exclude the original or appellate jurisdiction of the ordinary courts, unless there are very clear words in the enabling statute conferring the power to oust. In *Commissioners of Customs* v. *Cure & Deeley*[2] the Commissioners were empowered by regulation, if a person failed to lodge a purchase tax return, to make an assessment of the tax which appeared to be due and to demand payment thereof. The regulation was held invalid because the question of what tax was due was one of law and fact, not one for the discretion of the Commissioners, and it was one which it was ultimately for a court to decide, not the Commissioners. In *Chester* v. *Bateson*[3] the invalid regulation was one which forbade a landlord to take proceedings in a court to recover possession of his own house or to eject from it a tenant engaged in certain types of war work. The court interpreted the regulation to mean that a landlord could not seek from a court a decision as to whether the tenant was actually engaged in work of the specified kind. This interpretation was justified by a further provision that the institution of proceedings would constitute an offence punishable by imprisonment or fine. That it should be an offence to have bona fide recourse to courts of law was more than the judges could accept.

The second basic constitutional principle with which delegated legislation must comply is that, in the absence of a crystal clear statutory provision to the contrary, only Parliament has the power to levy taxes.[4] This was one of the objections to the regulation in the *Cure & Deeley* case. Parliament had enacted rules about liability to purchase tax, the proper meaning of which the courts could decide. The Commissioners could not, except by clear words, be given the power to decide conclusively that a citizen was liable to tax in a certain amount.

---

[1] *Minister of Health* v. *R. (on the Prosecution of Yaffe)* [1931] AC 494.
[2] [1962] 1 QB 340.
[3] [1920] 1 KB 829.   [4] Bill of Rights 1689 art. 4.

In *A.-G.* v. *Wilts United Dairy*[5] a regulation imposing a charge of 2*d* a gallon on milk, as a condition of the granting of a licence to purchase milk, was held to be an invalid taxing measure. In *Daymond* v. *Plymouth CC*[6] it was held by majority that very clear words would be needed to justify a water authority in levying a charge for services provided on persons whose property was not connected to sewer or water mains.

The fact that the power to make regulations which oust the jurisdiction of the courts or levy taxes can be conferred on a delegate by sufficiently clear words is a corollary of the omnicompetence of Parliament. On the other hand, by requiring very clear wording the courts can place a considerable practical constraint on the power of the legislature, and can set themselves up as guardians of the fundamental outlines of our constitutional arrangements.

(*b*) *Improper Purposes*

If a body has a power to legislate to achieve a particular purpose then legislation made for a different purpose will be *ultra vires*. So, for example, in *Arthur Yates & Co. Pty Ltd.* v. *The Vegetable Seeds Committee*[7] it was alleged that the Committee had made certain orders prohibiting the sale of seeds of particular descriptions, not for the statutory purpose of regulating quality and distribution, but to protect the Committee's own financial and trading interests. It was held that such an allegation, if true, would constitute a good ground for invalidating the orders. Improper purpose is not exactly the same thing as improper motive in that, provided the legislation furthers the express or implied statutory purpose, it does not matter what motivated the legislator to make it. But bad motive (such as fraud or oppression) on the part of the legislator may provide evidence of improper purpose.

(*c*) *Unreasonableness*

Delegated legislation can be struck down if it is unreasonable. The degree of control exercised under this head may vary according to the identity of the legislator. If it is a commercial body (such as a nationalized industry) the court, it has been said, should 'jealously watch' the exercise of its legislative powers to 'guard against their unnecessary or unreasonable exercise to the public disadvantage'.[8] But if the legislation was made by a public representative body such as a local authority the court would be slow to condemn the legislation as

---

[5] (1921) 39 TLR 781.   [6] [1976] AC 609.
[7] (1945) 72 CLR 37.   [8] *Kruse* v. *Johnson* [1898] 2 QB 91, 99.

unreasonable unless it was 'partial or unequal in [its] operation as between different classes . . . [or] manifestly unjust . . . [or] disclosed bad faith . . . [or] involved such oppressive or gratuitous interference with the rights of those subject to [it] as could find no justification in the minds of reasonable men.'[9] There is some authority for the view that delegated legislation made by Ministers is not subject to control under this head at all.[10] The argument for this is that the legislative activities of Ministers are subject to parliamentary control, both by virtue of the doctrine of ministerial responsibility and because ministerial regulations usually have to be laid before Parliament.[11] But neither of these checks is very efficient and they provide little justification for total ouster of judicial review.

It is very rarely that delegated legislation of any type is challenged under this head. In relation to both local authority and central government legislation this is, no doubt, partly the result of the fact that interested parties are usually consulted before the legislation is made.[12] In the case of local authorities many by-laws follow models drafted by central government departments; and by-laws are subject to ministerial confirmation.[13] This renders any distinction between local government and central government subordinate legislation of little value.

(d) Vagueness

It seems that subordinate legislation can be struck down if it is so vague either that it does not give those subject to it adequate guidance as to exactly what their legal rights and obligations under it are; or that it is impossible to say whether it is properly related to the purposes for which the law-making power was conferred.[14]

(e) Prior Consultation

One of the most obvious features of the parliamentary legislative process is that proposed legislation is usually subjected to a considerable amount of public discussion and scrutiny both inside and outside Parliament. Before drafting starts the government will usually

---

[9] Ibid.
[10] See *Sparks* v. *Edward Ash Ltd.* [1943] 2 KB 223, 229; but see Beatson & Matthews, *Administrative Law: Cases and Materials* (Oxford, 1983), p. 505.
[11] See p. 258 below.   [12] See further below.
[13] Local Government Act 1972 s. 236.
[14] *McEldowney* v. *Forde* [1971] AC 632.

consult interested groups[15] and will sometimes publish discussion documents (Green Papers) and White Papers (firmer statements of policy) on the subject matter of the legislation, which Parliament and outsiders can discuss and comment on. And although the content of the legislation will be largely decided by the government, parliamentary and concerted public pressure can sometimes force changes, even in legislation which is at an advanced stage of its progress through the legislative machine.

The process of making subordinate legislation is usually not nearly so public as this. It is certainly the case that the government and other bodies with legislative powers often consult widely amongst interested groups before making subordinate legislation.[16] An increasingly common pattern is illustrated by section 14 of the Building Act 1984. A non-governmental 'advisory committee' representative of relevant interests is set up, with a right to be consulted before regulations of substantive importance are made. The Minister is also given power to consult 'such other bodies as appear to him to be representative of the interests concerned'. Such procedures are designed to legitimate government action, to avoid disputes, and to reduce the chance of legal challenges to regulations in the future. But, unless the empowering legislation imposes a duty to consult, failure to consult does not render the legislation invalid.[17] Furthermore, the rules of natural justice do not, as we have seen, apply to the legislative process.[18]

Nor does delegated legislation pass through any significant public stage. Local authority by-laws will no doubt often be subjected to a certain amount of local scrutiny but they have to receive ministerial approval before they come into force and often this procedure is short-circuited by local authorities adopting model by-laws drafted by central government departments. Most central government legislation has to be laid before Parliament but, as we will see later,[19] most delegated legislation receives little or no discussion in Parliament. It would seem, therefore, that despite the volume and importance of delegated legislation, it is subject to very little public scrutiny, and such consultation as takes place is largely at the initiative of the law-maker and with bodies of its choice. This, coupled with the low-key nature

[15] Miers & Page, *Legislation* (1982), pp. 69–72. [16] Ibid., pp. 151–3.
[17] *Agricultural Training Board* v. *Aylesbury Mushrooms* [1972] 1 WLR 190.
[18] *Bates* v. *Lord Hailsham* [1972] 1 WLR 1373; but perhaps a regular practice of consultation might generate a legitimate expectation of being consulted; see p. 73 above.
[19] p. 259 below.

and the infrequency of judicial control of delegated legislation might lead one to expect considerable dissatisfaction with the system. But there seems to be very little dissatisfaction.

By contrast, in the United States the Administrative Procedure Act requires administrative rule-makers to give notice of proposed rules and to receive comments and objections. These provisions have been developed by the courts into an elaborate and demanding set of procedural requirements. In addition, the courts exercise extensive and detailed control over rules once they are made, not only to ensure that proper procedures were followed, but also to ascertain that the rules are supported by sound reasoning and that they do not conflict with the constitution. And yet administrative rule-making in the United States is a matter of acute and continuing controversy. It is worthwhile considering briefly why this might be so.[20]

Much rule-making in the United States is done by statutory regulatory agencies set up to administer government control over particular areas of economic and social activity. These agencies are manned largely by technical experts and are designed to be relatively independent of political influence and control. They have had considerable difficulty in establishing their legitimacy as legislators; there are two main reasons for this. First, many have felt that, while technical expertise is necessary to ensure that government regulations establish a regime of governmental control which is practicable and efficient, at the end of the day the extent to which and the way in which government should control the activities of its citizens is a political issue. Technical expertise does not help in the choice between different regulations which are equally acceptable on technical grounds. And sometimes there may be sound political reasons for preferring a technically inferior scheme.

The limited relevance of technical expertise also gives rise to the second reason for discontent. If governmental regulation does involve political choices, then it is undesirable that the decision-makers should be independent of the political process. And the more politically contentious the matters with which the authority has to deal, the more dissatisfaction there is likely to be with the technical solution, whatever it is. It is a plausible suggestion that the extensive and detailed system of judicial control over 'agency law-making' is a response to worries over the legitimacy of agency law-making. Requiring agencies to

---

[20] Here I rely heavily on Asimow (1983) 3 OJLS 253; see also Baldwin, *Regulating the Airlines* (1985), pp. 242–50.

publicize their proposals and hear and take account of objections injects a popular and political element into the law-making process; and judicial control adds a further element of publicity, as well as giving a say to groups who may not have been properly consulted earlier. Procedural requirements and judicial control are legitimizing techniques.

The position in Britain is very different. Here most delegated legislation is made by officials or bodies which are not, and are not seen as being or required to be, politically independent. And although rule-makers no doubt have the benefit of expert advice when deciding what rules to make, their function is seen as that of putting flesh on the bones of the *policy* objectives laid down by Parliament in the enabling legislation. In other words, delegated legislating is seen very much as a political activity. The legitimacy of political decision-makers in our system tends to derive more from the mode of their selection than from the substance of the decisions they make. We *expect* our delegated legislators to make rules which give effect to their declared policies, and we are not so concerned with influencing or controlling particular decisions, so long as we feel that the electoral process is reasonably fair and democratic.

There are two other reasons which may account for the lack of any real dissatisfaction with our system of control over delegated legislation. One is that, compared with the position in the United States, delegated legislation plays a relatively small part in our governmental arrangements. Although there is a lot of delegated legislation, much governmental activity is not conducted through rule-making. For example, in Britain public utilities tend to be nationalized and their activities are regulated by administrative techniques (such as auditing)[21] or parliamentary scrutiny by a select committee, whereas in the United States most utilities are in private hands and are regulated by legislative provisions. Another important alternative to rule-making is the encouragement of internal self-regulation by bodies such as the Stock Exchange. Sometimes pressure, in the form of threats of regulation by legislation, is applied to achieve the desired end. Such 'horse trading' can be a cause of political controversy if the government is perceived to have made compromises which would not have been made if legislation had been passed.

The other reason for apparent satisfaction is related and is that

---

[21] Auditing is also an important tool of central control of local government activity; see Garner, *Administrative Law* (6th edn., 1985), pp. 387–91.

in Britain we are much more tolerant of discretion in the governmental process than Americans are. We have already discussed the relationship between discretion and rules, and we have seen that the courts go to considerable lengths to prevent discretionary power being excessively rigidified and circumscribed by rules. The British administrative system is notable for its informality and this is particularly obvious in our approach to prior control over the delegated legislative process.

The main advantages of a more formal procedure of rule-making are said to be that it gives the citizen a greater chance to participate in decision-making and that it improves the quality of decision-making. On the other hand, unless participation leads to greater satisfaction with and acceptance of the outcome, it is of doubtful value. If the participants object to the rules made, despite extensive involvement, and feel that participation has only 'worked' if the result they favour is reached, then participation is in itself of limited value. There is little evidence that the formalized procedures used in the United States reduce dissatisfaction with the outcome. It may be that Americans are much less happy than the British about having their lives regulated by government at all, and that this, rather than the actual content of the regulation, is the main source of discontent. No amount of formalized procedure can overcome this problem.

As for the second alleged advantage, the concept of increased quality of rule-making is a very difficult one to pin down. If quality refers to technical matters such as drafting then participation of non-experts is unlikely to improve quality. If it is really a synonym for political acceptability then once again there is little evidence that increased popular participation increases acceptability.

There are considerable problems associated with more formal participatory forms of rule-making. They take a lot of time and money and so groups with the greatest resources have an advantage over less well-endowed interest groups. Furthermore, it is not clear that hearing a wide diversity of conflicting views makes it easier to frame a rule; the result may just be that the rule finally formulated fails to satisfy many of those views.

3. PUBLICATION

The Statutory Instruments Act 1946 requires statutory instruments once made to be printed and made available for sale to the public. Most subordinate legislation made by central government (but not local government) falls within the definition of 'statutory instrument' in the Act. It is, surprisingly, not clear whether failure to comply with the statutory requirement renders a statutory instrument unenforceable. This depends on the position at common law since the Act does not say anything on the matter. There is disagreement about whether at common law delegated legislation becomes enforceable as soon as it is made (in the case of statutory instruments this is when the instrument is laid before or approved by Parliament) or only when it is published.[22] The latter would seem preferable as a general rule, although there may be cases where it would be desirable for regulations to come into force as soon as they are made so as to minimize the possibility of large-scale evasive conduct in anticipation of a change in the law. It seems highly desirable that the matter be resolved by legislation.

4. DELEGATED LEGISLATION AND ADMINISTRATIVE CIRCULARS

Legislation may be defined as the laying down of general rules of conduct for the future. It differs from administrative action in that the latter tends to be more individualized as it concerns the application of general rules to particular cases. Legislation differs from judicial action in that the former is not directed at the resolution of disputes; and also in the respect that judicial decisions operate retrospectively whereas legislation usually does not.

Delegated legislation, in the sense we have been using that term so far, is legislation made under statutory powers to legislate contained in Acts of Parliament. Provided such legislation is made in accordance with any required statutory procedure and provided it is not *ultra vires* on any other ground, it will be legally binding and enforceable in the courts.

Legislation performs two major functions: to regulate the behaviour of citizens and to regulate the behaviour of governmental officials in the performance of their discretionary powers. Whereas the government can regulate the behaviour of citizens in a legally enforceable way (that is, a way which the courts will recognize as effective) only by means of binding rules of law (that is, rules duly made by Parliament or a delegate of Parliament), it is by no means the case that all the rules by which the exercise of governmental powers

[22] Lanham (1974) 37 MLR 510; Campbell [1982] PL 569.

are regulated are binding rules of law. Many of the activities of government officials are regulated to a greater or lesser extent by internal departmental memorandums often known as administrative circulars. These are often indistinguishable in form and content from delegated legislation but they are not made under statutory powers to legislate. This means that they do not have the force of law and that they are not subject to the various controls on delegated legislation.

Administrative circulars are by no means unimportant in the governmental process. In some areas, notably planning, central government wields extensive control over the exercise of powers by local authorities by means of such circulars. And in Chapter 4 we saw how, before 1980, the Supplementary Benefits Scheme was largely administered in accordance with administrative circulars.[23] Even now that an extensive set of regulations having legal force has been made, there is still a considerable body of administrative circulars instructing officials about the meaning and application of the regulations.

Although such circulars do not have the force of law and so are not directly enforceable in the courts, they are not totally ignored by the law. In the first place, we have already examined cases which concern the extent to which the courts are prepared to allow administrators to make administrative decisions in accordance with predetermined policies.[24] These policies will often be contained in administrative circulars. Conversely, we have also seen that there is some authority for saying that an administrative body having once adopted a particular policy may not be allowed to alter it without (at least) giving notice.[25]

Secondly, there are a few cases in which the courts have gone further and been prepared to quash a decision made as a result of some misapplication or misinterpretation of non-statutory 'rules'. One example concerns the Criminal Injuries Compensation Scheme[26] but this is probably not a generalizable example because it seems clear that although the scheme was non-statutory, it was intended to operate indistinguishably from a statutory scheme. Another example concerns the Immigration Rules,[27] but unfortunately there are conflicting authorities as to the ability of the court to intervene here.[28] There does

[23] pp. 67–8 above.   [24] pp. 71–2 above.

[25] pp. 73–4 above; see also *Vestey* v. *IRC (No. 2)* [1979] Ch. 198, 203 *per* Walton, J. (announced extra-statutory tax concessions).

[26] *R.* v. *Criminal Injuries Compensation Board, ex parte Lain* [1971] 2 QB 864.

[27] *R.* v. *Chief Immigration Officer, Gatwick Airport, ex parte Kharrazi* [1980] 1 WLR 1396.

[28] *R.* v. *Home Secretary, ex parte Hosenball* [1977] 1 WLR 766.

not seem to be much justification for the courts intervening when an administrative body changes the published rules without notice, but at the same time refusing to do so when it misapplies or misinterprets published rules. However, a major difficulty with non-statutory rules is that often they are not published (as the old Supplementary Benefits A-code was not) and this makes judicial control extremely difficult.

If, as is no doubt the case, a great deal of governmental activity is conducted more or less in accordance with internal circulars, especially at the lower echelons of decision-making (with senior officers having power to dispense with the policy guidelines when they see fit), a very important question arises. Since such judicial controls as there are over the making, interpretation, and application of rules apply only to delegated legislation, what is the reason and justification for allowing significant amounts of governmental power to be exercised in accordance with circulars not subject to such controls? And who or what determines which powers will be regulated by legislation and which by administrative circulars?

There is no apparent answer to the second of these questions. It is by no means the case that the more important areas are subjected to subordinate legislation and the less important to administrative circulars. The Immigration Rules are mere circulars; and much of the planning process is regulated by circulars. It seems largely a matter of *ad hoc* choice according to how the people involved when the decision is made see the relative values of discretion and published rules: delegated legislation tends to lay down rigid rules whereas guidelines contained in circulars must be applied flexibly.

As to the first question, several reasons might be suggested for the popularity of non-binding policy guidelines. A major advantage, from the government's point of view, of administrative circulars over delegated legislation is that while the former provide a framework for decision-making which promotes efficiency and uniformity, the fact that they are not binding allows them to be departed from when this seems right. This is particularly useful when the government has little experience of the area being regulated as the rules can be changed easily in the light of experience. Another obvious advantage for the administrator is exactly the fact that non-binding guidelines are not subject to the controls (such as the requirement of publication) over delegated legislation. The *disadvantages* of circulars affect the citizen rather than the government. If they are not published he has no way of knowing how he will be treated; and even if they are he has no guarantee that he will be treated in accordance with them.

It is not easy to justify the extensive use of circulars which are subject to minimal legal control. It might be thought that, if policy guidelines were to be enacted in delegated legislation, they would then operate as rigid rules at the cost of reduced flexibility in administration. But this does not follow. Delegated legislation can as easily consist of flexible standards as of rigid rules. While the law requires that rigid rules be embodied in legislation, it does not require that legislation consist *only* of rigid rules. On the other hand, if guidelines were embodied in delegated legislation they would be harder to change. On balance, however, this disadvantage of enactment seems outweighed by the advantages.

8

The Remedies: Uses and Availability

I. GENERAL INTRODUCTION

RULES about remedies are of more importance to the intending litigant in public law than they are in most areas of private law. In contract or tort, for example, the first question to be asked is whether the plaintiff has suffered some wrong at the hands of the defendant. Only if he has is it worthwhile considering what remedy, if any, would be suitable and available. In administrative law, on the other hand, it is necessary from the start to give at least as much attention to the question of remedies, as to the question of the strength of the applicant's case on the merits. By choosing the wrong remedy, or by pursuing one procedure rather than another in seeking his remedy, an applicant may lose his case, no matter how sound it might be as a matter of substantive law. Administrative law, it might be said, is more 'remedies-oriented' than private law.

It is worth examining briefly some of the possible explanations for this emphasis on remedial law. The first explanation is a very basic constitutional one. Private law concerns the rights and obligations of citizens against and towards one another. So it is clear that private citizens are the proper persons to 'enforce' private law. At the other end of the scale, although in many cases it is open to private individuals to prosecute for breach of the criminal law, it is generally thought, for various reasons, that usually it is best for public prosecutors to take such action. But, when it comes to ensuring that public bodies act within their powers, it is often much less clear how the law ought to be enforced. Should private individuals be given a remedy; or should some public official, such as the Attorney-General, enforce the law; or

would some parliamentary or internal administrative mode of enforcement be more appropriate? We have considered one aspect of this
question when we discussed the relevance of ministerial default
powers to the availability of an action in tort for breach of statutory
duty.

The origin of the idea that control of inferior governmental bodies
and officers by the higher echelons of government is in some way
particularly desirable can perhaps be found in the history of the so-
called 'prerogative' orders: *certiorari*, prohibition, and mandamus.[1]
These remedies are called 'prerogative' because they were initially
conceived of as being made available by the Crown for use by its
subjects to challenge and control the activities of governmental bodies.
The original nature of these remedies is still reflected in their form: all
applications for prerogative orders take the form: *R. v. A* (respondent
body or officer), *ex parte* (on behalf of) *B* (the real applicant). This is
now pure form, as the applicant initiates the proceedings, conducts
them in their entirety, and bears the costs of the action. It does,
however, serve as a reminder of our uncertainty about the extent to
which private citizens are the most appropriate persons to initiate
action in the courts to challenge governmental action.

This uncertainty about the proper role of litigation by private
citizens is also reflected in the requirement that a litigant who applies
for a prerogative order, must first seek the leave of the court to do so.
The function of the leave procedure is to protect public bodies from
harassment by citizens bringing cases of no merit. The respondent
does not have to appear in leave proceedings. In private law, by
contrast, it is for the defendant to take action to have the plaintiff's case
struck out if it is without substance. The leave procedure focuses
attention on remedies (more than on the merits) because 'leave' is
leave to apply for a *remedy*.

Another factor which draws attention to remedies in administrative
law is that all the remedies (except damages) are discretionary. There
are, in general, fairly well-defined principles upon which this
discretion is exercised, but no public law litigant can afford to ignore
the fact that usually he has no *right* to the remedy he seeks, however
strong his case on the merits.

In general terms, we can say that the remedies-orientation of

---

[1] See J. H. Baker, *An Introduction to English Legal History* (2nd edn., London, 1979)
pp. 56–9, 342–5.

administrative law is, in part, an expression of the limited role that common law and courts have to play in controlling government actions.

2. THE REMEDIES AND THEIR USES

In this book detailed consideration will not be given to the remedy called 'habeas corpus'. This remedy performs a specialized function outside the mainstream of the concerns of this book.

(a) Prerogative Orders

The remedies used in administrative law fall into two broad groups. On the one hand are the prerogative orders: *certiorari*, prohibition, and mandamus; on the other hand there are the 'private law' remedies of declaration, injunction, and damages.

(i) Certiorari

The function of *certiorari* is inextricably tied up with the theory of jurisdiction. In its terms an order of *certiorari* instructs the person or body whose decision is challenged, to deliver the record of the decision to the office of the Queen's Bench Division to be quashed (i.e. deprived of legal effect). However, modern theory draws a distinction between the effects of two types of error of law, which is relevant to the function of the order of *certiorari*. As we have already seen, there is some doubt as to whether the distinction between jurisdictional errors of law and errors of law on the face of the record, still exists in modern administrative law, but for the sake of this discussion we will assume that it does. The effect of jurisdictional error of law is said to be to render the affected decision void or a nullity, in the sense that the decision is treated as never having had any legal effect. A decision which has never had any legal effect cannot be deprived of legal effect, and so when we say that *certiorari* quashes a decision which is *ultra vires* what we really mean is that the order formally declares that, from the moment it was purportedly made (*ab initio*), the decision had no effect in law. Thus anything done in execution of it is illegal. This is the declaratory function of *certiorari*.

If *certiorari* only declares what is the case anyway, why would a person bother to seek such an order? Why not just ignore the decision and act as if it was never made? In practical terms, a person may be able to afford to ignore an order that he should do something, but not to ignore an order in pursuance of which an authority can do something detrimental to him. Furthermore, apart from the fact that it is often unclear, as a matter of law, whether a decision is *ultra vires* or not (and so it would be unsafe just to ignore it), it is not the case that an invalid decision is for ever invalid. A void decision can *become* valid, unless it is challenged within any time limit for challenges, by an applicant with sufficient standing, and unless a court exercises its discretion to award a remedy to the applicant. Once the decision 'matures into validity', as it were, acts already done in execution of it also mature into legality because maturity is retrospective.

This discussion applies not only to jurisdictional errors of law but to all heads of illegality which render a decision *ultra vires*, including breach of natural justice.

The effect of non-jurisdictional error of law is different; the affected decision has legal effect from the very beginning as it is wrong in law but not illegal. In relation to such decisions, therefore, *certiorari* really does quash the decision and deprive it of legal effect. The accepted theory is, however, that this quashing is not retrospective in effect but only prospective. Acts done in execution of the decision before the date of the quashing remain legal, but any such act done after that date would be illegal. This is the 'constitutive' use of *certiorari*. And, of course, unless an applicant with standing applies in time for *certiorari* and the court exercises its discretion in his favour, the decision, though wrong, will remain valid for ever. Decisions affected by non-jurisdictional error of law are sometimes called 'voidable' as opposed to 'void'.

(ii) Prohibition

The prerogative order of prohibition, as its name implies, performs the function of ordering a body amenable to it to refrain from illegal action. Its issue presupposes that some function of the body remains to be performed, and this sets an internal time limit after which the order could not issue (although an applicant can be denied the order because of undue delay even before the expiry of this limit). Prohibition is only available to restrain illegal action and so it plays no part in correcting errors of law within jurisdiction (on the face of the record) for which *certiorari* is the only remedy.

(iii) Mandamus

Certiorari and prohibition are concerned with control of the exercise of discretionary powers whereas the prerogative order of mandamus is designed to enforce the performance by public bodies of their duties. Mandamus sometimes issues in conjunction with *certiorari* to require a body whose decision has been quashed to go through the decision-making process again. In this type of case the duty which mandamus enforces is often not a statutory one but the common law duty, which every power-holder has, to exercise that power or to give proper consideration to the question of whether to exercise it or not.

(b) Private Law Remedies

The other group of remedies consists of the so-called private law remedies of declaration and injunction. These are called private law remedies because they were originally used only in private law but came to be used later in public law.

(i) Declaration

There are several reasons for this extension but the most important in the case of the declaration is that, being a non-coercive remedy (which means that failure to comply with a declaration does not amount to a contempt of court), it is very useful in situations where the seeking of a coercive remedy might be thought unnecessarily aggressive, and where the plaintiff is confident that the defendant will do the right thing once he knows what it is. It is sometimes possible to obtain a coercive order if a defendant deliberately refuses to comply with a declaration,[2] but this is exceptional and does not invalidate the general argument.

The declaration, as its name implies, only declares what the legal position of the parties is; it does not change their legal position or rights. The force of this statement can be illustrated by referring to the two functions of *certiorari*. The declaration is available to perform the declaratory function of *certiorari* (i.e. in relation to *ultra vires* decisions) but not to perform its constitutive function. So the declaration is not available as a remedy for error of law on the face of the record.[3]

(ii) Injunction

The injunction is important in public law mainly in the context of the rules of natural justice. The prerogative orders are not available

---

[2] *Webster* v. *Southwark LBC* [1983] QB 698.
[3] *Punton* v. *Ministry of Pensions and National Insurance (No. 2)* [1964] 1 WLR 226; it is not clear whether this rule is now obsolete as a result of the new procedural regime discussed in Chapter 10.

against domestic bodies, that is, bodies whose jurisdiction rests entirely on contract; but such bodies are often required to comply with the rules of natural justice and the injunction, being a private law remedy, can be used to enforce the rules against contractual bodies.

The injunction performs essentially the same function as the order of prohibition, namely to restrain a person or body from illegal action. It is possible to obtain a mandatory injunction which performs essentially the same function as an order of mandamus, that is to require a body to do its legal duty.

From this account it can be seen that, while there are five remedies, they only perform four functions: to 'quash' illegal or incorrect administrative decisions; to prohibit illegal administrative action; to require the performance of duties; and to declare the rights of the parties. This last function is in fact parasitic on the others, because the declaration can be used to 'state' non-coercively what any of the other remedies *require* coercively.

(c) Damages

Unlike the declaration and the injunction, which are private law remedies (i.e. remedies for the redress of private law wrongs) that have been extended to redress public law illegality, damages is a purely private law remedy. In other words, in order to obtain an award of damages it is necessary to show a private law wrong. The relevance of the remedy in public law is that public bodies can commit private law wrongs and so damages is a remedy available against public bodies. For example, damages for breach of contract can be obtained against a government department. Conversely, whereas a declaration or injunction is available to restrain a breach of natural justice or to declare the invalidity of a decision made in breach of the rules of natural justice, damages are not available for breach of natural justice, as such, because this is a wrong recognized only in public law. But, if a breach of natural justice also amounted to a breach of contract, damages might be available for the breach.

Because damages are available as of right once the substantive grounds for an award of damages have been established, the relevant 'law of damages' for the purposes of this book consists of the rules of contract, tort, and so on, which determine when private law wrongs have been committed. These rules are considered in later chapters.

3. AVAILABILITY OF THE REMEDIES

(a) *The Prerogative Orders*

(i) *The duty to act judicially*

We have already discussed this concept at length in the context of natural justice. It also constitutes (or, at least, used to constitute) a limitation on the availability of *certiorari* and prohibition (but not mandamus).[4] Just as in the context of natural justice, so here, Lord Reid's judgment in *Ridge* v. *Baldwin*,[5] by laying emphasis on the power to affect *rights* rather than on the duty to act judicially, was thought to have effectively expelled this latter difficult concept from the law. But the concept of judicial function still appears in the cases[6] and it may be that by using it the courts are trying to keep alive the idea that some decisions, even if they affect rights, are not suitable for review by the courts, that is, are non-justiciable.

The most important idea in this context is that of polycentricity.[7] Because judicial proceedings are essentially bipolar, they are designed to resolve disputes in terms of the interests of only two parties or groups represented by those parties. And, because judicial proceedings are adversarial, disputes are to be decided only on the basis of material which the parties choose to put before the court. If the problem is one which is felt to require, for its proper resolution, the consideration of interests of parties not before the court and not in formal dispute with one another, of persons who will be affected consequentially or incidentally by any resolution of the dispute between the parties, then a court is not an ideal body to resolve that dispute. And if a polycentric problem has been solved by suitable mechanisms of investigation, discussion, consideration of alternative solutions, compromise, and application of political principles of public interest, then it should not be challengeable in adversary bipolar litigation by one of the parties affected.

Lord Reid himself gave an example in *Ridge* v. *Baldwin*[8] of a motorway inquiry where 'the primary concern will not be the damage which its construction will do to the rights of individual owners of land' but where it will be necessary 'to consider all manner of questions and, it may be, a number of alternative schemes'. Now it is clear that the

---

[4] *R.* v. *Electricity Commissioners, ex parte Electricity Joint Committee Co.* [1924] 1 KB 171, 205 *per* Atkin, LJ.

[5] [1964] AC 40; see p. 110 above.

[6] See e.g. *R.* v. *Hull Prison Visitors, ex parte St Germain* [1979] QB 425.

[7] See pp. 100–2 above.   [8] [1964] AC 40, 72, 76.

rights of affected individuals are *relevant* to the decision whether to build a road, but, in adjudication, the rights of individuals are not only relevant to but are determinative of the outcome. If a polycentric decision is challenged by an individual on the ground that his rights did not determine the outcome in some relevant sense, the court should say that rights are not determinative in such cases and that it is not equipped to make polycentric decisions. This point is often made by saying that the public interest must in some cases prevail over the interests of the individual.

It might be thought that a conflict between the rights of an individual and the public interest is a bipolar one. But this idea attributes to the public interest a monolithic nature which it usually does not have. The public interest is in fact a compromise, the outcome of the resolution of a large polycentric dispute or set of disputes. The public interest is defined by political processes for resolving polycentric disputes and if, by means of the judicial process, the rights of individuals can prevail over that interest or can, as it were, operate as trumps over it, then the polycentricity of the public interest is ignored and denied.

In short, then, judicial review and judicial remedies should not be used to give to individual rights a determinative say in what are perceived as being essentially polycentric or multipolar disputes. It must be admitted, however, that even if this is the idea that the 'duty to act judicially' restriction was aiming at, such a conception of the proper role of judicial review has never been made explicit in English law. Lord Reid's example in *Ridge* v. *Baldwin* is probably more concerned with the procedures to be adopted at a motorway inquiry than with the question of the availability of judicial review, or the prerogative remedies as such.

Nevertheless, there are certain traces in the law of the idea of polycentricity. It probably provides the best theoretical justification of why the prerogative orders are not available to challenge the process by which delegated legislation is made.[9] The legislative process is so different from the judicial that it would be quite inappropriate to require legislators to observe judicial procedures or to act judicially. In practice the unavailability of the prerogative orders is less important

---

[9] *R.* v. *Hastings Board of Health* (1865) B. & S. 401; 122 ER 1243; *In re Local Government Board, ex parte Commissioners of the Township of Kingstown* (1885) 16 LR Ir. 150; (1886) 18 LR Ir. 509.

than it might seem, because, as we have seen, the substance of delegated legislation can be challenged on a variety of grounds by means of the declaration or injunction. But since delegated legislation usually deals with multipolar situations is it right that it should be challengeable at the suit of an individual? It is significant that most of the heads of review of delegated legislation protect basic constitutional principles rather than individual rights: the principle that access to the courts should always be open; the principle against non-parliamentary taxation; the principle that laws should be clear and published. The only ground which really entails an assertion of individual rights is that of unreasonableness, and it is significant that it is the status of this head of review which is most doubtful. It is by no means clear to what extent individual rights ought to be allowed to be determinative of the content of legislative schemes. It is probably safe to say that only in extreme cases concerning very fundamental interests of individuals will this head of review be available. Only then will a court be justified in focusing on the rights of an individual, at the expense of the multipolarity of the situation.

Another important case in this context is *R. v. Criminal Injuries Compensation Board, ex parte Lain.*[10] The question in this case was whether payments made by the Board to victims of crime were subject to judicial review. The difficulty was that Lord Reid's phrase 'power to make decisions affecting rights' was taken to refer to *legal* rights, whereas the Criminal Injuries Compensation Scheme was not set up by legislation but just as an administrative expedient, by means of internal departmental circulars. So payments made under the scheme were not, strictly, a matter of legal right but were *ex gratia*. On the other hand, the criteria on which payments were made were laid down in some detail and were very much like common law rules for the assessment of damages in tort. It seemed clear, therefore, that, whereas the essence of an *ex gratia* payment is that it is made regardless of any rules affecting the liability of the payee to pay and taking into account wider considerations, both political and practical, about the wisdom of making a payment, payments under the scheme were regulated by a set of (non-legal) rules which were and were meant to be regularly observed. So the Board, like the courts, was meant to be focusing on the individual before it, in deciding whether to make an award and how much to award, and their decisions bore none of the

---

[10] [1967] 2 QB 864, esp. p. 888 *per* Diplock, LJ.

marks of being multipolar. Therefore, these decisions were suitable
subjects for judicial review.

(ii) Mandamus

So far as mandamus is concerned, the main limit on its availability is
contained in the law we have already considered, as to when a judicial
remedy will be available to enforce the duties of a public body.[11] This
law draws mostly on the ideas of constitutional allocation of decision-
making powers and the controversiality of the duty in question.

(iii) Public bodies only

Certiorari and prohibition are only available against public bodies.
Private or domestic bodies which derive their powers solely from
contract are not amenable to these writs.[12] The analogous rule in
relation to mandamus is that the remedy will only lie to enforce public
duties, that is, duties owed to the public or a section of it. This would
exclude contractual duties. These limitations are technical and
historical. They are concerned with drawing the line between public
and private law. As we will see later, the line between public and
private law is no longer drawn in terms of remedies available.

Some particular cases have been the cause of considerable
discussion. In *R. v. Aston University Senate, ex parte Roffey*[13] it was
assumed, without discussion, that *certiorari* and mandamus would, in
appropriate cases, be available against the Senate for failure to comply
with the rules of natural justice in deciding to send a student down for
academic failure. This assumption led to an academic disputation
between Professor Wade,[14] who argued that the Senate was a private
body and that the rights of students were purely contractual; and
Professor Garner,[15] who argued, to the contrary, that the Senate was a
public body and that the students had rights based on their status
(a public law notion). Two issues are at stake here: should students be
seen as having a status the protection of which (and the responsible
exercise of which) the public are interested in, or should their position
be seen as depending solely on the private law of contract. Secondly, to

---

[11] Chapter 6.
[12] *R. v. Criminal Injuries Compensation Board, ex parte Lain* [1967] 2 QB 864, 882 *per*
Lord Widgery, CJ.
[13] [1969] QB 538.
[14] (1969) 85 LQR 468; (1974) 90 LQR 157; cf. Russell, LJ in *Herring* v. *Templeman*
[1973] 3 All ER 569, 585. See also *R. v. Post Office, ex parte Byrne* [1975] ICR 221.
[15] (1974) 90 LQR 6.

what extent should the activities of universities be seen as a matter of public interest, rather than just a matter between the university and its students. This debate is of limited practical importance in that, even if the Senate is not a public body and even if the rights of students are purely contractual, the rules of natural justice can apply and be enforced by means of the declaration and injunction. On the other hand, as we will see, the distinction between public and purely private bodies is still important from a procedural point of view.

(iv) The Crown

Prerogative orders are not available against the Crown or any servant of the Crown acting in his capacity as such.[16] Section 21 of the Crown Proceedings Act 1947 also prevents injunctions being awarded against the Crown or against any officer of the Crown, if the effect of this would be to grant injunctive relief against the Crown. The appropriate remedy against the Crown is the declaration. If one assumes that the Crown will always act in accordance with the law as declared by the courts, without the need of coercion, the only serious limitation which this situation presents is that, since there is no such thing as an interim declaration (that is, a declaration which operates temporarily pending the final determination of matters in dispute at the trial), interim relief is not available against the Crown.

The reasons for the unavailability of the prerogative orders and injunctions against the Crown are technical and constitutional. In theory the Crown is the applicant for every prerogative order; therefore, it would be incongruous if coercive relief were available against the Crown at its own suit. Further, it would be unseemly that the Crown should be liable to be held in contempt of its own courts for disobedience of a prerogative order or an injunction.

Are there any good reasons of substance for this immunity? This depends in part on what we mean by 'the Crown'. We will discuss this question in greater detail in Chapter 14. The most important point here is whether Ministers are part of the Crown for the purposes of the immunity. If so, it would mean that Ministers and their departmental officials, and servants acting on their authority, would never be amenable to a coercive order when performing official functions. This would seem to follow from *Merricks* v. *Heathcote-Amory*,[17] but there are very many cases in which prerogative orders have been awarded

---

[16] *R.* v. *Secretary of State for War* [1891] 2 QB 326, 334.
[17] [1955] Ch. 567.

against Ministers, without any qualm or discussion of the matter. The widest definition of the Crown in the cases is that of Lord Diplock in *Town Investments Ltd.* v. *Department of Environment*[18] who says of the term that it is 'appropriate to embrace both collectively and individually all the Ministers of the Crown and parliamentary secretaries under whose direction the administrative work of government is carried on by civil servants in the various government departments'. This case did not concern the availability of coercive remedies against the Crown and it may be that this statement is of no relevance in that context. Certainly, once the Crown has been depersonalized to the point where it is synonymous with 'the government', it is simply absurd to say that coercive remedies designed to control government activity should not be available against the Crown which *is* the government.

(v) *Expertise, etc.*

It is sometimes seen as a good ground for denying a judicial remedy that the decision challenged is of a technical nature, beyond the competence of the courts. Thus, the courts have refused to review decisions about the grading of examination papers by university examiners.[19] A related argument of autonomy would justify refusal to interfere with the internal disciplinary machinery of a prison; interference might upset the delicate balance of authority within the closed community of the prison. So, it would be improper for a court to review disciplinary decisions made by a prison governor, but the argument does not apply in the same way to decisions of Boards of Prison Visitors, which are independent external bodies designed to be detached from the day-to-day affairs of the prison.[20] These arguments apply equally to any judicial remedy.

(vi) *Master and servant*

Public law remedies are not available in respect of contracts of service to restrain termination of the master/servant relationship.[21] We noted the basic reason for this in the context of natural justice: the courts are unwilling indirectly to enforce contracts for personal service.[22] This rule is distinct from the rule that prerogative orders are

---

[18] [1978] AC 359, 381.
[19] *Thorne* v. *University of London* [1966] 2 QB 237; cf. pp. 107–8 above.
[20] *R.* v. *Hull Prison Visitors* [1979] QB 425; *R.* v. *Deputy Governor of Camphill Prison* [1985] 2 WLR 36.
[21] *R.* v. *BBC, ex parte Lavelle* [1983] 1 WLR 23.   [22] See pp. 106–7 above.

only available against public bodies, since it applies even where the employer is a public body.

(b) Private Law Remedies

There are very few relevant restrictions here. We have noted the unavailability of injunctions against the Crown. We have also noted the unavailability, for technical reasons, of the declaration in respect of patent errors of law.

9

Standing

1. INTRODUCTION

In order to be entitled to a remedy to restrain a public law wrong, an individual must show that he has sufficient standing (or *locus standi*). The requirement of standing indicates that the law's primary concern is not to control government illegality, as such, but rather to control it at the suit of persons affected by it in a particular way. The rules about standing need to be considered in two sections: private law actions, and public law actions.

2. PRIVATE LAW ACTIONS

We will discuss the distinction between public law actions and private law actions in detail later. Here an example will suffice: a challenge to a decision of a private body, such as a trade union, the jurisdiction of which depends solely on contract, is a private law action. The only remedies which can be sought in private law actions are private law remedies, that is declarations, injunctions, and damages. Damages, as we have seen, can only be sought in respect of private law wrongs; declarations and injunctions can also be sought in respect of public law wrongs, such as breach of natural justice. It should be noted that it follows from this that an action in respect of a public law wrong can be a private law action, for present purposes, if it is against a private body.

The requirement of standing only applies to actions in respect of public law wrongs. The reason for this is not entirely clear. There are certain rules of private law which resemble rules of standing: for example, duty of care rules in the tort of negligence, and rules of privity in contract. But these are not seen as separate from the rules which define the wrong, but as part of the definition of the wrong. In public law, on the other hand, rules of standing are seen as rules about entitlement to complain of a wrong, rather than part of the definition of the wrong. The explanation for this may be that public law wrongs are first and foremost wrongs against the public; they infringe the public's right to be lawfully governed. The government, as representative of the public, is the proper guardian of the public interest, but the government allows certain individuals, affected by the wrong to the public interest, to bring action to redress the wrong. Thus the wrong is defined in terms of the public interest, whereas the right to sue in respect of it is described in terms of the individual's interest in the matter. This explanation might be thought to fit in with the prerogative nature of the original public law remedies. It would also explain why the Attorney-General, as representative of both government and people, always has standing to seek redress for public wrongs (although in practice he never does sue where the respondent is a department of central government).

This is a very government-centred view of the matter. It sees judicial review as a concession by government to its subjects, and standing as a major tool for keeping that concession within manageable and acceptable bounds, and for protecting government from undue harassment by its subjects. As we will see later, there is good reason to believe that this is the way in which at least some English judges view standing rules.

A litigant who seeks redress for a public law wrong in a private law action must establish, in order to have standing, that the public law wrong has invaded some legal right of his, recognized in private law, or has caused him some special damage.[1] Typical legal rights are property rights and contractual rights. For example, a breach of natural justice by a trade union in depriving an official of office is actionable, if at all, as a breach of the contract between the union and the official. By contrast, a private citizen has no legal right which would give him standing to seek to prevent a post office union (a private body) from acting illegally by boycotting mail to a foreign country.[2]

Special damage is a more difficult concept. In general terms, special damage is damage over and above that suffered by the public at large, or some significant section of it affected by the decision. For example, a boycott of mail to a foreign country adversely affects all persons who might wish to use the mail service to that country. It would inflict

---

[1] *Boyce* v. *Paddington Corporation* [1903] 1 Ch. 109; *Gouriet* v. *Union of Post Office Workers* [1978] AC 435; *Barrs* v. *Bethell* [1982] Ch. 294; *Ashby* v. *Ebdon* [1985] 2 WLR 279. It may be that if a public law action is brought by ordinary writ procedure (see p. 167 below) the standing rule is the same as that for a public law action brought under RSC Ord. 53 (see p. 159 below): *Steeples* v. *Derbyshire CC* [1985] 1 WLR 256, 293–6.
[2] *Gouriet* [1978] AC 435.

special damage on a person who had just posted a business letter, the purpose of which would be defeated by any exceptional delay. Special damage is not defined in terms of the right of the plaintiff which has been invaded, but in terms of the effect on him of the challenged action. It seems that the requirement of special damage may be satisfied by potential damage, and it may be possible to rephrase the requirement in terms of the plaintiff having a special *interest in or concern with* the challenged action. So, for example, it may be that a keen walker would have a special interest in a stretch of country where he frequently walked, which would entitle him to challenge a decision to grant planning permission to develop it, whereas an ordinary member of the public or even of some environmental group in a different area might not have. The question of whether someone has suffered special damage or not depends on the facts of the particular case, and so is very much in the discretion of the court.

There is a procedure by which a plaintiff in a private law action may be able to seek redress for a public law wrong, even though he cannot establish sufficient standing in accordance with the above rules. This is called the relator procedure (*Attorney-General (ex relatione A)* v. *B*). It will be recalled that the Attorney-General always has standing to sue in respect of public law wrongs. If a private individual without standing can persuade the Attorney-General to 'lend his name' to the action, it can go ahead. The relator, as the real complainant is called, conducts the proceedings and bears their cost, but the Attorney-General is the nominal plaintiff. The most famous recent attempt to use this procedure is *Gouriet* v. *Union of Post Office Workers*.[3] In that case Gouriet sought an injunction to restrain the union from instructing its members to boycott mail to South Africa, as a protest against the South African government's policy of apartheid. The Attorney-General refused to lend his name to the action, and the House of Lords held that this refusal could not be challenged in an action for judicial review. One of the arguments used to justify this result was that the Attorney-General's decision could and should be questioned, if at all, only in Parliament. This is somewhat unrealistic because, provided the government has a majority in the House of Commons, any parliamentary challenge to such a decision on political grounds is unlikely to be successful. The situation in the *Gouriet* case was a politically sensitive one and this may well justify the court's refusal in

<hr>

[3] Ibid.

that case to review the Attorney-General's decision, but it is not clear that such refusal would be justified in every case.

Another difficulty in the *Gouriet* case was that the applicant sought an injunction to restrain a threatened breach of the criminal law. The basic principle of English criminal law, that a man should be presumed to be innocent until he is proved *to have committed* a criminal offence, produces another principle. This is that, except in very special cases, injunctive relief will not be granted to restrain threatened breaches of the criminal law before they are committed. In general, such an injunction will be granted only when offences have been committed in the past and it appears that mere prosecution will not deter further breaches of the law in the future.[4]

3. PUBLIC LAW ACTIONS

Public law actions may be actions in respect of public law wrongs, or (perhaps) in respect of private law wrongs, where the case has some significant public law element. All applications for a prerogative order are public law actions. We will discuss the definition of public law actions in more detail later. The standing rule for public law actions is laid down in RSC Ord. 53 r. 3(7).[5] Order 53 contains the procedural rules governing applications, *inter alia*, for prerogative orders. The rule says that the court shall not grant leave to apply for judicial review (as the Order 53 procedure is called) unless the applicant has a sufficient interest in the matter to which the application relates. It is worth noting that, in its terms, this rule applies only to applications for leave. As we will see later, the applicant in a public law action must first seek leave to apply for judicial review, and only when leave has been granted will his application actually be heard. The rules contain no provision about standing at the hearing stage, but the basic test of sufficient interest does appear to apply at the hearing stage, as well as at the leave stage.

Before the provision contained in rule 3(7) was enacted, the law governing standing to apply for prerogative orders was, in simplified terms, as follows: any person could apply for *certiorari* or prohibition,

---

[4] *Stoke on Trent CC* v. *B. & O. (Retail) Ltd.* [1984] 2 WLR 929. This case was an action by the local authority under s. 222 of the Local Government Act 1972 which gives local authorities standing to sue in their own name, where the authority considers it expedient for the promotion or protection of the interests of inhabitants in its area.
[5] See also Supreme Court Act 1981 s. 31(3).

provided he had a genuine grievance or, in other words, provided he was a person aggrieved by the challenged decision.[6] A genuine grievance did not have to be financial. It could, for example, consist of a complaint that a rating list had been prepared on an unfair basis, in the sense that another ratepayer's property had been undervalued, even if a revaluation would not lead to a reduction in the complainant's rate bill.[7] The crucial difference between special interest, or special damage, and genuine grievance was that a special interest was one greater than that of other affected people generally, whereas a genuine grievance need be no different in type or intensity than that of other affected persons.

The statute in pursuance of which the challenged action was done would provide guidance to the court as to what grievances were to be considered as giving a genuine cause for complaint. For example, an inhabitant of Glasgow would be unlikely to be held to have a genuine interest in a planning decision in Oxford. Persons without a genuine grievance have been called 'busybodies', as people who interfere in things which do not concern them. Usually the statute would provide only limited guidance on the question of genuine grievance, and the court would have quite a bit of freedom in deciding which grievances were genuine.

The law regarding mandamus was less clear. There was authority for the view that the test was 'person aggrieved'. But there were also cases which held that the applicant for mandamus must show that some legal right of his had been infringed by the challenged decision. For example, in *R.* v. *Hereford Corporation, ex parte Harrower*[8] it was held that electrical contractors, as such, had no right to complain that the council had not followed proper tendering procedures in letting out a contract for the installation of central heating.

It is not yet clear what impact the enactment of rule 3(7) has had on

---

[6] *R.* v. *Paddington Valuation Officer, ex parte Peachey Property Corporation* [1966] 1 QB 380.

[7] *Arsenal Football Club* v. *Ende* [1979] AC 1. This was actually an application under a statutory provision to have a decision quashed. The prerogative orders are, of course, common law remedies, but many statutes also contain provisions allowing decisions of administrative authorities to be challenged on specified grounds. Such provisions are sometimes said to make available a remedy of 'statutory *certiorari*'. The standing rule for such remedies is usually that any 'person aggrieved' may apply. This rule appears to be indistinguishable from that for common law *certiorari*, except perhaps in the respect that in an application for statutory *certiorari* the statutory context would clearly be paramount in defining 'genuine grievance'.

[8] [1970] 1 WLR 1424.

these rules.[9] The leading case on the interpretation of the rule is *R*. v. *Inland Revenue Commissioners, ex parte National Federation of Self-Employed and Small Businesses Ltd.*[10] (the *Fleet Street Casuals* case). In this case the applicant challenged a tax amnesty granted by the Revenue to casual workers in Fleet Street: the Revenue had agreed not to seek to recover unpaid tax, provided the workers ceased their tax evasion tactics in the future. It was held that the applicants lacked a sufficient interest in the matter because the Revenue had acted within the discretion permitted to it in the day-to-day administration of the tax system. Some of the judges thought that one effect of rule 3(7) was to abolish the distinction between mandamus, on the one hand, and *certiorari* and prohibition on the other, but at least two of their Lordships were less certain on this point.

Other important points emerge from this case. First, the question of what is a sufficient interest is partly a question of legal principle—what do earlier cases say about standing?—and partly a question of fact to be decided in the light of circumstances of the case before the court. So it is impossible to be entirely sure, in advance of litigation, whether any particular applicant has a sufficient interest. Secondly, the question of sufficient interest has to be judged in the light of the relevant statutory provisions—what do they say or suggest about who is to be allowed to challenge decisions made under the statute?—and also in the light of the substance of the applicant's complaint. Looking at the substance of the complaint has a number of purposes. There is no point granting leave to a person with sufficient interest if it is clear, for example, that he has a hopeless case on the merits which is bound to fail; or that the case raises only non-justiciable issues. Secondly, whether the applicant's interest is sufficient depends to some extent on the seriousness of the alleged illegality. Whatever the applicant's interest, the more serious the illegality, the more likely that interest is to be sufficient.

This last aspect of the case raises a fundamental question about the nature and function of standing rules. There is a sense in which standing is a preliminary question, separate from that of the substance and merits of the applicant's case: standing rules determine entitlement to

---

[9] It has clearly had no direct impact on the genuine grievance rule for statutory *certiorari* (see n. 7 above) since the phrase 'person aggrieved' is contained in the statute. But in practice the difference between 'genuine grievance' and 'sufficient interest' in this context is probably unimportant.

[10] [1982] AC 617.

raise and argue the issue of illegality, and it makes little sense to say that entitlement to argue the merits of the case depends on whether one has a good case on the merits. Only if the chance of failure at the end of the day approaches certainty should the likely outcome affect the question of access to the court.

But this argument assumes that there is some value in separating the issue of entitlement to apply for judicial review, from the question of entitlement to a remedy at the end of the day. A counter argument might be that standing rules are just one mechanism for weeding out hopeless and frivolous cases at an early stage and protecting government bodies (rightly or wrongly) from harassment by 'professional litigants' (who else would expend the time and resources necessary to mount a hopeless case?). If this assertion is correct, then it would not matter if the standing requirement was abolished entirely, provided some other mechanism was put in its place for weeding out hopeless and crank cases. The requirement of obtaining leave performs this function, and we will see later that some judges seem to discern quite a direct relationship between relaxation of standing rules and strict enforcement of the leave requirement. So we might conclude that there is no need to have stringent standing rules (or, indeed, any standing rule at all) if other means to weed out hopeless cases are provided. The 'sufficient interest' test as interpreted in the *Fleet Street Casuals* case can be seen as giving partial effect to such an argument.

This explanation assumes, however, that the requirement of sufficient interest is a liberal standing rule, in the sense that it makes access to the courts to challenge administrative action very easy, and so shifts the burden of weeding out weak cases to other mechanisms. Since there are as yet very few cases which discuss the rule in detail, it is hard to say how liberal it will turn out to be. The most important point to note is that the phrase 'sufficient interest' is very vague and leaves it largely up to the court to decide what interests are sufficient. If the substance of the complaint is to be relevant to this issue, the courts are given even more leeway in judging whether a particular interest is sufficient. It *is* clear that the requirement of standing has not been abolished—rule 3(7) has been re-enacted in the Supreme Court Act 1981 s. 31(3)—and the main effect of the rule seems to have been to equip the court with a flexible and unpredictable tool for refusing a remedy.

We have seen that, according to the *Fleet Street Casuals* case, the question of sufficient interest is to some undefined extent a question of legal principle. What are the principles involved? There are not very many, in fact. It is clear that *ratepayers* have standing to challenge a wide variety of decisions, including expenditure decisions, by local authorities; whereas it is clear from the *Fleet Street Casuals* case that the right of taxpayers to challenge decisions of the Revenue, let alone of central government, is limited. It will be recalled that local authorities owe a fiduciary duty to their ratepayers in the use of rate revenue, and the right of ratepayers to challenge local authority decisions is no doubt a corollary of this duty. Central government, by contrast, owes no special legal duties to taxpayers in the use of the 'tax pound'. There has been quite a bit of litigation in the United States in which taxpayers have sought to challenge some use to which taxes have been put. The American cases draw a distinction between genuine personal interest (which gives a right to sue) and generalized grievances about the way the country is being run (which do not). In England the courts are almost certain to take the view that the way taxes are spent is a political question which the courts are not the proper bodies to consider, and that no taxpayer has sufficient interest to raise this matter in court.[11] Is the difference between the challengeability of central and local government spending decisions justified?

Neighbours have sufficient interest to challenge planning decisions in respect of neighbouring land. In one case an applicant for a street trader's licence was held to have standing to challenge the grant of the licence to a *competitor*. In terms of that aspect of the *Fleet Street Casuals* case which relates sufficient interest to the facts and merits of the applicant's case, it is probably correct to say that ratepayers challenging decisions of local authorities, competitors challenging decisions affecting their business activities, and neighbours challenging planning decisions would be held to have a sufficient interest, unless other facts of the case provided very strong ground for denying the existence of such an interest. By contrast, taxpayer standing is likely to be heavily dependent on the detailed facts. Broad 'standing categories' of this nature are clearly desirable because they inject a degree of certainty and predictability into the question of standing.

Some other recent cases deserve mention. It has been held, for example, that a gypsy, living on a caravan site provided by a local authority under statute, has sufficient interest to challenge a decision

---

[11] But a taxpayer might have standing to challenge decisions affecting spending on technical grounds which do not question the substance of the spending decision: *R. v. Her Majesty's Treasury, ex parte Smedley* [1985] 2 WLR 576, 581, 583–4.

by the authority no longer to provide the site or any alternative; and to challenge a decision by the Minister not to exercise his statutory default power. Of considerable importance is a series of cases which introduce the concept of 'legitimate expectation' into the law of standing. A legitimate expectation, as we have seen, arises when a government agency, by its words or conduct, leads the citizen reasonably to expect that it will act in a particular way. If the agency then acts differently it may be held to have acted unfairly and illegally, at least if it has not given the citizen a chance to make representations as to why he should be treated in the way he expected he would be. Such legitimate expectations are not rights in the classic sense, but it has been held in a number of cases that, if a person claims that he has a legitimate expectation, this will give him standing to make an application for judicial review, unless his claim is totally frivolous. One case concerned a change in the criteria according to which immigrant children whom British residents wished to adopt would be given leave to enter Britain.[12] In another it was said that the legitimate expectation of a prisoner that he would be allowed maximum parole, if no disciplinary award of forfeiture of remission of sentence had been made against him, gave him sufficient interest to challenge the award.[13] A third case concerned changes in the policy guidelines governing release of prisoners from gaol before expiry of their sentences.[14] These cases are significant because they illustrate one of the ways in which standing is related to the merits of the case. The notion of legitimate expectation concerns whether the applicant has a case on the merits, but the claim that such an expectation exists, provided it is not prima facie ludicrous, will give the claimant standing to argue the merits of his claim.

Finally, it seems clear that the meaning of 'sufficient interest' is related to some extent to the ground on which the decision is being challenged. For example, it is likely that the only person who would be held to have sufficient interest to challenge a decision, on the ground of breach of natural justice, would be the person denied a hearing, because the rules of natural justice are designed to protect individual rights. But if the ground of challenge was unreasonableness, then a wider range of affected persons would probably be able to demonstrate sufficient interest, because the notion of unreasonableness defines the

[12] *R. v. Home Secretry, ex parte Khan* [1984] 1 WLR 1337, esp. 1345A–B *per* Parker, LJ.
[13] *O'Reilly* v. *Mackman* [1983] 2 AC 237, 275 *per* Lord Diplock.
[14] *In re Findlay* [1984] 3 WLR 1159, 1173.

limits of legal action (and in one sense everyone has an interest in the government acting legally) rather than the limits of individual rights.

The same point can be made in a different way. Defining sufficient interest is relatively easy where one or more persons are more seriously affected by a decision than people generally. But where a decision affects everyone in general and no one in particular it is much harder to define sufficient interest. The cases of the neighbouring landowner, the competitor, and the gypsies, mentioned above, fall into the former category. The cases of the ratepayer and the taxpayer, as well as the environmental pressure group[15] mentioned earlier, fall into the latter category. The *Fleet Street Casuals* case is primarily concerned with this type of case, and it shows how difficult the question is of who ought to be allowed to challenge, in the courts, governmental action which affects society generally. The question raises acutely the issue of the proper constitutional and political role of the courts.

4. THE FUNCTION OF STANDING RULES

What is the function of standing rules? We have mentioned one function already: to protect public bodies from harassment by professional litigants. Others have been suggested: to ration scarce judicial resources; to ensure that the argument on the merits is presented in the best possible way, by a person with a real interest in presenting it; to ensure that people do not meddle paternalistically in the affairs of others; to ensure that the applicant has a *personal interest* not just an *ideological concern* in the outcome. This last function is important in the task of establishing the boundary between the judicial and the political realms, and of keeping the courts out of political fights. Ideology is properly pursued in political forums, not in the courts.

A useful way of approaching the issue of functions is in terms of the three models of administrative law which we considered in Chapter 1. If one views the aim of judicial review as the protection of the individual, this would suggest and justify standing rules which require the applicant to show that he as an individual is specially affected. On the 'protection of interests' view of judicial review, standing rules would only require that the plaintiff establish that he

---

[15] It appears that an interest or pressure group will have standing if its members have a sufficient interest, and the status of the group entity as representative of its members can be established expressly or impliedly from the actions of the members.

shares (or perhaps represents) some *interest* or point of view not generally accepted by the decision-makers who represent the majority. If one adopts the 'public interest' view of administrative law (according to which the most important thing is that administrative illegality should be rooted out) one might support an absolutely minimal standing requirement such as 'taxpayer' or 'citizen', or even no requirement at all ('any person'). The ultimate logic of the public interest approach is the abolition of standing rules: the only question to be answered on this approach concerns the merits of the arguments about illegality. By retaining standing rules but injecting into them substantive issues, the House of Lords in the *Fleet Street Casuals* case has produced a confusing amalgam.

The Application for Judicial Review

I. INTRODUCTION

ONE of the results of the emphasis on remedies in administrative law is that the procedure for applying for those remedies (which is separate from the procedures which are used in ordinary private law actions) is central to an understanding of the position of the public law litigant. A new procedural regime was introduced in 1978, the impact of which is only now being seen and appreciated. Although the new regime extends to public law remedies and some of the procedural features of private law actions, the fact that there is still a separate procedural regime for public law remedies is of great importance.

The public law procedure is found in Order 53 of the Rules of the Supreme Court (RSC), some provisions of which have been re-enacted in statutory form in section 31 of the Supreme Court Act 1981. Order 53 lays down the procedure for what are called Applications for Judicial Review (AJRs). The AJR is not itself a remedy but rather a procedural umbrella under which can be sought, in any combination which is compatible with their nature and function, any of the prerogative orders plus declarations and injunctions. A claim for damages can also be made under the umbrella of an AJR.

The AJR procedure is the *only* procedure by which the prerogative orders can be sought. But since the declaration and injunction are remedies in private law as well as in public law, there is also a procedure contained elsewhere in the Rules (which I shall refer to as the 'ordinary writ procedure')[1] for applying for these remedies in cases not covered by Order 53. Rule 1(2) of Order 53 provides that the AJR

---

[1] This phrase is inaccurate. Private law proceedings can be begun by writ or by originating summons. The latter procedure is appropriate in cases in which there are no substantial disputes of fact. In procedural terms, the AJR procedure is very like the originating summons procedure. The justification for contrasting the AJR with ordinary writ procedure is that it is the differences between the AJR procedure and writ procedure which give such importance to the existence of a separate procedure for public law cases. The main point is that although AJR procedure is like originating summons procedure, public law cases are not necessarily cases in which disputes of fact do not arise.

procedure *may* (but need not) be used by an applicant who seeks a declaration or an injunction in what can loosely be called 'cases in public law'.

In short, we can say that, in relation to applications for a declaration or injunction, the AJR procedure is meant for use in public law cases while the ordinary writ procedure is meant for private law cases in which the plaintiff seeks redress for a public law wrong (as well, of course, as cases in which he seeks redress for a private law wrong). Although rule 1(2) provides that the AJR procedure *may* be used when applying for a private law remedy in public law cases, and not that it *must* be used in such circumstances, the House of Lords has held that applications by ordinary writ procedure for declarations or injunctions in public law matters will normally be struck out as an abuse of the process of the court (the plaintiff will, in effect, be non-suited) except in a few cases which we will discuss shortly (the 'exclusivity principle').[2]

2. PUBLIC LAW

What is meant by 'public law cases'? There is, unfortunately, no simple answer to this question. The law is in a state of rapid change and development, because it is only since the introduction of the 1978 procedural reforms that the courts have had to draw the distinction between public law and private law in any systematic way. A number of different criteria can be discerned in the cases for deciding whether a case is a public law one, and hence whether the appropriate procedure for bringing it is the AJR procedure.

(a) The Statutory Criteria

The first we might call the 'statutory criteria' because they are contained in Ord. 53 r. 1(2) and in section 31(1) of the Supreme Court Act 1981. These provisions 'define' public law in terms of the matters in respect of which, and the persons and bodies against which, the prerogative orders may be awarded. So, for example, it has been held that AJR procedure need not be and ought not to be used when the respondent is a domestic tribunal[3] or when the applicant is a servant alleging that he has been wrongfully dismissed by his employer,[4]

---

[2] *O'Reilly* v. *Mackman* [1983] 2 AC 237.
[3] *Law* v. *National Greyhound Racing Board* [1983] 1 WLR 1302.
[4] *R.* v. *BBC, ex parte Lavelle* [1983] 1 WLR 23; cf. *R.* v. *East Berks HA, ex parte Walsh* [1984] 3 WLR 818.

because in neither case would a prerogative order have been available before the procedural reforms were introduced. However, it is not yet clear from the cases whether declarations and injunctions can only be sought by AJR procedure in cases where a prerogative order could in theory be awarded instead, or whether the limitations on the availability of the prerogative orders only define in a general way the scope of Order 53. (Conversely, it is not clear whether one effect of the rule is to make declarations available for error of law on the face of the record.)[5] In other words, it is unclear whether the scope of public law exactly coincides with the scope of the prerogative orders. If it does, then some strange results follow: for example, that challenges to delegated legislation are not public law matters for the purposes of the rule.

(b) The Rights Criterion

The second criterion of public law in the cases might be called the 'rights criterion'. According to this criterion AJR procedure must be used when the rights which the applicant seeks to vindicate are public law rights as opposed to private law rights. So in *O'Reilly* v. *Mackman*[6] it was held that a prisoner who was seeking to challenge (for breach of natural justice) a decision of a Board of Prison Visitors, which had the effect of depriving him of a remission of sentence, had to use AJR procedure, because he had no private law right to a remission, but only a legitimate expectation that the remission would be granted if no disciplinary sentence of forfeiture of remission had been made against him. This legitimate expectation sounded in public law, not private law. In *Cocks* v. *Thanet DC*[7] it was held that an applicant who wanted to challenge a decision of a local authority, that he was intentionally homeless and so not entitled to he housed, had to use AJR procedure because his only rights in respect of the decision were public law rights, namely that the decision would be made in accordance with the rules of public law. By contrast, in the same case it was held that, once the council had decided that he was entitled to be housed, the right to be housed was a private law right which did not have to be enforced by AJR procedure, but could be enforced in the County Court.

Consider also *Wandsworth LBC* v. *Winder:*[8] here the council passed a

---

[5] See p. 147 above.
[6] [1983] 2 AC 237; 'legitimate expectations' are public law rights in the relevant sense.
[7] [1983] 2 AC 286.   [8] [1984] 3 WLR 563.

resolution increasing council house rents. The applicant thought that
it was *ultra vires* and refused to pay the increased rent. When the
council sought to evict him for non-payment of the extra rent he
pleaded in defence that the resolution was invalid. The House of
Lords held in effect that, since the applicant was arguing that he had a
contractual right under his lease to remain at the lower rent, he was
asserting private law rights and so could raise the defence in the
possession proceedings in the County Court, and did not have to raise
it by means of an AJR. Similar reasoning seems to have been used in
Irish Dairy Board v. *Milk Marketing Board*[9] in which the Court of Appeal
held that if the applicant has a *right* to be awarded a remedy (all the
public law remedies are discretionary), then his claim is in private law
and he need not use the AJR procedure.

The distinction between public law and private law interests seems
to rest on the assumption that the latter are in some way more
important and more worthy of protection than the former. AJR
procedure incorporates certain procedural protections for public
bodies (discussed later on in this chapter) which ordinary writ
procedure does not, and the rule that a claimant asserting public law
interests can only use AJR procedure puts him at a disadvantage,
justifiable only on the assumption that public law interests do not matter
as much as private law rights and, therefore, do not deserve as much
legal protection. But when one considers the subject matter of some of
the public law interests which have generated litigation (e.g. remission
of sentence, obtaining council housing) this assumption appears
absurd. The fact that the public law applicant is usually challenging the
exercise of a *discretionary* power does not mean that what is at stake for
him is any less important than the sort of interests protected by private
law.

Assuming that the underlying rationale of the rights criterion is to
force certain litigants to use the less advantageous Order 53
procedure, it might seem to follow that, if an applicant chooses to bring
an AJR even though his case raises no public law issue, there would be
no particular reason to stop him. However, it appears that if there is an
alternative to an AJR available to the plaintiff, which the court
perceives to be more appropriate and convenient, then the applicant
whose case raises no public law issue will not be allowed to have

---

[9] [1984] 2 CMLR 584; cf. *Wandsworth LBC* v. *Winder* [1984] 3 WLR 1254,
1261F–G.

recourse to Order 53.[10] This approach suggests a second underlying rationale for the rights criterion, namely to channel certain types of cases to the judges who regularly hear AJRs, but to channel cases of other types to other tribunals perceived to be more suitable for hearing them.

(c) The Substantive Criterion

A third criterion might be called the 'substantive criterion'. According to this criterion the AJR procedure need not be used if the case, even though against a public authority, raises no 'public law issues'. An example is *Davy* v. *Spelthorne BC*[11] in which the council issued a notice requiring the plaintiff to cease using certain premises as a concrete works. The plaintiff thought that the notice was invalid but agreed not to appeal against it, provided the council did not enforce the notice three years. The council agreed, but later sought to enforce the notice on the basis that the agreement was a void fetter on the exercise of its statutory powers. The plaintiff sought an injunction (by ordinary writ procedure) to restrain enforcement of the notice, and damages, which were claimed on the basis that the council had negligently advised the applicant as to his rights under the planning legislation. The claim for an injunction was apparently based on the alleged breach of contract, but it entailed a claim that the enforcement notice was invalid, and the Court of Appeal held that it would therefore 'operate in public law' and so ought to have been sought by AJR procedure.[12] The claim for damages, although arising out of the public activities of a governmental body, was made in tort, on the assumption that the enforcement notice was valid, and was held (by the House of Lords) to be a private law claim rightly made by ordinary writ procedure. (Order 53 r. 7 allows a claim for damages to be brought under AJR procedure.) The council had, in effect, simply given the plaintiff negligent legal advice.

It appears that if the plaintiff can frame his case in private law, for example, in tort, the courts will be very unwilling to hold that the case raises public law issues so that the plaintiff must use AJR procedure (even though a claim for damages can be brought under Order 53). In one case, for example, the owner of an automotive workshop sued a

---

[10] Contrast *R.* v. *East Berks HA, ex parte Walsh* [1984] 3 WLR 818, in which an application to an industrial tribunal in respect of alleged unfair dismissal was possible, with *R.* v. *Home Secretary, ex parte Benwell* [1984] 3 WLR 843 in which, if the applicant had not been allowed to make an AJR, he would have had no available means of redress.

[11] [1984] AC 262.   [12] (1983) 81 LGR 580.

local authority in nuisance.[13] The ˌlocal authority owned a field
adjacent to the workshop on which some gypsies were squatting. The
road which gave access to the workshop crossed this field and the
behaviour and habits of the gypsies made use of the road so unpleasant
that the plaintiff's business suffered. The defendant obtained a court
order for expulsion of the gypsies, but did nothing to enforce the order
for five years. The main reason for the delay was that the council was
under pressure from the County Council and from Whitehall, not to
do anything about the gypsies until some more general solution to the
gypsy problem, which was not confined to the council's area, could be
found. The court thought that, although a delay of five years was
unreasonable, the council, being a public body, was entitled to spend
more time than a private landowner, faced with a similar situation, in
deciding what to do because, being a public body, it was under a duty
to consult widely before acting. The court held that the plaintiff was
entitled to damages, but this conclusion was reached entirely on the
basis of private law principles of the law of nuisance. The court denied
that any public law principles were relevant to the decision of the case.

Similarly, in *Wandsworth LBC* v. *Winder*, mentioned above, it was
held that, even though the central issue in the case was the validity of
the resolution increasing rents, nevertheless the defendant's defence
was based on his pre-existing contractual rights, arising from his
occupation of his council flat and from the previously established rent.
It might be, therefore, that provided an applicant can show that some
private legal right of his is in issue then he need not use AJR
procedure, even if the interference with his right raises significant
substantive public law issues. The substantive criterion, therefore,
seems to operate subject to the rights criterion.

The substantive criterion may not, however, always operate in
favour of the applicant. In a recent case it was held that no issues of
public law are raised by the allegedly unfair dismissal of a senior
psychiatric nursing officer employed by the NHS.[14] The fact that the
applicant was a senior officer in a public hospital was not seen as
making his dismissal a matter of public law, even if it did make it a
matter of public interest: 'public law' and 'public interest' are not
coextensive. Nor did the fact that the restrictions on the power of
dismissal, which the applicant claimed had been ignored, had a
statutory basis, import the necessary public element; all the statute did

---

[13] *Page Motors Ltd.* v. *Epsom & Ewell BC* (1982) 80 LGR 337.
[14] *R.* v. *East Berks HA* [1984] 3 WLR 818.

was to require conditions of service, negotiated by a statutory negotiating body, to be incorporated in the applicant's terms of service, which had been done. Once incorporated these terms were purely contractual and breach of them solely a matter of private law. Public law issues would arise if the power of dismissal was directly regulated by statute, or if the employer refused to incorporate the agreed terms in the conditions of employment. As a result of this reasoning it was held that the applicant was not entitled to bring an AJR to challenge his dismissal, but should have complained to an industrial tribunal. On the other hand, it has also been held that dismissal of a prison officer in alleged breach of the Code of Discipline does raise issues of public law.[15] The judge seems to have been moved to reach this decision not so much by any real difference between the terms and conditions of service of nurses and prison officers, or the way the conditions were imposed, but by the fact that, whereas the nurse could alternatively complain of his dismissal to an industrial tribunal, the prison officer could not, so that unless he could bring an AJR he would have no avenue of redress.

(d) *The Procedural Criterion*

A fourth criterion of when AJR procedure is applicable might be called the 'procedural criterion'. This is very different from the other three criteria. They specify that AJR *procedure* ought to be used (or need not be used, or, occasionally, may not be used) when the applicant's case possesses some particular *substantive* characteristic. The procedural criterion, on the other hand, says that AJR procedure ought to be used when the particular *procedural* features of Order 53, which distinguish it from ordinary writ procedure, are appropriate, and need not be used when they are not needed.

The aim of the procedural peculiarities of Order 53 is to protect public bodies from being harassed in the performance of their public functions by, and from having to spend time and money in defending, trivial or vexatious claims.[16] There are three main features of the AJR procedure which serve to cast a protective wall around public bodies. The first is the requirement of leave to apply for judicial review. This

---

[15] *R.* v. *Home Secretary, ex parte Benwell* [1984] 3 WLR 843.

[16] There is a serious question of policy as to whether and to what extent public bodies ought to be so protected. The House of Lords seems now to be drawing back from the extreme 'protectionist' position of Lord Diplock in *O'Reilly: Wandsworth LBC* v. *Winder* [1984] 3 WLR 1254, esp. 1261D–E but only in relation to the vindication of private law rights.

requirement gives the court control over the proceedings from the very start and because the respondent does not have to appear at the leave stage, it is relieved of the need to take any steps to get weak claims struck out. The second protective feature of AJR procedure is the fact that Ord. 53 r.4 imposes a very short time-limit in which an AJR must be made: subject to a discretion to extend the period, the application must be made promptly and at any event within three months from the date when the grounds for the application arose. The chief function of the short time-limit is to prevent public programmes from being unduly held up, by litigation challenging the legality of such programmes.[17] The third protective feature of AJR procedure is the fact that the facilities provided in Order 53 for pre-trial fact-gathering, in the form of interrogatories and discovery of documents, are less freely available than under ordinary writ procedure.

This third feature requires a little more explanation. It is often said that Order 53 procedure is designed to be speedy and that cases raising significant disputes of fact are not suitable for resolution under Order 53.[18] Thus there are no pleadings (which are designed to clarify issues of fact in dispute) in an AJR and the evidence is given in writing on affidavit rather than orally. Cross-examination of the maker of the affidavit is possible but not usual. Interrogatories and discovery of documents are procedures designed to help in the resolution of factual disputes by ensuring that all relevant documents and information are disclosed, and in ordinary writ procedure they are available to the parties without the consent of the court. Under Order 53 these procedures can only be used if the court so orders. These limitations on the availability of the interlocutory procedures are presumably designed to prevent AJRs becoming bogged down by complex factual arguments, thus unduly delaying public programmes.

In these three respects, therefore, Order 53 procedure is less advantageous to the applicant than ordinary writ procedure: under the latter there is no requirement of leave, there is no fixed time-limit, and facilities for pre-trial gathering of evidence are better. The procedural criterion in a pure form would say that, if in a particular case there is no need to protect the respondent from harassment and there is no danger of undue delay to public works, then AJR procedure need not be used. For example, it was said in *Davy* v. *Spelthorne* that, since the

---

[17] And sometimes to promote certainty in commercial matters: *R.* v. *Companies Registrar, ex parte Esal Ltd.* [1985] 2 WLR 447.

[18] See especially Lord Scarman in *IRC* v. *Rossminster Ltd* [1980] AC 952, 1025–6.

plaintiff's claim was not holding up anything the council wanted to do, there was no need to require him to use a speedy procedure.[19] In regard to the limited interlocutory facilities under Order 53, it was said in *R.* v. *Jenner*[20] that an applicant ought not to be required to use AJR procedure if his claim raised difficult factual issues which would be better dealt with by a fuller procedure. As for the requirement of leave, the courts seem to take the view that this can be dispensed with if the plaintiff is seeking to protect his private law rights against government infringement but not if he is seeking to protect his public law rights.

Another aspect of the procedural criterion is captured in the phrase 'abuse of the process of the court'. This was the phrase used by Lord Diplock in *O'Reilly* v. *Mackman*[21] in laying down the exclusivity principle, and it was thought particularly appropriate in that case because the time-limit for an AJR had long passed (by a matter of years)[22] and the applicant clearly chose ordinary writ procedure to evade the Order 53 time-limit. However, the main criterion for whether a failure to use AJR procedure will be seen as an abuse of process appears to be whether the applicant is seeking to protect private law rights or public law rights. So, in *Wandsworth LBC* v. *Winder*, it was said that, since Winder was seeking to protect his private law rights, it could not be said that he was abusing or misusing the process of the court, by raising the invalidity of the resolution in a defence to a County Court action brought against him by the council, even though the time-limit for direct challenge by way of AJR had long since expired.

(e) A Clash of Criteria?

The reader might detect that there is a potential for conflict between the first three criteria of the appropriateness of Order 53 procedure and the procedural criterion. The requirement of leave is designed to weed out frivolous, vexatious, or hopeless cases; but there is no guarantee that private law claims will not sometimes be frivolous, vexatious, or hopeless. Nor is there any reason to think that private law claims will not sometimes hold up public programmes if they are allowed to be brought after the short time-limit in Order 53. Finally, there is no reason to think that public law claims for which Order 53 must be used may not sometimes raise difficult factual issues. Cases in

[19] [1984] AC 262, 274 *per* Lord Fraser of Tullybelton.
[20] [1983] 1 WLR 873.　　　[21] [1983] 2 AC 237.
[22] Although it is hard to see that the delay did the respondent any harm.

which a breach of natural justice or a jurisdictional error of fact is alleged will often raise acutely difficult issues of fact. Conversely, private law claims do not necessarily raise factual issues.

In short, there is no reason to think that the procedural features of Order 53 are ideally suited for all public law cases, or conversely that the procedural features of ordinary writ procedure are necessary for private law claims. The exclusivity principle, therefore, seems to be based on a false premise, namely that AJR procedure is necessary and desirable for dealing properly with all public law cases (however these are defined).

3. THE EXCLUSIVITY PRINCIPLE AND ITS EXCEPTIONS

As we have noted, it has been held that, despite the permissive wording of rule 1(2), an applicant for a declaration or injunction in a public law matter must normally use Order 53, if he is not to risk being non-suited. This makes it vital to him to know what we mean by public law matters. The position of the litigant who begins his case under Order 53 and is then told that he ought to have used ordinary writ procedure is not so bad because Ord. 53 r. 9(5) may allow the case to continue as if it had been started by ordinary writ procedure.[23] It is always safer, therefore, to use AJR procedure if there is doubt about whether one's case is a public law case or not. But this course of action brings with it the three disadvantages of AJR procedure already discussed.

What is the theoretical justification for this procedural minefield? The protection of public authorities from excessive litigation, it seems. But what theory of judicial review underlies this approach? It is hard to find one. One might cynically suggest the 'doorman theory' by which the courts mount guard to keep undesirables from troubling the men in Whitehall and their political superiors. On this view the demands of administrative efficiency and convenience take precedence over the rights and interests of citizens. This seems inimical to any image of the courts as guardians of the law; they become enemies rather than champions of open and legally responsible government.

There are, it seems, a few exceptions to the exclusivity principle. In *O'Reilly* v. *Mackman*[24] Lord Diplock gave two exceptions: where none

---

[23] But there may be a catch-22 lurking here in cases raising complex factual issues: these may preclude the use of AJR procedure, but may also lead the court to refuse to exercise the discretion under r. 9(5) on the basis that it would be better if the case were started afresh by writ: *R.* v. *East Berks HA* [1984] 3 WLR 818, 835 *per* May, LJ.

[24] [1983] 2 AC 237.

of the parties objects to the use of ordinary writ procedure; and the case of a collateral challenge to an administrative decision, that is, a challenge which arises out of and incidentally to a claim for infringement of a private law right. The case of the gypsies is an example: this was a claim in nuisance based on the exercise by the council of its decision-making powers.

At first sight it is not easy to see why the fact that an administrative decision is challenged collaterally should justify not using AJR procedure. The collateral challenge exception may simply be a restatement of the rights criterion: if private rights are in issue, Order 53 need not be used.[25] The procedural restrictions contained in Order 53 are the *price* of being allowed to enforce public law rights. The generous standing rule of 'sufficient interest' under Order 53 is traded off against the procedural disadvantages of the AJR.

But it should also be borne in mind that the most common case of a collateral challenge will be an action for damages. Such actions often involve significant factual disputes, and it is certainly arguable that it should not be an abuse of the process of the court not to use Order 53 in such cases, because the proper resolution of such disputes ideally requires the use of pleadings, oral evidence, and full interlocutory facilities at the automatic disposal of the parties, none of which is a feature of AJR procedure. The trouble with this argument is that there is no reason to think that direct challenges to governmental action may not also raise difficult factual issues. In *O'Reilly* v. *Mackman* itself, the challenge to the decision of the Board of Visitors raised difficult factual questions about what happened at the hearing. It would seem, therefore, that the exclusivity principle rests on two false and related assumptions: that all private law claims need and deserve the fuller procedure available by ordinary writ; and that all public law claims require and deserve only the more truncated procedure available under Order 53. These assumptions are clearly wrong and this suggests that a more fundamental reappraisal of AJR procedure is warranted.

4. FURTHER PROCEDURAL REFORMS

We have seen that the procedural protections in Order 53 achieve three purposes: the requirement of leave serves to filter out hopeless or

---

[25] But see *Wandsworth LBC* v. *Winder* [1984] 3 WLR 1254, 1260B–D.

frivolous claims; the strict time-limit serves to prevent public works being held up for too long by the threat of litigation; and the court's control over the interlocutory procedures ensures that actions against public bodies do not get bogged down. The last purpose, as we have noted, comes into direct conflict with the demands of justice in cases involving substantial disputes of fact. Indeed, AJR procedure is modelled on originating summons procedure, which is designed for cases which do not raise substantial factual disputes. We have noted, too, that direct challenges as well as collateral challenges to administrative decisions can raise factual disputes; this is true not only of direct challenges by way of application for a declaration or injunction (for which there is an alternative procedure), but also of challenges by way of an application for a prerogative order (for which there is no alternative to AJR procedure). In such cases there seems little justification for not allowing full use of pleadings, oral evidence, and interlocutory facilities at the automatic disposal of the parties, subject only to the demands of public policy as embodied in the strict time-limit in Order 53 and in the requirement of leave.[26]

This could be achieved by assimilating public law procedure, as it applies both to the prerogative orders and the private law remedies, more closely to private law procedure. Under such a scheme there would be two procedural tracks for actions against public bodies: one suitable for cases raising substantial factual disputes and one suitable for cases raising no such disputes. In this respect, public law procedure would not differ from private law procedure. But the special position of public authorities would be recognized by providing that the applicant would not be given a free choice between procedures as he is in private law. Every applicant for a remedy against a public body[27] would need to obtain leave to apply for the remedy. At the leave stage the court would first consider whether the case raised any public law issues. If not, the applicant's case would proceed by private law procedure and he would have a choice of procedural track. If the case did raise public law issues, the court would have to decide whether the applicant had sufficient standing, whether the case was brought in time, and whether

[26] I assume for the sake of the present argument that *some* special procedural protection for public bodies is justified, on the ground that individuals ought not to have, in effect, a temporary veto on public programmes. But not all will agree with this assumption; my only answer to them is that the validity of special protection is so widely accepted that any reform which did not accept it in some form would be unlikely to be well received.
[27] There would, undeniably, be some difficulties in defining 'public body'.

the case was a hopeless, frivolous, or vexatious one. If the court decided that the case should go ahead, it would then have to decide by which procedural track it should proceed. If the case raised factual issues, then the fact-oriented procedure should be allowed, unless there were compelling reasons of time why the extra delay this would cause was unacceptable. The court should take account of the fact that it could minimize the delay by setting a timetable for the action.

It might be argued that this scheme puts the claimant who at present could use private law procedure (that is, the claimant who brings a private law action against a public body) at a disadvantage, because under the new scheme he would have to seek leave and would possibly be subject to very restrictive time-limits. But the requirement of leave need not be too burdensome if an expeditious procedure for cases of emergency is provided; and the question of time-limits could be dealt with by making it clear that a short time-limit should be imposed only if public works would otherwise be held in undue suspense.

This proposal is a sort of half-way house. It is an attempt to preserve the special protections for public bodies contained in Order 53, while at the same time limiting the application of those protections to cases where they are necessary and suitable. There is, however, a view which supports an even more radical approach, which would remove the protections for public bodies and assimilate public law procedure fully to private law procedure. Why, after all, should public bodies be specially protected from the grievances of citizens who feel strongly enough to litigate?

5. OTHER FEATURES OF AJR PROCEDURE

There are several other features of the AJR procedure which should be noted. The first is that applications for leave are made ex parte, that is, in the absence of the respondent decision-maker. This further protects the respondent from trouble, by enabling the court to reject cases it considers hopeless or frivolous, without the respondent having to expend time or money in defending them in any way. Secondly, we have noted that a claim for damages arising out of the matter to which the AJR relates (i.e. collateral challenges) can (although they need not) be joined with the AJR. This is a purely procedural matter. Damages can only be awarded under Order 53 if, had the claim for damages been made by ordinary writ procedure, an award of damages would have been made. In other words, rule 7 does not in any way alter the substantive law governing entitlement to damages. And an applicant whose claim for damages raises complex factual issues might be wiser to make his claim for this relief by ordinary writ procedure.

Thirdly, under rule 9(4) the court may, in an application for *certiorari*, in addition to quashing the decision, remit it to the decision-maker with a direction to reconsider it in accordance with the decision of the court. The provision is designed for cases in which the only error in the decision is one of law. If the decision were merely quashed, the body would have to go through the whole decision-making process again, including the finding of any relevant facts; but under the remittance procedure it can confine itself to reconsidering the impact on the decision of the error of law. This saves time and money. The power to remit turns the review procedure in these cases into something very like an appeal. Instead of the court substituting the legally correct result, this is left formally for the decision-maker to do; but the latter's only job is to give formal effect to what the court has decided.

Finally, it should be noted that it is open to the court on an AJR to grant what is called interim relief. This means, in effect, that the court can order the respondent to take no further action adverse to the applicant, until the legal position is settled by the court. Order 53 r. 3(10) provides that the granting of leave to apply for *certiorari* or prohibition automatically operates as a grant of interim relief; and also that, in other cases, the court may grant such interim relief as it has the power to grant in ordinary cases. In practice the latter means that the court may grant an interim injunction; there is no such thing as an interim declaration because a declaration by its nature is said to be a final statement of what the rights of the parties *are*. This means that there is no form of interim relief available against the Crown, which is amenable neither to the prerogative orders nor to injunctions.[28]

6. A GENERAL ADMINISTRATIVE COURT?

Except in criminal matters, most applications for judicial review are heard by single judges of the Queen's Bench Division. This arrangement is the result of a 1980 amendment to the 1978 scheme. Under the latter, applications were heard by the Divisional Court of the Queen's Bench Division, and one of the arguments in favour of

[28] *R. v. Home Secretary, ex parte Mohammed Yagoob* [1984] 1 WLR 920; *R. v. Home Secretary, ex parte Kirkwood* [1984] 1 WLR 913.

this arrangement and of having a special procedure for all public law cases was that the Divisional Court would become a specialist administrative law court. The hope was that this would improve the quality of administrative law decisions, and lead to more rapid and rational development of public law. This objective has been preserved, despite the 1980 changes, because under the new arrangement a panel of judges is allocated to hearing cases on what is called the 'Crown Office List', that is, applications for judicial review.

The whole thrust of the procedural changes since 1977, therefore, has been to develop and emphasize the distinction between public and private law. It is not yet by any means clear what the exact distinction between public and private law is. This is partly because judges do not seem to have a clear conception of the underlying rationale of the distinction. But the procedural importance of the distinction guarantees that much effort will have to be put into elaborating it. It is a pity, to say the least, that the development of expertise in administrative law has been purchased at the cost of a procedural regime which depends on such a complex notion of the distinction between public and private law, and which, by reason of the exclusivity principle, contains the possibility of the failure for technical reasons of meritorious cases.

Compensation as a Public Law Remedy

1. DAMAGES NOT A PUBLIC LAW REMEDY

THE main remedy for breaches of *private law* rules by public bodies is damages. The basic *public law* rule is that damages (or, more widely, monetary compensation) is not available as a remedy for public law wrongs. The reason for this is not easy to discern: why should a citizen, injured in a pecuniary sense by a public law wrong, have to be satisfied with having the decision against him reversed, if reversal does not undo the pecuniary injury? The explanation may lie in the fact that the awarding of damages is not a discretionary remedy and so the courts do not have as much control over the award of this remedy as over the public law remedies. Another possible explanation is related to the nature of judicial review. One of the characteristics of judicial review is that the supervising court does not substitute its decision for that of the public authority; rather it leaves it to the body to make good its illegal behaviour by making a fresh decision which complies with the requirements of the law. To award damages, on the other hand, is in a sense to substitute a decision for that of the public authority. A strict analogy with judicial review would perhaps give the decision-maker a power (and a duty) to award compensation after it had remade its decision, if it turned out that the applicant had suffered loss as a result of the initial illegal decision (although there are difficulties in this solution which we will consider in a moment).

Whatever the explanation, a plaintiff is only entitled to an award of damages against a public authority if he can show that he has suffered a private law wrong, most commonly a tort or a breach of contract. Sometimes public law wrongs also amount to private law wrongs; but illegality in the public law sense is not equivalent to wrongfulness in the private law sense, and a public law wrong may not involve any private law wrongfulness.

The question to be considered here is whether monetary compensation ought to be made available as a remedy in public law, and if so, on what basis? There seems no reason not to allow that monetary compensation may, at least in some cases, be a suitable remedy in public law. The second question is, therefore, the more important of the two. There are two main theories which have been suggested as providing a suitable basis for an award of monetary compensation: the illegality theory and the risk theory.

2. COMPENSATION FOR ILLEGAL ACTION

Under the illegality theory, as the name implies, the ground for the award of damages is that the defendant has acted illegally, that is, *ultra vires*. The main problem with this theory is that, because of the nature of judicial review for illegality, it would be extremely difficult, if not theoretically impossible, for a plaintiff to prove a causal link between the illegal action and his loss. Suppose a plaintiff suffers loss as a result of an illegal administrative decision. The decision is quashed and the authority makes a fresh and legal decision. That decision might be the same as the first one and cause the plaintiff the same loss. In fact, one would expect a public authority always to be inclined to search for a way to reach the same decision legally the second time round, if only to save face; and the incentive to do so would be even greater if it were likely to be required to pay damages should it decide that its earlier loss-causing decision ought to be changed.

Most grounds of public law illegality do not necessarily rule out the making of the same decision again. A decision can be illegal because, for example, it was made in contravention of the rules of natural justice; or because relevant considerations were ignored in making it; or because the authority was unduly influenced by some external factor, such as the opinion of some other authority or an agreement with a third party. None of these grounds of illegality rules out the possibility that exactly the same decision might be reached, even if natural justice were complied with, or all relevant considerations were taken into account, or the authority were to ignore all undue fetters on its discretion. So, until the decision is made again, it is not possible to say whether the loss would not have been suffered but for the illegal decision. A solution might be to postpone the decision on the issue of damages until after the authority has deliberated again. The danger of this is that the fear of an award of damages against it would unduly encourage the authority to reach the same decision again, thus creating an appearance of bias. Whether this is a real practical difficulty would depend on whether the desire to save face would not anyway have this effect of encouraging the same decision to be made again, even if there were no risk of a damages award.

On the other hand, public authorities do not usually commit illegal acts deliberately, and if an atmosphere of opinion were created in which compensation for illegality would be seen as being simply compensation for loss, and not as carrying any stigma of fault, or as being designed to perform the function of deterring illegal conduct, public authorities might be able to put the chance of an award out of their mind in deciding the applicant's case the second time round. There is a danger of viewing compensation for illegality too much in terms of a traditional tort model, rather than in terms of distributing widely and thinly the financial ill-effects of governmental 'mistakes'. In a less than perfect world it is inevitable that government authorities will sometimes act illegally, and there may be a lot to be said for bringing the 'loss distribution' insights of modern tort theory to bear on the way we perceive public law compensation. The fact that the government pays the compensation should not lead us to think of the government as an ordinary defendant. We could see it as providing an insurance fund against loss caused by (usually) unintentional failure to keep within the bounds set by the principles of *ultra vires*. On the other hand, it may be that this is wishful thinking and that, in practical terms, the award of damages for illegality is incompatible with the theory of judicial review, because it cannot be reconciled with the idea that the ultimate decision must usually be left to the public authority.

In some cases the ultimate question is only in theory left to the public authority; for example, in the case of review for jurisdictional errors of law or fact. Here the court *does* substitute its decision for that of the deciding authority in all but strict theory, at least in circumstances in which it is clear that, if the authority had got the law or the facts right, its decision would have been different and could only have been one way. In such cases there is no impediment to an award of damages, because the finding of fact or the decision of law by the reviewing court will necessitate a particular decision by the authority when it reconsiders the matter.

There are certain other circumstances in which this problem of unduly encouraging an authority to reach a particular decision does not arise and in which a scheme of compensation might work: where there is no question of a decision being remade, notably where the time-limit for challenging an allegedly illegal decision has run out; or where a citizen has suffered loss by relying on a representation by a public body that it will act in a particular way, in circumstances where the law will not require the body to make good its representation because it has undertaken to act illegally. In such cases the problem of causation does not exist, because the decision in question will not be reconsidered. The problem with drawing distinctions between cases in this way is that the chance circumstance that one's case falls into one of these categories, does not seem to justify the difference between compensation and no-compensation for illegality.

3. COMPENSATION FOR RISKS

The risk theory is a theory which operates independently of any concept of fault or illegality. The idea here is that citizens would be entitled to compensation for loss caused by the conduct of a particular activity, regardless of whether that activity was conducted legally or illegally, in a faulty way or absolutely blamelessly. In terms of the law of tort, the risk theory contemplates either a strict liability scheme of compensation, in which the government bears the initial burden of compensation, or a no-fault scheme in which the individual is insured against loss by some form of insurance (perhaps tax-based) taken out by him. Under the risk theory, therefore, compensation might be awarded for public law wrongs, but it might also be awarded for action which is perfectly legal in the public law sense.

There are situations in which, by statute, compensation is already payable on a risk theory.[1] For example, under the Land Compensation Act 1973 property owners are entitled to compensation for depreciation in the value of their land caused by such things as noise, vibration, smells, and fumes, resulting from public works. The underlying reasoning is that, since the public is presumed to benefit greatly from the building of a motorway (for example), private citizens who suffer as a result of its construction should not have to bear their loss for the sake of that wider public interest. The risk theory, therefore, requires an important value judgment in relation to any particular governmental

[1] For discussion of a couple of other compensation schemes, run by the government for citizens who suffer financial loss as a result of decisions or actions of government officials or employees, see Harlow & Rawlings, *Law and Administration* (1984), pp. 409–18. Government departments sometimes also make *ad hoc ex gratia* (i.e. without admission of liability) payments of compensation to citizens who have suffered loss as a result of government decisions or actions. The Ombudsmen (see Chapter 21) also sometimes successfully advise government bodies to pay monetary compensation to victims of maladministration; for a case-study see Harlow & Rawlings op. cit. chapter 8.

activity: if that activity inflicts loss of certain type on private individuals, should those individuals be expected to bear it or should the government pick up the bill? A court might not be thought to be a particularly suitable body to make such a decision because, in many situations, the decision, whichever way it goes, will be politically highly contentious.

It is worth noting, however, that one of the ideas behind the risk theory, namely that losses should be borne by the party best able to absorb them with least dislocation and disruption, is a very popular one in the (private) law of torts, where the theory of fault liability is, in some areas at least, in something of a decline. And since government is responsible for, or influences in important ways, a very large number of activities, there may be sound political arguments for thinking seriously about a more extensive and rationalized set of 'risk theory schemes' of compensation for loss caused by governmental action. It may be, of course, that what we really want is that some losses so caused should be compensated for if they result from illegal action, and some other losses compensated for regardless of whether they result from illegal action or not. The category into which particular losses are put will depend on the value we put on the interests which the governmental action in question has interfered with, weighed against the value we put on the end which the governmental action was designed to serve. In some cases we might be happy for courts to do the weighing exercise involved, and, to the extent that we are, we could have a 'common law' of public law compensation. But if the decisions involved are perceived as being too politically sensitive for the courts, some legislative intervention might be necessary to establish the desired framework of value judgments.

12

Exclusion of Remedies

1. EXPRESS OUSTER

THE courts have generally taken an uncompromising attitude towards express legislative provisions designed to exclude judicial review. Judicial review is seen as a basic right of all citizens, which the legislature will be taken to have excluded only by the very clearest words. This attitude seems to be the result of viewing administrative law as chiefly designed to protect the rights of the individual from unlawful interference by government. So, in the context of delegated legislation, it has been held that a provision in a statute (now never used by the legislature) that regulations made under the statute will take effect as if enacted in the statute (that is, they will be unchallengeable as if they were made by Parliament) does not prevent the courts holding the regulation to be *ultra vires*.[1] And in *Anisminic* v. *Foreign Compensation Commission*[2] it was held that a provision, which sought to immunize decisions of the Commission from legal challenge by way of judicial review, was ineffective to exclude the quashing of an *ultra vires* decision: its only effect was to prevent a decision being quashed for error of law on the face of the record. The excluding provision was drafted in what appeared to be very clear and unambiguous terms and, although in theory the decision left intact Parliament's power to exclude judicial review, Parliament has not since made use of clauses explicitly purporting to exclude judicial review entirely, probably realizing that, since the court was able to find a way around the provision considered in *Anisminic*, it would probably find a way around almost any provision which purported to protect illegal decisions from challenge. The courts clearly see their role in judicial review of administrative action as being of fundamental constitutional importance.

More common now are provisions which purport to set a time-limit on judicial review. It has been said by the courts that there are good reasons of public policy to enforce such time-limits: public programmes

---

[1] *Ex parte Yaffe* [1931] AC 494.   [2] [1969] 2 AC 147; see p. 13 above.

ought not to be suspended or held up indefinitely for fear of a challenge at some later date.[3] The most common statutory period for the challenge of administrative decisions is six weeks. It will be recalled that Order 53 imposes a time-limit of three months on applications for judicial review, subject to a discretion to extend the period 'for good reason'. This provision operates subject to any statutory time-limit. There can be no sound objection to time-limits of some sort, but six weeks (or even three months) seems an unnecessarily and even unfairly short time. Such limits might be acceptable if the only persons entitled to challenge governmental action were persons directly affected. But, as we have seen, the law in some cases allows anyone with a genuine interest to make an application for judicial review, and it may take such persons a considerable time to find out about the decision they want to challenge.

2. IMPLIED OUSTER

Besides explicit exclusion of remedies, remedies can be impliedly excluded. A couple of relevant principles deserve mention. The first is the general rule that since the prerogative orders are discretionary remedies, they will not be awarded if there is some more convenient remedy available.[4] The main application of this principle arises out of the fact that the prerogative orders are supervisory remedies concerned only with legality (or patent error of law) and not with broader questions of the merits or policy of a decision. If the statute under which the decision was made provides for a full appeal to some other body, which can, on appeal, deal with questions of the merits and of policy which the applicant wishes to raise and which the court cannot deal with, then the applicant should pursue the avenue of appeal, rather than seek judicial review.

Order 53 rule 3(8) provides that, where *certiorari* is sought to quash any decision which is subject to appeal and a time-limit is fixed for that appeal, the court may adjourn the application for leave to seek *certiorari* until the appeal is heard or the time limit for appealing has expired. This is a sensible way of resolving any difficulty caused by the application of the above principle.

The second principle is that, if the statute which creates the right

---

[3] *R.* v. *Environment Secretary, ex parte Ostler* [1977] QB 122.

[4] *R.* v. *Hillingdon LBC, ex parte Royco Homes Ltd.* [1974] QB 720; *R.* v. *Epping & Harlow General Commissioners, ex parte Goldstraw* [1983] 3 All ER 257.

which the applicant seeks to enforce also provides a remedy for its enforcement, that remedy is the only one available. Thus, in *Barraclough* v. *Brown*[5] the statute gave a right to sue in the County Court for the recovery of costs of dredging a canal. It was held that the High Court could not award a declaration that the dredging costs were recoverable from the defendant. The rule is based on an implied presumption that Parliament intended the statutory remedy to be the only one. The rules which we have already considered, about the use of ministerial default powers in relation to statutory duties, are an application of this rule. But the principle only applies if the judicial review remedy sought by the applicant performs the same function as the statutory remedy. In *Barraclough* v. *Brown* it did, as the function was the recovery of the money. A ministerial default power performs the same function as an order of mandamus: the securing of the performance of the duty. However, it does not perform the same function as an order of *certiorari* to quash the decision of the authority as to what it will do in fulfilment of its duty, since this leaves it up to the authority to decide again what it will do.[6] Nor does a supervisory remedy perform the same function as an appeal on the merits; the former is concerned with legality only. So, the principle that a prerogative order will not be awarded if there is a more suitable remedy is not an application of this principle, but simply a sort of discretionary restraint on the part of the courts.

3. THE CONSTITUTIONAL FUNCTION OF THE RULES

The rules about express exclusion of judicial review are rules by which the courts seek to prevent the legislature from immunizing the activities of the executive from judicial scrutiny. They, therefore, mark the limits, as it were, of the willingness of the courts to accept political control of administrative action and represent an important practical limitation on the freedom of Parliament to pass what law it chooses. It is often said that an excess of faith in the doctrine of ministerial responsibility to Parliament has made the courts unduly unwilling to develop a strong law of judicial review. This may be true in relation to the grounds of review; perhaps they are not sufficiently intrusive into the administrative process. But it does not seem to be fair comment in

---

[5] [1897] AC 615.
[6] *R.* v. *Environment Secretary, ex parte Ward* [1984] 1 WLR 834, 845E–F.

relation to the courts' obvious determination to keep judicial review open as one avenue of control of administrative activity.

The rules about implied exclusion of review tend to raise, more directly, questions about the suitability of the judicial process as opposed to the other avenues open for the control of administrative misconduct. In other words, these rules tend to rest on ideas of justiciability and the proper scope of judicial review. We have discussed this aspect in detail in the main context in which it is important, namely control of the exercise of statutory duties.[7]

---

[7] Chapter 6.

THE APPLICATION OF PRIVATE LAW RULES AND CONCEPTS IN PUBLIC LAW

13

Introduction

So far we have been concerned with rules of law which relate primarily, though not exclusively, to the governmental activities of public bodies. These rules can be loosely called rules of public law. In this section we will be concerned with rules of private law and, in particular, the way in which these rules are modified in their application to public bodies performing governmental functions. It should be noted that, in this context, the terms 'public law' and 'private law' are not used in the technical sense which they bear in the context of RSC Ord. 53, but in a looser sense. Thus, private law rules are simply rules which govern the relations between citizens amongst themselves; public law rules are rules which primarily govern relations between private citizens and the government.

There is a strong tradition in English law of seeing private law rules as the paradigm governing not only relations between citizens, but also relations between citizens and the government. We have already discussed Dicey's idea that the 'rule of law' required that governmental officials should be answerable for their actions, to the same extent and according to the same rules as private individuals. It is clear that this approach is inadequate as a complete theory of governmental liability, if for no other reason than that there are many grounds of public law illegality which have no application or relevance to the conduct of private individuals. But we might defend Dicey from further criticism by saying that his theory primarily concerned the application, to the activities of government officials, of private law rules *of liability* for loss or damage caused.

At the time Dicey was writing, this view of the liability of governmental bodies was not entirely implausible, and so influential has Dicey's approach been that it is probably true to say that there is a basic principle in English law concerning the liability of public bodies, that rules of private law liability apply to the activities of public bodies and officials in the same way and to the same extent as they apply to the activities of private citizens, unless some good reason can be found why they should not. It seems clear, as we will see later, that private law rules are not always appropriate in public law contexts, in an unqualified form. But it may well be that the best starting-point is a presumption that they do apply, leaving it to the public body to adduce some good reason why they should not. In some instances, the legitimate demands of public policy may require that the government be subject to lesser obligations than a private individual, who has no responsibilities to the public generally.

But there is another side to the coin of the government's special position as 'guardian' of the public interest. Especially in contractual contexts the government wields such economic and psychological power that it may be argued that ordinary citizens dealing with the government, require greater protection from the effects of inequality of bargaining power than they do when they are dealing with each other. This might imply that in some cases the government should be subject to greater restrictions than private citizens, not less. Privilege, it might be thought, should not exist without countervailing responsibilities. At this level of generality such arguments are very difficult to assess, and it is only by discussing specific areas of the law that their force or lack of it can be appreciated.

Perhaps the most important point to make at this stage is that the traditional Diceyan view rests on what might now be thought a rather outdated picture of the nature of government and the way it operates. It sees government as made up of a collection of rather autonomous and personally responsible individuals, who differ from private citizens only in the respect that, when a government official acts, he does not do so on his own behalf, but on the behalf of others, as a sort of agent. Today, on the other hand, we view government much more as a corporate entity which stands over against individuals and, to some extent, operates antagonistically to them, on behalf of a set of interests that are often opposed to the interests of individuals as perceived by themselves. Government is seen as rather impersonal and sometimes hostile, whereas Dicey seems to have conceived of it as a more personal and benign force. This change is not unrelated to the dramatic increase, during the last 100 years, in the scope of governmental activities in the social and economic spheres. Government is now very intrusive in the lives of ordinary citizens and this fact throws doubt on the value of Dicey's approach as a complete theory. At the same time, there seems no reason to abandon the basic premise that in the absence of countervailing considerations the government should be at least as liable in contract, tort, and so on, as private citizens.

14

The Crown and Crown Proceedings

SOME of the rules relating to the civil liability of public authorities are couched in terms of and apply to 'the Crown'. This term does not by any means embrace all governmental bodies, and so it is important to determine exactly what the term means. This is so, in particular, because the Crown enjoys certain privileges which other persons and bodies do not enjoy. For example, under section 21 of the Crown Proceedings Act 1947 a court cannot grant an injunction or make an order of specific performance against the Crown. The only remedy certainly available against the Crown is the declaration. One result of this is that, since there is no such thing as an interim declaration, interim relief cannot be obtained against the Crown. Again, section 40(2)(*f*) of the same Act preserves the principles of statutory interpretation that the Crown may take the benefit of a statute, even if the statute does not specifically mention the Crown as a beneficiary; and that the Crown is not subject to any statutory obligation or burden, even if the statute does not specifically relieve it of the obligation or burden.

I. DEFINITION OF THE CROWN

The privileged position of the Crown dates from a period when the monarch personally wielded a great deal of political and governmental power. When, as a result of the constitutional changes of the seventeenth and later centuries, many of the powers of the monarch were transferred to Parliament and to Ministers, a distinction developed between the Crown in a personal sense (the monarch), and the Crown in an impersonal, governmental sense. This would suggest that, in historical terms at least, the Crown in this latter sense encompasses all persons and bodies who exercise powers which were at some time exercised by the monarch. But the term in its modern sense clearly does not extend this far. For example, Her Majesty's judges of the High Court in theory dispense royal justice, but judges are not thought of as being comprehended by the term 'the Crown'.

And because of the development of the doctrine of parliamentary supremacy over all other organs of government, including the monarch, Parliament is not thought of as being a part of the Crown, even though it was a major beneficiary of the shift of powers from the monarch.

This would seem to leave the executive branch of central government (local government has always been subordinate to and separate from central government, whether in its present form or in its monarchical form). By the 'executive branch of central government' is meant Ministers of State and the departments for which they are constitutionally responsible. There are dicta in a recent House of Lords case[1] which support exactly this definition of the Crown. Also there is an older High Court decision to the effect that an injunction may not, because of section 21(2) of the Crown Proceedings Act, be awarded against a Minister performing functions in his capacity as Minister, because the effect of such an award would be to grant injunctive relief against the Crown.

2. THE CROWN AND REMEDIES

On the other hand, it may be that the term 'the Crown' does not bear the same meaning in every context. To start with, it never seems to have been questioned in practice, in the last fifty years or so, that prerogative orders can be awarded against Ministers acting in their official capacity, or against those acting on their behalf. More importantly, if it were the case that the only remedy available against Ministers was the declaration, this position would represent a serious, indeed a ludicrous, gap in the scheme of public law remedies. Public law is designed specifically for the control of governmental activity, and that its main remedies should not be available against the core of central government would be absurd.

However, if we say that Ministers and their departments fall outside the definition of the Crown for remedial purposes, it becomes unclear what the term does refer to in that context. This was the difficulty faced in *Merricks* v. *Heathcote-Amory*[2] in which the plaintiff sought an

---

[1] *Town Investments Ltd.* v. *Department of Environment* [1978] AC 359, 381 *per* Lord Diplock.
[2] [1955] Ch. 567; cf. *R.* v. *Home Secretary, ex parte Mohammed Yaqoob* [1984] 1 WLR 920; *R.* v. *Home Secretary, ex parte Kirkwood* [1984] 1 WLR 913.

injunction to restrain the Minister of Agriculture from presenting a potato-marketing scheme to Parliament for approval. The Minister was clearly not acting in his personal capacity; and it was held that, if he was acting on behalf of the government, which he obviously was, then the provisions of section 21 of the Crown Proceedings Act precluded the award of an injunction. The plaintiff attempted to argue that the Minister was in fact acting in a third intermediate capacity as a Minister, but not as a representative of the Crown; or, in other words, that his functions as Minister attached to his office, as such, and not to his office as a manifestation of the Crown. The court rejected this argument and held that there was no such intermediate capacity.

The only way of squaring this decision with the apparent availability of prerogative orders against Ministers, despite the fact that theoretically they are not available against the Crown, is to say that this decision is wrong; or, possibly, to say that it was justified by the express provisions of the Act of which there is no equivalent in respect of the prerogative orders. The wide dicta in the *Town Investments* case[3] could then be interpreted strictly, in the light of the facts of that case, as concerning only the question of when the Crown will be held to be the contracting party in respect of a contract made by a Minister. In that case it was argued (for the purposes of determining the applicability of rent control provisions) that since the lessee of certain premises was nominally the Environment Secretary but the premises were in fact occupied by Civil Servants from a different department, the premises were not occupied by the tenant. The House of Lords held that although the lease had been signed by (the predecessor of) the Environment Secretary, the lease had been made by him for and on behalf of the Crown, so that the real lessee was the Crown acting through the Secretary; and, since the building was occupied by Crown servants, it was occupied by the lessee.

In saying that Ministers and their departments are all part of the Crown, the judges were making a point about the nature of central government, namely that it is in one sense an indivisible entity, even though made up of a number of identifiably distinct units. This theory fits in well with the constitutional doctrine of corporate ministerial responsibility and was particularly useful in this case because it meant that the lessor could not ignore anti-inflation legislation in fixing the rent.

[3] n. 1 above.

3. THE APPLICATION OF STATUTORY PROVISIONS TO FRINGE BODIES

A context in which the issue of defining the Crown often arises is whether a particular statutory provision applies to a particular non-departmental or quasi-governmental body. This question is particularly important, first, in relation to government involvement in economic and commercial activities through the media of public investment or nationalization; and, secondly, in relation to public non-departmental bodies (such as the Commission for Racial Equality), and private bodies (such as the Law Society, in its role as administrator of the Legal Aid Scheme) which perform administrative functions of public importance.

A number of factors emerge from the cases as being important. First, the degree of control which the organs of central government exercise over the body has to be considered. For example, in *BBC* v. *Johns*[4] it was held that the BBC does not enjoy Crown immunity from taxation; the Court of Appeal stressed the fact that the BBC was set up as an independent entity and that this was no doubt for the exact purpose of avoiding both the appearance and the actuality of central government control over its activities. Conversely, in *Pfizer Corporation* v. *Ministry of Health*[5] it was held, in effect, that the supply of drugs to the NHS is supply 'for the services of the Crown'. The question in this case was whether the NHS had certain rights under patent legislation, and the fact that the decision benefited the NHS financially may have been an important factor in leading the court to it. But it is perhaps also relevant that although the NHS is made up of a system of statutory corporations, these are subject to a high degree of central government control and are directly, and almost entirely, dependent on the government for finance. Statutory corporations which operate in a more commercial way would be less likely to be seen as being part of the Crown in any sense.

A second factor is whether the function which the body performs is one which we would call governmental. For example, in *BBC* v. *Johns* it was argued that wireless telegraphy was a governmental function but the court rejected this argument. The classification of functions as being proper or appropriate to central government is a highly ideological one, as the recurrent debates over private education and medicine illustrate. The task the courts have set themselves seems to be to judge, in the light of prevailing political ideology, and the nature

---

[4] [1965] Ch. 32.   [5] [1965] AC 512.

of the immunity or benefit claimed in the name of the Crown, whether a particular function should be held to enjoy that immunity or benefit. So, for example, if the provision of basic health care is thought to be a function of such public importance that it should be primarily in the hands of the government, rather than of private enterprise, then this could provide an argument for interpreting legislation in such a way as to relieve the NHS of an obligation to pay royalties to a private drug manufacturer for the use of drug patents. It may be that there are some functions, such as defence of the realm, which would, at all times and according to all political theories, be considered as part of the proper role of central government, but most functions are more difficult to categorize because the way they are perceived tends to change with time, and according to changing views of the nature and proper province of government.

A third factor is the relationship between the claimed benefit, or immunity, and the particular ground on which it is claimed. For example, in *Tamlin* v. *Hannaford* [6] it was held that the British Transport Commission was not part of the Crown but rather was an independent commercial entity. Thus, it was not entitled to ignore the provisions of the Rent Acts in ejecting a tenant from its premises. But even if the Commission had been held to be an arm of central government, this by itself should not justify it in ignoring legislation designed for the protection of tenants. The Commission did not need such immunity for the proper conduct of its statutory functions. In an Australian case [7] the question was whether a statutory body, charged with the job of investing the assets of a superannuation fund for government employees, had to pay stamp duty in respect of transactions entered into by it in pursuance of its statutory functions. One judge drew a distinction between this issue and the question of whether, for example, landlord and tenant legislation would apply to acquisition, by the Investment Trust, of office accommodation. He seems to have thought that the latter was less central to the functions of the Trust and, therefore, less likely to give rise to entitlement to any immunity or benefit.

Finally, specific statutory provision can decide the issue of immunity. The Act which establishes the Advisory, Conciliation, and Arbitration Service (ACAS) [8] provides that the functions of the service

---

[6] [1950] 1 KB 18.
[7] *Superannuation Fund Investment Trust* v. *Commissioner of Stamps* (1979) 26 ALR 99.
[8] Employment Protection Act 1975, Schedule 1 para. 11(1).

are performed on behalf of the Crown, notwithstanding the fact that, in the performance of its central functions, it is to be free of ministerial direction. This led Lord Scarman in *UKAPE* v. *ACAS*[9] to say that injunctive relief was not available against the service. This is an interesting case because, given the nature of the service and the functions it performs, it is, as the legislation recognizes, highly desirable that the service should be independent and free from outside influence, so that it can truly mediate between the parties in dispute. So, judged by the criterion of central government control, ACAS would not qualify as a Crown body. On the other hand, the conciliatory nature of the service's activities makes the use of injunctive relief in connection with them wholly inappropriate; agreement between the parties, not coercion by one of them, is the essence of the exercise. So there are good grounds for according the Service immunity from injunctive relief, but they are not captured by the formula that ACAS 'performs its functions on behalf of the Crown'.

The conclusion we should perhaps draw from all this is that there are sometimes good grounds for relieving governmental bodies of certain obligations, such as an obligation to pay tax, or to give them some immunity, such as freedom from injunctive relief. But these grounds have little to do with the fact that the body is or is not part of *central* government, or subject to central government control. They have much more to do with the nature of the activity or function in question, and its relationship to the benefit or immunity claimed. It is, therefore, not helpful to express a conclusion about immunity in terms of whether a body is or is not part of the Crown. It would be better if the terminology were jettisoned and the real issues underlying it were faced squarely. This would also reveal common threads running through the law. For example, just as the exercise of discretion in the areas of defence and foreign affairs is usually held to be immune from judicial review, so the demands of defence and foreign relations may sometimes provide good grounds for immunity in matters of civil liability, not because defence and foreign relations are peculiarly activities of central government (which, of course, they are), but because the courts, by reason of their procedures and particular expertise, and for the sake of preserving their political independence, are unsuitable forums for judging the demands of defence and foreign relations.

[9] [1980] 1 All ER 612, 619*j*.

Much governmental behaviour which is alleged to be tortious or in breach of contract is done in the exercise of some discretionary power. The same basic issues of justiciability arise whether the act is challenged directly, by judicial review, or collaterally, in proceedings in tort, or for breach of contract. It is historical accident that collateral challenges have become complicated (in a way that direct challenges have, by and large, not) by the notion of *Crown* immunity, as opposed to immunity related to subject matter.

15

Liability in Tort

1. THE CROWN

THE Crown Proceedings Act 1947 provides in section 2 that the Crown shall be liable in tort to the same extent 'as if it were a private person of full age and capacity' in respect of vicarious liability, employers' liability, and occupiers' liability. There are a number of qualifications and exceptions to this general provision the most important of which are: (a) statutory immunities or limitations of liability accruing to any government department or Minister also accrue for the benefit of the Crown; (b) the Crown is not liable for breaches of statutory duties resting only on its officers and not on other persons (this limitation is actually implicit in the general principle in section 2, because if ordinary persons do not have the duty the Crown could not, by definition, be liable in respect of breach of duty *as if it were* a private person). The limitation is related to the rule that mandamus is not available to enforce duties owed by servants of the Crown exclusively to the Crown; (c) no statutory obligation binds the Crown unless the statute in question specifically so provides; (d) injunctions are not available against the Crown; and (e) the Crown cannot be sued in respect of the judicial activities of its officials.

The assumption underlying this general provision is that, prior to the Act, the Crown enjoyed a general immunity from liability in tort. Governmental bodies other than the Crown never enjoyed such an immunity, nor did the immunity of the Crown prevent a person suing personally the Crown servant or agent who committed the tort. The general principle now is that all governmental bodies may be sued and held liable in tort, in the same way and to the same extent as private individuals. This might be called 'the assimilation principle'. A classic example of the principle at work is *Cooper* v. *Wandsworth Board of Works*[1] in which the plaintiff successfully sued the defendant in tort for trespass to land, when it demolished part of a house in pursuance of an invalid demolition order. Again, trespass to the person is the most

---

[1] (1863) 14 CBNS 180.

important tort used for judicial control of police activities. (The latter fall outside the scope of this book for the technical reason that the police are not strictly part of the executive branch of government but have independent status. In fact, the police constable is in some ways the paradigm case for the Diceyan Rule of Law theory: the police constable is a public official, answerable in the courts for his conduct in his private capacity).

2. THE DEFENCE OF STATUTORY AUTHORIZATION

The *Cooper* case illustrates clearly a defence which is more often available to governmental officials and bodies than to private individuals, in answer to claims in torts such as trespass and nuisance, in which the tortiousness consists in the deliberate doing of a particular act, such as arresting a suspected criminal, or establishing a dangerous installation, such as a prison or an infectious diseases hospital, without lawful justification. That defence is statutory authorization. The relevant question to be asked by the court when the defence is pleaded is whether the act which constitutes the tort was authorized by statute. In *Cooper*, if the demolition order had been valid, it would have authorized the demolition and constituted a good defence to the claim in trespass. In general terms, a plea of statutory authorization in a trespass action will be successful if the defendant can show that the trespass resulted from the performance of a statutory duty or the *intra vires* exercise of a statutory or prerogative power.

3. NEGLIGENCE AND STATUTORY POWERS

(a) The Basic Principle

The basic idea that a governmental body may escape liability in tort if the tort was the result of the performance of some statutory function, also applies to the tort of negligence. But negligence as such is not, by its very nature, capable of being authorized in advance. In fact, the basic principle of the law is that statutory functions must be exercised without negligence. The leading cases which establish this proposition[2] date from the nineteenth century and were actions against non-governmental statutory corporations. But they are now treated as establishing a general rule governing the exercise of statutory functions by

[2] *Mersey Docks Trustees* v. *Gibbs* (1866) LR 1 HL 93; *Geddis* v. *Proprietors of Bann Reservoir* (1878) 3 App. Cas. 430.

governmental as well as non-governmental bodies. The starting-point
of English law is, therefore, that governmental bodies are subject to the
law of negligence just as private citizens are. We will examine later the
way this principle operates in relation to liability for negligent exercise
of a statutory duty. We are here concerned with its application to the
exercise of statutory discretionary powers.

(b) *The Public Policy Defence*

The leading case on this subject is *Anns* v. *Merton LBC* [3] in which the
plaintiffs were owners of a flat which suffered structural damage
because the foundations of the block in which it stood were
inadequate. The House of Lords was asked whether the council,
which had statutory powers to regulate building in its area and to make
inspections to ensure compliance with building regulations, could be
held liable in negligence, on the assumption (a) that the foundations of
the building had not been inspected at all to ensure that they complied
with regulations concerning foundations; or (b) that an inspection had
been made but so carelessly that the inspector did not notice that the
foundations did not comply with the regulations. The judgment of
Lord Wilberforce lays the basis of the law governing the liability of
governmental bodies for negligence in the exercise of statutory powers;
but it is, unfortunately, not entirely clear at all points and the following
account is, to some extent, an interpretation of what was said in *Anns*.

The starting-point is the basic rule that, unless some good reason to
the contrary can be found, a governmental body is subject to the
ordinary law of negligence. Whether such good reason exists or not is
ultimately for the court to decide. A good reason will exist if the
defendant can establish, first, that the action or decision complained of
and alleged to be negligent was done in furtherance of some public
interest or policy, the pursuit of which was committed by the
legislature to the defendant, by giving it statutory powers to further
that interest or policy; and, secondly, that the act or decision was *intra
vires*. Some explanation of this statement is needed.

Governmental bodies are very frequently given statutory powers to
enable them to further specified policy objectives. The rules according
to which the courts exercise control over the use of such powers are
contained in the doctrine of *ultra vires*. Just as a prerogative order or a
declaration or injunction will not be awarded unless it can be shown

[3] [1978] AC 728.

that the respondent has acted *ultra vires*, so damages in tort cannot be awarded unless the exercise of power which allegedly constitutes the tort (a private law wrong) is also an illegal act in the public law sense, that is, unless it is *ultra vires*. The requirement that the defendant governmental body, if it wishes to displace the operation of the ordinary rules of negligence, must show that in doing what it did it was exercising a statutory power in furtherance of some public policy, brings into operation the public law rules of *ultra vires*. The requirement that the plaintiff then show that the defendant's action was *ultra vires* immunizes the latter from liability to pay damages in tort for *intra vires* action, just as the doctrine of *ultra vires* immunizes governmental bodies from the award of a prerogative order in respect of *intra vires* action, when a decision is directly attacked by way of application for judicial review.

It can be seen from this account that the ordinary law of negligence is modified, in its application to governmental bodies, so as to take account of the public law doctrine of *ultra vires*. Although the law starts from the position that the liability of governmental bodies is governed by private law rules, once this starting-point is abandoned and public law rules are taken into account, then if the private law and the public law rules clash the latter prevail. This means that even if, according to private law rules, the act of a governmental body constitutes a tort, it will not be actionable if, according to public law, the act is a lawful one.

(c) When is the Defence Available?

The crucial question, then, is how to decide when the public law rules of *ultra vires* have to be introduced into the question of the liability in negligence of a governmental body. The answer which has already been implied is that the doctrine of *ultra vires* is relevant when, in exercising a statutory power, the defendant was furthering some public policy. No attempt will be made to give a definition which will enable such situations to be identified in advance, mainly because such a definition does not exist. The reason why no such definition exists can be appreciated if one asks why the doctrine of *ultra vires* is thought to be relevant in some negligence cases. The doctrine of *ultra vires* serves two main functions: first, it prevents governmental bodies from exceeding their powers, whilst still leaving them a wide area of freedom by defining illegality in terms of action so unreasonable that no reasonable authority could have decided upon it. Secondly, so far as the courts are concerned, the doctrine of *ultra vires* embodies a principle of restraint on their part in controlling government activity. In the context of negligence actions, therefore, there will be a good reason for the court not to award damages in respect of governmental action, even if it is a private law wrong, if the policy considerations which support the doctrine of *ultra vires*—the desirability of leaving administrative bodies relatively autonomous in the exercise of their powers, the constitutional position of the courts, and the limitations of adversary procedure for investigating and deciding complex policy issues—seem relevant to evaluation of the legality of the action, and the action is, judged by the rules of *ultra vires*, within the powers of the authority. No definition of such cases can be given because, at the end of the day, it all depends on how suitable for judicial adjudication the court perceives the policy issues in the case to be. The best we can do is to look for illustrations of the process at work in the cases, and this is what we will now do.

In *Anns* there was no good reason why the council ought not to have been held liable in negligence in the ordinary way, if an inspector had looked at the foundations, but had carelessly failed to notice their inadequacy. It is hard to conceive that such negligence on the part of the inspector could be said to have been done in legitimate furtherance of some public policy. But, if no inspection had been made, this might have been because, for example, the council had decided that it could only afford to inspect every third building site and the site of the plaintiff's flat was not one of these. If the court felt that this decision about the allocation of resources raised issues of policy for the council to decide, then an action in negligence would not succeed, even assuming that the decision not to inspect amounted to negligence, unless the decision was *ultra vires*.

In *Dorset Yacht Co. Ltd.* v. *Home Office*[4] Borstal boys escaped from Brownsea Island in Poole Harbour, where they had been taken on a training exercise; in the process of escaping they damaged a yacht belonging to the plaintiff. It was alleged that the escape was the result of negligence, on the part of the prison officers, in carrying out their instructions as to supervision of the boys. If this could have been proved, there would have been no good reason of policy why the Home Office as employer should not have been held liable for their negligence. But if the boys had escaped, not because of any negligence on the part of the officers, but simply because the island was a low-

[4] [1970] AC 1004.

security location, and the decision to send the boys to such a location had been made because it had been thought that it would further their rehabilitation, then a court would be likely to say that such questions of penal policy were for the prison authorities to decide, subject only to the doctrine of *ultra vires*.

In another case[5] markings on a road which indicated traffic priorities at an intersection were obliterated when the road was resurfaced. The markings were not repainted immediately and the council decided 'as a matter of policy' not to erect temporary priority signs at intersections in such circumstances. It was held that the council was liable in negligence for creating a danger and not taking reasonable steps to remove it. There was no good policy reason why the ordinary rules of negligence should not apply. In *Vicar of Writtle* v. *Essex CC*[6] a youth on remand was placed in an open community home. The social worker who sent him there knew that he had a propensity to wander and to light fires, but decided not to tell the house parent, allegedly because he thought that this silence was in the best interests of the child. The boy escaped and set fire to the plaintiff's church. It was held that the ordinary law of negligence applied to the case and that there was no good policy reason which could justify the decision of the social worker not to pass on the information. Again, in *MHLG* v. *Sharp*[7] where a land registry clerk gave an inaccurate certificate, which failed to state that the plaintiff held a charge over the subject property, the ordinary law of negligence applied; the case had no policy ramifications at all.

The position we have, therefore, is that, when faced with an allegation of negligence, a governmental defendant might defend itself either by showing that it was not negligent; or, in some cases, by showing that the allegedly negligent act was done in *intra vires* exercise of a statutory power and in furtherance of a public policy which the court finds unsuitable for consideration by it, except in accordance with the doctrine of *ultra vires*. If the court decides that the case is one in which the doctrine of *ultra vires* is relevant and that the defendant acted *ultra vires*, the only line of defence left to the defendant would be to disprove negligence on its part. Because the test of whether an act is *ultra vires* is not the same as the test of whether an act is negligent, the fact that it is *ultra vires* does not mean that it is negligent, although it may make proof of negligence easier in some cases.

[5] *Bird* v. *Pearce* [1979] RTR 369.
[6] (1977) 79 LGR 656.
[7] [1970] 2 QB 223.

(d) The Policy–Operational Distinction

In *Anns* v. *Merton LBC*[8] cases in which the defendant cannot convince the court that its act or decision raises policy issues which the court ought not to consider except in accordance with the doctrine of *ultra vires*, were called cases of 'operational negligence' or 'negligence at the operational level'. By this is meant simply cases in which no issue of policy arises which is beyond the court's competence; the ordinary law of negligence operates because the defendant has adduced no ground on which its operation ought to be displaced. If the defendant can convince the court that its action raises issues of policy to which public law rules should apply, then, using the terminology adopted in *Anns*, the case would be one of alleged negligence at the 'policy' or 'planning' level.

It should not be concluded from this terminology that the planning level concerns decisions and the operational level the execution of decisions. The distinction turns on whether issues of public policy of a certain type are raised by the alleged negligence. For example, the decision to establish a system of open prisons, for reasons of penal policy, might be held to be a 'policy' decision. The fact that a prisoner escaped during the execution of that decision would not mean that the case was at the operational level, unless the reason why the prisoner escaped was simple negligence by a prison officer. If the escape resulted from the nature of the prison, rather than from any negligence in the running of it, the case would raise the same policy issues as the decision itself to set up the prison.

(e) General Criteria of Policy

It is clear that the court exercises a very important function when it decides whether the policy issues raised by a negligence action make the public law rules of *ultra vires* relevant. The importance of the function has led to attempts to lay down principles as to when a case will be held to raise policy issues. It is sometimes said that decisions about how to spend limited public funds are actionable in negligence only if *ultra vires*. But this is not correct as a general principle. No doubt one reason why the council in *Bird* v. *Pearce*[9] decided not to provide temporary signs was to save money. But the interest of motorists in personal safety is so great that it should prevail over such considerations of public finance. Again, the management of a

---

[8] [1978] AC 728.   [9] [1979] RTR 369.

government factory would not be allowed to plead that negligent failure by it to provide a safe system of work, in pursuance of a decision about how to spend limited funds, was a protected policy decision. The interest of the workers in personal safety would outweigh considerations of economy or the need to observe 'cash limits'. The basic question is not whether the decision is one about spending, but whether the interest which loses out in the financial carve-up is one which the court is prepared to allow the authority to starve of funds, or whether the court considers that interest to be so important that funds ought to be found to protect it.

Again, it is sometimes suggested that decisions which involve a conscious taking of risk should be actionable in negligence only if *ultra vires*. A conscious decision to take a risk in setting up an open prison, for the sake of the rehabilitation of prisoners, would fall into this category. But once again, this criterion does not exclude the factory manager, who consciously decides to take the risk created by an unsafe system of work, for the sake of some other goal, such as productivity; or the local authority, which consciously decides to save money by not erecting temporary road signs. Whether the ordinary law of negligence applies depends on what the risk is and what the other goal is.

(*f*) *Negligence and Ultra Vires at the Operational Level*

After this lengthy exposition of the way in which public law affects the liability of governmental bodies in negligence, a number of other points about the subject need to be made. The first is this: it is sometimes said that *no* action against a government body for negligence in the exercise of a statutory power, will succeed unless the exercise of power was *ultra vires*, and that this is true as much at the *operational level* as at the policy level. In theory, this approach is undesirable because it turns the law on its head: instead of subjecting governmental bodies to ordinary tort liability unless good reason to the contrary is shown, it subjects the application of ordinary tort rules to the public law of *ultra vires* in *every* case. In practice, however, it does not matter which view of the operational level is adopted. Either the ordinary law of negligence applies or, if it also has to be shown that the authority acted *ultra vires*, mere negligence is treated at this level (but not at the policy level) as a head of *ultra vires*.

(*g*) *Liability for Non-Feasance*

A second point to note is that *Anns* contemplates the imposition on governmental bodies of considerable liability for non-feasance, as opposed to misfeasance. There is a general principle in the law of torts that, in the absence of a pre-existing positive duty to act, mere failure to act will not incur liability. The line between misfeasance and non-feasance is not an easy one to draw, but the sort of situation in which *Anns* contemplates the imposition of liability for non-feasance can be illustrated by reference to the case itself. The council had a statutory power, but not a duty, to inspect foundations. If councils could be held liable for negligent inspection of foundations, but not for complete failure to exercise their power to inspect, there would be a great temptation for them to sit back and do nothing. But public law imposes on the holder of a discretionary power a duty to give proper consideration to whether the power should be exercised, or not, and in what way. If a governmental body decides, for no good reason, not to exercise a power, or fails to consider whether it will exercise it or not, it acts *ultra vires*, and if it has acted *ultra vires* it can be sued in negligence in respect of its failure to act.

The liability of public bodies for non-feasance may go further than this. In *East Suffolk Rivers Catchment Board* v. *Kent*[10] the plaintiff's land was flooded when a tidal wall burst; the defendant, acting under statutory powers, made negligent attempts to repair the wall. If the work had been done properly the flood could have been abated in fourteen days; but as it was, it took 178 days. The plaintiff sued for damages in respect of the extra 164 days' flooding. The board was held not liable on a number of grounds, but the decision was disapproved in *Anns* and it seems likely that today the Board would be held liable.

The important point is that it is unlikely that a private individual who gratuitously came to the aid of a landowner in such a situation, would be held liable if his efforts were unsuccessful, even if this was owing to his incompetence. But because the Board had a statutory power to repair, they also had a common law duty to repair carefully. This approach may indicate a recognition that, in many situations, the citizen is in a relationship of dependence on public authorities, and that the power and control which such bodies exercise, justify requiring more of them, by way of positive action, than would be required of fellow citizens. In one Australian case[11] there are hints that a local authority, with a statutory duty to give information about land to a purchaser, may also be under a duty to warn him of defects in the

[10] [1941] AC 74.
[11] *Wollongong City Council* v. *Fregnan* [1982] 1 NSWLR 244.

land, which it knows about, even though the council has no statutory duty to disclose such defects, and is not in the habit of disclosing them. A gratuitous private adviser clearly has the option of remaining silent, but a public adviser may be under a duty to reveal information of which it is aware and which is of great importance to its citizens.

(*h*) *Negligence at the Policy Level*

A third point worth making concerns what it means to say that a decision at the policy level is negligent. It will be recalled that, at this level, *ultra vires* and negligence are two different things, and the fact that a decision is *ultra vires* does not necessarily mean that it is negligent. If the court holds that the decision is *ultra vires* because it is so unreasonable that no reasonable authority properly understanding its powers could have made it, then it is very likely also to be held to be negligent. Again, if an authority takes into account, in reaching its decision, matters which it clearly ought not to have taken into account, then it may be held to have acted negligently.

A general matter, which needs to be taken into account here, arises out of *Dunlop* v. *Woollahra Municipal Council*[12] in which the council, before passing a resolution fixing the maximum number of storeys of new buildings in a particular street, consulted a competent solicitor as to whether the resolution would be valid. The resolution was later held to have been invalid; and it was clearly a policy decision on a matter within the province of the council. So, a negligence action was allowable, but the Privy Council held that the council, by consulting the solicitor, had taken all the care that could be expected to ensure that the resolution was valid. It seems, therefore, that public bodies can protect themselves from many actions in negligence by taking sound legal advice before they act.

It was also decided in this case that mere failure to give a hearing, as required by the rules of natural justice, could not, by itself, amount to negligence. The reason for this appears to be the lack of a foreseeable risk of injury as a result of a failure to hear the plaintiff: the failure to hear would render the decision invalid; the plaintiff was in as good a position as the council to know this; an invalid decision would not affect his legal rights and he could simply ignore it. This line of reasoning is of enormous potential significance: by relying on the fact that an *ultra vires* decision is a nullity, it could have the result that a

---

[12] [1982] AC 158.

negligence action would never succeed in respect of an *ultra vires* policy decision. Although correct in theory, the argument seems unrealistic in pratice. The only way to be sure that the failure to give a hearing (or any other sort of allegedly *ultra vires* conduct) has rendered the decision invalid is to test the matter in litigation, and a prudent plaintiff would be very unwilling to build in disregard of an official building regulation until he was sure, both that its imposition was invalid, and also that the council could not easily render it valid by remaking the same decision by proper procedure.

4. NUISANCE

The role of statutory provisions as defences to claims in nuisance has recently been restated in succinct form.[13] The law is complicated by rules about the effect of the presence or absence in the statute of (a) provisions enabling compensation to be paid to victims of nuisances created by the exercise of statutory functions; and (b) provisions expressly imposing, or expressly exempting the authority from, liability in nuisance. Since the effect of such provisions is strictly a matter of statutory interpretation, we can pass over them and concentrate on the basic common law rules about the effect of statutory authorization of the activities giving rise to the nuisance.

The position is as follows: if the statute authorizes (or requires) the doing of a specific act, and the doing of that act necessarily or inevitably creates a nuisance no matter how carefully it is done, then the nuisance is authorized and cannot form the subject of a successful tort action. But if the nuisance is the result of negligence in doing the authorized act, then an action in nuisance may lie, because the nuisance will not be inevitable.

If the statute authorizes a class of acts and leaves it up to the authority to decide which of those acts it will perform (in other words, if the statute gives the authority a discretion), and if the discretion could have been exercised in such a way as not to create a nuisance, then an action for damages (or an injunction) may lie, if a nuisance is created by the exercise of the statutory discretion.[14] This is so, even if the authority executed the course of action it decided upon without

---

[13] *Department of Transport* v. *North West Water Authority* [1984] AC 336, 344 *per* Webster, J (QBD); approved by HL [1984] AC 336, 359–60.
[14] *Managers of Metropolitan Asylum District* v. *Hill* (1881) 6 App. Cas. 193; *Allen* v. *Gulf Oil Ltd.* [1981] AC 1001.

negligence; but, of course, the basic rule, that statutory powers must be exercised without negligence, applies here as well, and if the nuisance is the result of negligent exercise of a statutory power, a plea of statutory authorization would fail. The impact on this rule of the doctrine of *ultra vires* and its interrelationship with the law of negligence has not yet been considered in a nuisance case, but one would expect the picture here to end up looking much the same as that in negligence actions: if an authority pleads that it was exercising a statutory power, then, if the nuisance-creating action was at the operational level, the authority would have to prove that it exercised its power without negligence. If the action was at the policy level then, provided it was *intra vires*, the defence would succeed. If it was *ultra vires* the authority would have to disprove negligence.

5. BREACH OF STATUTORY DUTY

It is, of course, illegal in a public law sense for a governmental body to breach any of its statutory duties. In strict public law terms breach means non-performance, and the chief remedy for non-performance is mandamus. We have already discussed the law governing the availability of mandamus, and the relationship between it and non-judicial remedies for breach of statutory duty.[15] We have also noted that, although, in theory, a duty has either been breached or it has not, in some cases the open-textured language in which a duty is cast may, in practice, give the duty-bearer an amount of discretion as to how he will perform his duty.

The present concern is with actions for damages in tort for breach of statutory duty. The basic private law rule is that such an action will lie for damage inflicted by the breach of a statutory duty (whether negligently or, if the duty is cast in stricter terms than a duty of reasonable care, without negligence) only if the duty is owed to individuals generally (as opposed to society as a whole), or to the plaintiff in particular, or as one of a particular group of people. The law on this point is complex and students should refer to a torts textbook for greater detail.

One view is that this rule also applies to actions against governmental authorities for breach of duties of a public nature, and the bulk of the case law supports this view. But one writer[16] maintains that a plaintiff

---

[15] Chapter 6.
[16] Wade, *Administrative Law* (5th edn., 1982), pp. 666–7.

who sues a public authority for breach of statutory duty, need only show that he has suffered damage as a result of the breach. A midway position might be that the plaintiff who sues a public authority must establish, either that the statute intended individuals to have a right to sue, or that he suffered special damage as a result of the breach.[17] (If this were the law, it would bring actions for breach of statutory *duty* into line with actions for public nuisance which protect public *rights*).

An important point to make in this context concerns the notion already discussed of *ultra vires* breach of statutory duty. In *Meade* v. *Haringey LBC*[18] it was held that an action in tort for breach of the statutory duty of an education authority to provide educational facilities would lie, in respect of a decision not to open a school because of a strike by ancillary workers, only if the decision was *ultra vires*. The duty to provide educational facilities is a vague one and leaves a lot of discretion to local education authorities. By contrast, in *Reffell* v. *Surrey CC*[19] in which a child was injured when her hand went through a glass swing-door which she was trying to control, it was held that the school authority was in breach of its statutory duty to ensure* that school premises are safe. Now, this duty, too, is a rather open-textured one, and could be interpreted so as to leave to school authorities a considerable degree of discretion to decide how much to spend on safety and the level of safety to be aimed at. It was held, however, that the duty was an 'absolute' one, in the sense that it was for the authority to secure the safety of pupils, and that the test of breach was objective, in the sense that it was for the court, not the authority, to decide what 'reasonable safety' meant. There was no evidence in the case as to whether the council, which, according to the judge, appreciated the risk presented by such doors (which existed in a number of older schools), had consciously decided, for reasons of economy or otherwise, not to replace such doors or modify them to render them safe. The judge surmised that the council simply waited for a major refurbishment of old schools, or for a breakage, before replacing such doors. Such an approach may have been *ultra vires*, but the clear implication of the case is that, even if the council had genuinely decided not to replace all such doors immediately, an action for breach of statutory duty would still have lain, because the authority's duty was to secure safety, not to make a valid decision whether to secure it or not.

---

[17] See *Booth* v. *National Enterprise Board* [1978] 3 All ER 624.
[18] [1979] 1 WLR 637.   [19] [1964] 1 WLR 358.

It is suggested, on the basis of these and other cases, that we can say that the distinction between the operational and the policy levels of administrative activity is relevant in actions for breach of statutory duty. If the duty is an open-textured one, which leaves the authority a degree of discretion as to how to perform its duty, then if the exercise of this discretion raises policy issues which the court feels have been committed to the authority's decision (as in *Meade* where the Court of Appeal was unwilling to interfere with the decision of the authority as to how it would deal with a delicate situation of industrial dispute), then a tort action for breach of statutory duty will lie only if the discretion has been exercised *ultra vires*. But, if the breach of duty raises no policy issues which the court feels incompetent to decide (as in *Reffell* where the safety of the children was seen as paramount), then an action will lie for breach of statutory duty, provided only that the ordinary rules of private law governing actions for breach of statutory duty are satisfied.

6. MISFEASANCE IN A PUBLIC OFFICE

All the torts we have considered so far have their origin in and derive their basic characteristics from private law. There is one tort which can be called a public law tort, because it applies only to the activities of public officials. This tort is called 'misfeasance in a public office'. There is little English case law about this tort, but there are quite a few Commonwealth decisions. There has been considerable discussion of the exact origins and status of this tort, and of technical points, such as the meaning of the term 'public office'. The only point which needs to be made here is that the balance of authority (including a dictum of the Privy Council)[20] is that the tort is only committed if the official whose action inflicted injury on the plaintiff acted with 'malice', which seems to mean, deliberately with the intention of injuring the plaintiff, or at least recklessly as to such an outcome. As a result, the tort is of quite limited value and importance as a means of controlling the ordinary run of unintentional governmental illegality.

[20] In *Dunlop* v. *Woollahra MC* [1982] AC 158.

16

Government Contracts

1. THE CROWN

THE basic principle, that government should be subject to the ordinary law of the land, lies at the bottom of the law of government contracts, both in respect of contracts made with governmental bodies generally, and in respect of contracts made with central government (the Crown) in particular. Prior to 1947 the fiat (or leave) of the Attorney-General had to be obtained by a litigant who wished to bring an action for breach of contract against the Crown, but this special procedural protection for the Crown was abolished by section 1 of the Crown Proceedings Act 1947. There is also a provision in the Act (s. 17) which overcomes technical obstacles to suit which may arise if the department of central government which the plaintiff wishes to sue is not strictly a legal person (that is, if it is not incorporated). The 1947 Act has, therefore, removed procedural obstacles to suing central government for breach of contract.

The only major respect in which central government is in a protected position, in a procedural sense, is that the ordinary process of executing judgments for the payment of money is not available against organs of central government.[1] This means that government property cannot be seized and sold to provide money to satisfy any judgment against central government. But the Act does provide an alternative procedure, by way of certification by the court of the amount due to the plaintiff, backed up by a statutory direction that the appropriate government department 'shall . . . pay' the sum due plus interest. In constitutional terms, the disbursement of money by the executive is subject to a parliamentary vote of funds for disbursement. In practice, however, a specific appropriation for the purpose of paying damages would not usually be necessary. Save in totally exceptional and politically contentious cases, central government is expected to meet its legal liabilities, and individual departments would usually have sufficient contingency funds available to do so.

[1] Crown Proceedings Act 1947 s. 25(4).

In 1865 it was held that the availability of funds to meet contractual obligations was of basic significance, not just at the stage of meeting judgments for breach of contract, but also at the stage of formation of contract. In *Churchward* v. *R*:[2] it was held that, unless at the time a contract was made sufficient funds had been voted by Parliament to meet the government's obligations under that contract, no valid contract came into existence. In other words, the existence of a valid contract was contingent upon the availability of funds for its performance. It followed that, in such cases, the government could not be sued, or held liable, for breach of contract if it did not perform its contractual obligations. Although there is no modern English authority on the point, it seems likely that English courts would accept the theory laid down in an Australian case[3] that the availability of funds is relevant to the performance of the contract and to the enforcement of any judgment for damages for breach, but that lack of funds does not prevent a valid contract being made.

2. PRECONTRACTUAL NEGOTIATIONS

Just as the central focus of the private law of contract is breach of contract—questions of formation and validity of contract only arise when a party fails to perform his part of the contract—so the most developed part of the law relating to government contracts concerns the liability of the government for breach of contract. It should be noted, in the first place, that section 21 of the Crown Proceedings Act provides that an injunction or a decree of specific performance cannot be awarded against the Crown and so, as against central government, but not as against other governmental bodies, the only available remedy is a declaration or damages. In practice this restriction is not of great importance: government will usually perform its obligations once a court has decided what they are; and anyway, except in respect of contracts for the sale of land, specific performance and injunction are only rarely available, as a matter of private law, for breach of contract. We will discuss the theory behind this restriction in greater detail later.

This concentration on questions of liability for breach coupled with the fundamental principle of English law of freedom of contract—that is, that parties are entitled, subject to any relevant legal qualifications, to make what contracts they like with whomever they choose—has two

---

[2] (1865) LR 1 QB 173.
[3] *New South Wales* v. *Bardolph* (1934) 52 CLR 455.

important consequences. The first is that the *law* of government contracts is concerned almost entirely with the extent of government privilege, that is, with those situations in which government bodies can escape the normal legal consequences of breaches of contract by them. The law has much less to say about governmental behaviour at the precontractual or negotiating stage, at which the authority decides with whom it will contract and at which the contents of the contract are settled between the parties. This is particularly so in relation to contracts made by central government, because the contracting powers of central government are basically the same as those of any private citizen. There are, to be sure, a great many internal departmental guidelines concerning the making of contracts by departments, but these will in general have no legal force, and so could not form the basis of an application for judicial review if a prospective contracting party felt that the guidelines were unreasonable, or had been applied or ignored in an unreasonable way.[4] In practice, a great many government contracts are made in standard form. There are two main sets of standard contract terms, one for construction contracts, and the other for supply contracts. Contracts of central government typically contain a number of special terms; for example, terms giving the government more control over performance than is usual in contracts between private parties; and giving the government certain powers of unilateral variation; and making provision for recovery of excess profits made by the contractor.

The position of other governmental bodies, including local government, is more restricted, because their contracting powers, like all their other powers, derive from statute and so may be limited by statutory provisions. Relevant statutes may restrict the sort of contracts which the body can enter. For example, there are provisions in planning legislation which arguably impose restrictions on the sorts of deal which authorities can make with developers in return for the grant of planning permission. Such provisions are, however, exceptional. But statutes conferring the power to contract will rarely, if ever, say anything about precontractual behaviour, and the ordinary common law (or lack of it) will apply. The behaviour of a local authority in the negotiating phase might be subject to a certain degree of legal control,

---

[4] There is some authority—*HTV Ltd.* v. *Price Commission* [1976] ICR 170—which might be used to support an argument that departure from established guidelines might be held unlawful, even though the guidelines were not strictly legally binding. But this is unclear.

as in *R.* v. *Hereford Corporation, ex parte Harrower,*[5] in which it was held that the applicants were entitled to apply for mandamus to force the local authority to comply with its own standing orders, regulating the process by which tenders for contracts were to be invited. Most local authorities adopt uniform standing orders published by central government, and these contain provisions on contracting. In addition, central government may issue circulars to local authorities recommending the adoption of particular contract terms. In practice, local authorities normally use a standard form of building contract published by the RIBA. Finally, the contracting practices of nationalized industries are subject to relatively little central control, so as to preserve their freedom of commercial judgment.

In short, although the power to make contracts is similar in its basic characteristics to many other governmental discretionary powers, because it is a power which is shared with private individuals, it is not subject to the ordinary law of judicial review of governmental discretionary powers. Rather, it is protected from significant control by the common law principle of freedom of contract.

The common law has very little to say about the conduct of parties in contractual negotiations, or about the content of contracts. The Unfair Contract Terms Act 1977 probably does not apply to the Crown, although it would probably apply to other governmental bodies, at least to the extent that, in making the contract, the body could be said to be acting in the course of a business. The exact scope of the incipient doctrines of inequality of bargaining power and economic duress is unclear, and their application to government contracts even less clear. It is just possible that the idea of unfairness (that is, inconsistency) in the exercise of governmental powers might have some role to play in controlling governmental precontractual behaviour.[6] But, on the whole, the law has made no attempt to deal with the question of inequality of bargaining power generally, or to consider its relevance to the unique position of government as a contracting party. This is, no doubt, partly a result of the fact that disagreements between the government and its contractors are usually resolved by mutual accommodation, without recourse to the courts. But this in turn means that matters which are often of great public importance are not subjected to public scrutiny. It should not be thought, however, that inequalities in the government–contractor relationship always inure

---

[5] [1970] 1 WLR 1424.
[6] See n. 4 above.

for the benefit of the former. A good example relates to recovery of excess profits, especially in relation to defence contracts made with monopoly suppliers. Such contracts usually contain a provision for recovery, but it seems clear that, in practice, excess profits are often successfully concealed, and retained by the contractor. The established procedures for the recovery of such profits do not involve recourse to the courts.

A second important consequence of the lack of legal control of government contracting is that government can use contractual provisions to achieve policy objectives, which would otherwise have to be pursued by means of primary or delegated legislation, and so with the approval (or lack of disapproval) of Parliament. The most notorious example of this was the use, by the Labour Government in 1978, of contractual provisions and of its right to choose with whom it would contract to enforce its pay policy. But such practices have a long and not unrespectable history; governments, for a very long time and without opposition, have included provisions as to pay (setting minima rather than maxima) in its contracts with private contractors. It can be seen that such use of contracts (the provisions of which need not be subjected to parliamentary scrutiny and which are not subject to judicial control) to achieve governmental policy objectives (whether social or economic) raises fundamental constitutional questions about the relationship between the executive and Parliament. If neither Parliament nor the courts are to have any significant degree of control over governmental precontractual behaviour, there is effectively very little control *of any sort*, beyond the fear of electoral consequences (and in the absence of publicity there are unlikely to be such consequences), on this form of central governmental activity.

3. LIABILITY FOR BREACH OF CONTRACT

As has been said, the law of government contracts is most highly developed in respect of the liability of the government for breach of, or failure to perform, its contractual undertakings. It must be stressed at the outset, however, that, as noted above, it is extremely rare for government contracts to be the subject of litigation. Disputes are usually resolved by informal negotiation between the government and the contractor.

The basic principle is easy to state, but not so easy to apply: because government bodies have to consider the wider public interest, there may be circumstances where the demands of public policy provide good grounds for a government body to refuse to perform its contractual obligations to the other contracting party. In such cases the interests and rights of the individual contractor are subordinated to the demands of public policy. In other words, the law recognizes what might be called a public policy defence, or immunity, which governmental bodies can sometimes plead in actions against them for breach of contract. The difficulty is to define the scope of this defence or immunity, to specify when it will be available.

The other side of the same coin is that it is illegal for a governmental body to fetter its statutory discretions by contract or undertaking. It is important to note at this point that the principle refers to both contracts and undertakings. Here we are concerned with contracts, but undertakings which are not contractually binding should not be ignored, because we have already seen that failure to perform such undertakings can be held to be *ultra vires*.[7] In *The Amphitrite*[8] the owners of a foreign ship sued the government for failure to honour a promise to release the ship from British waters after it had discharged its cargo. The judgment of Rowlatt, J is unclear as to whether the promise was contractually binding or not. If the case stands for the proposition that non-contractual undertakings can never be binding, it may now be incorrect. It has long been recognized that the courts are sometimes reluctant to find the requisite intention to create legal relations in relation to agreements between government and citizen. But it does not follow from this that government bodies ought never to be prevented from going back on non-contractual undertakings, which have raised legitimate expectations and induced reliance, when there is no good policy reason for allowing the government to dishonour its undertaking. But on the facts of *The Amphitrite* it seems clear that a plea of the exigencies of war would be treated by a court as justifying the government action, regardless of whether the promise was contractual or not.

As we have already seen,[9] the rule against fettering requires the court to make a value judgment about the relative claims of the individual contractor and the demands of public policy, which the discretion is designed to serve, and in the light of this value judgment to decide whether the contract or undertaking is an illegal fetter on the proper exercise of the discretionary power. The question facing the

---

[7] pp. 73–4 above.   [8] [1921] 3 KB 500.
[9] pp. 76–7 above.

court is not essentially different from that facing a court confronted with a plea of public policy in defence to an action for breach of contract. The only difference lies in the way the question is typically raised in practice. The fettering principle is usually relevant when a party seeks to force the government body to exercise its discretion, rather than to perform its promise not to exercise its discretion; or to challenge the exercise of a discretion which has been exercised in accordance with or contrary to the demands of a contract or undertaking. The plea of public policy as a defence typically arises in cases in which the contractor seeks to enforce the contract or to recover damages for breach of contract. It is important to realize that the same basic issue ties the two areas together, because it serves to show that any sharp division between the so-called public law obligation not to fetter the exercise of discretions and the private law contractual obligations of governmental bodies, is unwarranted. The law of government contracts is basically an application of public law principles to the ordinary law of contract, leading to certain modifications of private law principles in their application to governmental activities.

Most of the cases relevant to this topic have already been discussed in the chapter on control of discretionary powers. Brief mention need be made of only two cases. *The Amphitrite*[10] has always been the source of much disagreement amongst writers. The most extreme proposition for which it may be taken to stand is that a defence of public policy can be established merely on the government's word that the demands of public policy justify non-performance of its undertakings. Such an interpretation is out of line with the case-law generally. It seems clear that the courts retain for themselves the final power to judge the validity of a plea of public policy. In some areas, such as the conduct of war, the courts will no doubt exercise their power in a very restrained way and will usually accept government certificates as to the demands of public policy, on the ground that the exercise of the power to wage war is unreviewable in the courts (this explains *The Amphitrite*).

But there is no general rule that pleas of public policy cannot be questioned and evaluated by the court. This emerges quite clearly from *Commissioners of Crown Lands* v. *Page*[11] in which it was held that the requisitioning of premises in 1945 could not be held to be in breach of the implied covenant of quiet enjoyment in the lease. Devlin,

[10] [1921] 3 KB 500.
[11] [1960] 2 QB 274.

LJ was clearly not prepared to allow decisions about the demands of the conduct of the war to become the subject of judicial inquiry, but denied that this gave the government a general privilege to escape from any contract, which it happened to find disadvantageous, by pleading the public interest. The court will scrutinize the plea and, if it feels competent to do so, will judge its merits. In one sense there is always a legitimate public interest in the government not being bound to a disadvantageous contract, but against that interest must be weighed the contractual rights of the contractor. A contract is a technique by which parties can restrict their freedom of action in the future and a party to a contract cannot be free to ignore that restriction as it wishes.

4. ULTRA VIRES AND LIABILITY FOR BREACH OF CONTRACT

An attempt should now be made to state more explicitly the relationship between the doctrine of *ultra vires* and the common law rules of breach of contract. In the first place, it should be noted that the rule, that government bodies must not fetter the exercise of their discretionary powers by contract, implies a legal limitation on the contracting powers of a governmental body which does not attach to the contracting powers of private individuals or corporations. Secondly, it should be recalled that if the contracting powers of the body in question derive from statute, then the statute might impose limitations on those powers, and failure to observe those restrictions may mean that the body has exercised its discretionary contract-making power *ultra vires*.

More difficult to disentangle is the relationship between the doctrine of *ultra vires* and a plea of public interest in answer to a claim for breach of contract. It might be thought that, as a matter of general principle, a governmental body could not be held liable in contract in respect of the exercise by it of its governmental powers, unless that exercise of power was *ultra vires*. Clearly, if a breach of contract consists of the *ultra vires* exercise of a discretionary power, the governmental body would not be allowed to argue that its breach was justified by the public interest. But in many contract cases the exact problem is that there is a conflict between two valid exercises of different discretionary powers, that is, the contract-making power and some other power. Only if the contract is declared to be a void (and thus *ultra vires*) fetter on the other discretionary power will no such clash arise. In such cases, the question which the courts seem to ask themselves, when faced with a plea of public interest, is whether the public interest pleaded is of sufficient importance that it should be held to outweigh the interests of the private contractor. For example, in *The Amphitrite*[12] and *Commissioners of Crown Lands* v. *Page*[13] the defendant's plea involved an appeal to the exigencies of war, and it is a well-established principle that the courts will not review the exercise of the (prerogative) power of waging war. By contrast, in *Dowty Boulton Paul* v. *Wolverhampton Corporation*[14] and in the *Birkdale Electricity Supply Company*[15] case, the court seems to have decided that the public interest pleaded was not sufficient to justify treating the government body, as a contracting party, differently from a private contracting party, and allowing the interests of the private contractor to be overridden.

It is clear, therefore, especially from the *Dowty Boulton Paul* case, in which the decision of the local authority was directly challenged and held to be valid,[16] but was also held to amount to a breach of contract,[17] that a plaintiff who sues for breach of contract in respect of the exercise of a discretionary power, need not prove that the exercise was *ultra vires*. Contractual rights are deemed worthy of protection, even against *intra vires* acts, if the public interest being served by the exercise of the power is not seen as sufficiently important to justify infringing the strong principle that contracts ought to be performed.

5. THE EFFECT OF A PLEA OF PUBLIC POLICY

Perhaps the most contentious issue in this area is the *effect* of a plea of public policy. It is possible to approach this question in a technical fashion, by seeking private law analogies. For example, it is possible to treat at least some cases (involving, for example, declaration of war after the contract was made) in terms of the doctrine of frustration and, if this analogy is used, a readjustment of the affairs of the parties along the lines provided for in the Law Reform (Frustrated Contracts) Act 1943 would be justified, that is, restitution of benefits given and received, subject to a claim for expenses incurred. But, if there is seen as being an implied term, entitling the governmental body to refuse to

---

[12] [1921] 3 KB 500.   [13] [1960] 2 QB 274.   [14] [1971] 1 WLR 204.
[15] [1926] AC 355.
[16] *Dowty Boulton Paul Ltd.* v. *Wolverhampton Corporation (No. 2)* [1976] Ch. 13.
[17] [1971] 1 WLR 204.

perform if public policy so demands (as in *Commissioners of Crown Lands* v. *Page*), the justified result may be to leave the losses where they fall.

If a contract is held to constitute a fetter on the exercise of a discretionary power, the obvious analogy is with a contract which contains a covenant in restraint of trade. This analogy would then lead to questions about whether the void provision was severable from the rest of the contract, and also questions about *restitutio in integrum*.

But it may be that a better approach than searching for private law analogies would be an approach which, while recognizing that there may be good grounds of public policy which justify releasing governmental bodies from contractual obligations, deals with the question of monetary compensation for the disappointed contractor more flexibly. Restitution of benefits conferred on the governmental body by the other party would be fair and reasonable, to the extent that this is possible. It may be, too, that if a contracting party has incurred irrecoverable expenses in performance of the contract, he should be entitled to compensation for these reliance losses. Should the contractor ever be entitled to damages for profits which he expected to make out of the contract? There might be an argument for saying that, although a contractor should never be expected to bear actual losses for the sake of the public interest, he should not be allowed to make a profit at its expense. The most flexible of all approaches would be to leave the question of the availability and amount of monetary compensation to be decided by the court, in the light of the circumstances of each individual case and of the interests of both the public and the private contractor. But courts are unlikely to be prepared to get involved in the fine discriminations and policy judgments which such an approach requires. It would probably be better if the legislature laid down some general principles.

The argument for monetary compensation for contractors, whose claims are met by a successful plea of public policy, is strengthened if it is recalled that often the action in breach of contract will be *intra vires*. The appropriate question is, who should bear the risk that the public interest may justify and demand non-performance? When the question is put in this way the answer, fairly obviously, is 'the public'.

17

Restitution[1]

A FEW words should be said about the application of restitutionary rules to public authorities. The law of restitution deals with situations in which the defendant has acquired some benefit at the expense of the plaintiff and it can be said that the benefit has been unjustly obtained. Suppose a public authority charges a citizen for a service, which it is under a duty to provide free of charge, or for some lesser amount than it actually charges. If the authority threatened to withhold the service if the charge was not paid, then the law of restitution would consider that the charge had been unjustly extracted and would allow the citizen to recover it.[2] But what if the authority makes no such threat? Suppose that it believes, wrongly, that it is entitled to make the charge and the citizen does not realize that he need not pay? Here public law and private law principles conflict. Public law says that the authority has acted *ultra vires*, but the private law of restitution does not in general allow recovery of benefits conferred as a result of a mistake of law. And, as we have seen, monetary compensation is not available as a remedy for *ultra vires* action as such.

If the private law of restitution would not impose liability if the defendant were a private citizen, should it do so against a public authority? Should the ordinary citizen be expected to find out for himself whether the authority is entitled to charge? Often it will be a difficult question of law whether the authority is entitled to charge. Would it not be fairer to allow the citizen to recover the money, if it turns out that the payment was not due, even though he did not resist it at the time, but relied on the authority's interpretation of his obligations? After all, if he had resisted, the authority might have refused the service unless he paid, and thus given him a right to recover. Should he be in a worse position just because he did not resist? The justification for such an approach would be that the ordinary citizen is at a great disadvantage when faced with official

---

[1] Birks [1970] CLP 191.
[2] cf. *Congreve* v. *Home Office* [1976] 1 QB 629 (threat to revoke TV licence unless extra licence fee paid).

demands for money, and is not realistically in a position to resist.

The sort of situation primarily under consideration here is one where an authority makes a demand for payment for a public service. But the question of restitution of payments made to public authorities can also arise in 'private law' contexts, for example, if the authority as landlord makes an improper claim for rent. Perhaps the special rule, suggested above, should only apply where the authority is acting in a governmental capacity. One can reasonably expect those who have commercial dealings with public authorities to organize their affairs in accordance with the ordinary law. On the other hand, when discussing the contractual liability of public authorities we noted an argument that, even in relation to ordinary commercial contracts, the strong economic position of public authorities should be reflected in special obligations. Perhaps public authorities should always bear the burden of ensuring that they act legally, even in ordinary commercial contexts.

Sometimes a decision that a demand for payment was unlawful and unjust will have very wide effects, as similar payments may have been made by many citizens.[3] If an authority is required to repay a large number of small payments, the total impact on its finances might be very great. Is this a good reason to refuse restitution? It is not generally thought a good reason not to overturn decisions of the Inland Revenue, that the impact on the public purse will be significant. A wrongful demand for payment for a public service is similar to a wrongful tax demand. It is unlikely that a court would be very sympathetic to an argument that to declare the demand invalid would damage public finances. A court would be more inclined to leave it to the legislature to reverse the decision by legislation, if thought fit.

[3] See e.g. *Daymond* v. *South West Water Authority* [1976] AC 609.

18

Estoppel

1. INTRODUCTION

IN private law estoppel is a many-faceted principle. For example, the doctrine of promissory estoppel in contract law prevents a contracting party, under certain circumstances, from enforcing his strict legal rights under the contract, because he has promised that he will not enforce them; the doctrine of proprietary estoppel in land law disentitles a person (*A*), under certain circumstances, from denying that another (*B*), who has acted to his (*B*'s) detriment in reliance on a belief that he owns certain property, actually has an interest in the property because *A* has fostered in *B* a belief that he (*B*) has the interest. A closely related concept of private law is that of waiver: for example, by his conduct, a party to a contract may be held to have waived his right to have the contract performed on a particular day. These examples of estoppel and waiver have one basic characteristic in common: they are all cases in which, for some reason, a party is denied the right to assert (or 'is estopped' from asserting) what are admitted to be his strict legal rights. So, all cases of estoppel involve a contrast between strict law and some notion of equity, which relieves a party of the strict legal consequences defined by a contract or title-deed.

It is suggested that no attempt should be made to draw detailed analogies between any particular type of estoppel or waiver in private law and the doctrine of estoppel in public law. The analogy should be taken no further than the common characteristic noted at the end of the last paragraph: the doctrine of estoppel in public law is primarily concerned with whether a public body ought to be denied the right to rely on and assert the fact that one of its decisions or actions is *ultra vires* and, therefore, not binding on it. In other words, the primary role of estoppel in public law is to provide a means of creating exceptions to the doctrine of *ultra vires*. Looked at in this way, it can be seen that it may be more appropriate to look for private law analogies, not in private law rules of estoppel, but in rules of company law. Like those of public statutory bodies, the powers of companies are limited, and there are rules of private company law about when a company can be bound to a course of action, even though that course of action is, as a matter of strict law, beyond its powers. On the other hand, it may be better, in this area, not to look for private law analogies at all, but just to seek to understand the public law doctrine of estoppel in its own terms.

I have just said that the public law doctrine of estoppel is concerned primarily with situations in which strict adherence to the doctrine of *ultra vires* can be dispensed with. But the language of estoppel is also used in another context. As a general principle, an *intra vires* decision is binding on the authority which makes it. But the law does apparently recognize that the demands of public policy can sometimes justify a public authority in changing or revoking some *intra vires* decision made by it, if circumstances change. The question of whether an authority can alter or revoke an *intra vires* decision is sometimes put in terms of whether it can be estopped from revoking or changing the decision. These two different contexts in which the term 'estoppel' is used in public law, should be kept distinct. The latter is really just another way of talking about the head of *ultra vires* which I have called 'unfairness'.

2. ESTOPPEL AS AN EXCEPTION TO THE DOCTRINE OF ULTRA VIRES

(a) Limited Nature of the Exception

Suppose that a local authority purports to exercise a statutory power in such a way as to provide a benefit for one of its citizens; and that this exercise of power is *ultra vires*, but that the citizen could not reasonably be expected to know this. A strict application of the principle of *ultra vires* would force us to say that the local authority would act illegally if it provided the promised benefit and that it could not be forced to provide it, no matter how unfair this might seem to the citizen involved and no matter how much loss he had suffered in reliance on the purported exercise of power.[1] To what extent is the law prepared to relieve parties of the strict consequences of the doctrine of *ultra vires*?

It must be said that most of the cases display a distinct unwillingness to allow any exceptions to the principle of *ultra vires*, beyond those which are necessary to deal with the most obvious cases of injustice. And it must also be said that even those exceptions which are recognized are largely the work of Lord Denning, MR, only accepted

[1] *Rhyl UDC* v. *Rhyl Amusements Ltd.* [1959] 1 WLR 465.

with a greater or lesser degree of reluctance by other judges. The House of Lords has not yet given comprehensive consideration to the matter. Why is there this reluctance? The first reason is obvious and is as valid in private law as in public law. The logic of any distinction, between the strict legal position and equitable exceptions to or relief from strict law, requires that the exceptions be kept within relatively narrow and well-defined limits, if they are not to threaten the general principle with extinction.

But there are other reasons which relate more specifically to the position of public authorities. First, most of the powers of executive government are statutory in origin and, thus, limited in scope. In fact, one of the basic ideas behind the doctrine of *ultra vires* is that all statutory powers have limits, and that the power to decide those limits must reside in some person or body other than the power-holder. It would make a nonsense of the idea of powers limited by statutory provision, if the courts had too extensive a power to dispense with those limits in the name of some idea of (non-statutory) justice. A second reason is implicit in the first and it relates to the idea of separation of powers. The doctrine of *ultra vires* serves to define the boundary between the powers of the legislature, the courts, and the administration, in deciding what the government can and cannot do. If the courts could freely dispense with the requirements of the doctrine of *ultra vires*, this would entail a considerable shift of power to the courts, and away from the legislature and the administration. For example, suppose that a planning officer of a local authority purports to grant planning permission, even though he has no authority to do so. The council later refuses permission. It might be thought that the aggrieved citizen ought to use the statutory method of appeal to the Secretary of State against refusal of planning permission, rather than go to the courts and seek to have the purported grant by the officer upheld, on the basis of the doctrine of estoppel. An appeal would allow the merits of the application for planning permission to be properly considered.

Thirdly, it is basic to the very structure of public law and governmental activity that, sometimes, the interests of private individuals must suffer at the expense of some larger interest defined by government policy. Therefore, it cannot be a ground for attacking government action, *just* that it caused injury to a private citizen. Conversely, it could not be a ground for waiving the doctrine of *ultra vires*, *just* that not to do so would cause injury to the plaintiff. If the doctrine is to be waived, there must be some additional ground. This need to find some additional ground itself produces a bias in favour of a narrow doctrine of estoppel in public law.

Fourthly, and related to the last reason, the mere fact that a private citizen will suffer injury if the doctrine of *ultra vires* is not waived in his favour, cannot by itself justify such waiver, because to allow an *ultra vires* decision or action to stand might inflict injury on the public interest (which the doctrine of *ultra vires* is designed to serve), or on specific third parties. If an *ultra vires* grant of planning permission is allowed to stand, persons who own property adjacent to or near the applicant's land may suffer by not having the planning law enforced. A fundamental difference between the way we perceive private law and the way we perceive public law, is that private law situations are basically bipolar, whereas public law ones involve interests beyond those of the two parties (the government body and the citizen) actually in dispute. It is true, of course, that the resolution of private law disputes does often affect third parties; but we are generally prepared to ignore these external effects as unimportant. In public law, however, the public interest and the interest of particular third parties always have to be considered of great importance in any dispute between a citizen and a government body.

(b) The 'Delegation' Exception

In *Western Fish Products Ltd.* v. *Penwith DC* [2] Megaw, LJ said that there are two types of exceptions to the basic principle that a statutory body cannot be estopped from asserting that a particular action, which the plaintiff seeks the performance of, would be *ultra vires*. The first exception deals with cases where the power to make a decision on a particular matter resides in one officer or body, but a decision on that matter is made by another officer on behalf of that body or officer, in such circumstances that it reasonably appears to the plaintiff that the officer has the power to make the decision on behalf of his superior. In some cases, of course, administrative agencies have the power to delegate their decision-making powers. [3] If this has been duly done, then the decision of the delegate is as binding on the authority as would be the same decision made by the authority itself. But if the authority has no power to delegate its discretion, or has such a power but has not properly exercised it, then the doctrine of *ultra vires*, in the

[2] [1981] 2 All ER 204.
[3] See p. 78 above.

form of the rule against delegation, renders the decision of the supposed delegate illegal and not binding on the principal body.

There is authority,[4] which was accepted in *Penwith*, for the proposition that, if there is evidence, such as a well-established practice of (unlawful) delegation, which would justify a person dealing with the delegate in thinking that the delegate had the power to make the decision, then the employing agency could be estopped from asserting the lack of authority. It is not enough that the decision is made by a person holding a senior office; this by itself would not justify a person in assuming that the officer had authority. There would have to be some more positive ground for making this assumption. The Court of Appeal rejected wide dicta of Lord Denning, MR[5] to the effect that any person dealing with officers of a government department, or local government authority, is entitled to assume that they have the authority which they appear to have, to make the decisions which they purport to make.

Two points should be made about this rule. First, this exception is sometimes referred to in terms of whether the officer had 'ostensible', or 'apparent', or 'usual' authority to make the decision in the plaintiff's favour. These phrases come from the private law of agency, and refer to situations in which a principal can be bound by the acts of an agent who has no actual authority to bind his principal, if the principal represented or put the agent in a position where he could make it appear that the agent had the authority claimed. There is a clear difficulty in applying these agency rules to public law situations: they potentially conflict with the rule against delegation. In public law terms, an agent with no actual authority is an unlawful delegate; in public law, appearances are strictly unimportant and cannot make good a lack of actual authority. Appearances will be important in public law only in a very narrow range of circumstances. It is better, therefore, not to use the language of agency to describe this exception to the strict application of the rule against delegation, but rather to define the exception simply in terms of the conditions which have to be fulfilled to establish it.

The second point to make is this: as just noted, the exception allows citizens to rely on appearances only in a very limited class of cases. This might be satisfactory when the citizen in question is a well-

[4] *Lever (Finance) Ltd.* v. *Westminster Corporation* [1971] 1 QB 222.
[5] Similar dicta appear in *Robertson* v. *Minister of Pensions* [1949] 1 KB 227, disapproved in *Howell* v. *Falmouth Boat Co.* [1951] AC 837.

educated and articulate individual, or a corporation, and can make the enquiries necessary to satisfy himself that the officer, with whom he is dealing, has the authority he claims or appears to have. But the ordinary citizen, dealing with a government department or local authority, would not necessarily think to question the authority of the desk officer nor know how to ascertain the true position. It was this, perhaps, which led Lord Denning, MR in *Robertson*[6] to make the sweeping statements he did. There a citizen relied, to his detriment, on an assurance by a government department (which it had no power to make) that he was entitled to a military pension.

(c) The 'Formality' Exception

The second exception is exemplified by *Wells* v. *Minister of Housing and Local Government*[7] in which a planning authority was not allowed to rely on the fact that a particular, formal procedural requirement for the grant of planning permission had not been complied with, because the authority itself had waived that requirement by initially ignoring non-compliance with it. In *Penwith*[8] Megaw, LJ said that the operation of this exception would depend on the construction of the statute. By saying this, his Lordship may have wanted to convey the idea that, whether a procedural requirement could be waived or not would depend on the importance of that requirement in the total context of the statutory scheme of procedure. A similar idea is embodied in the distinction between mandatory and directory procedural requirements.[9] It should be noted, however, that if the requirement waived is merely directory, then the breach of it does not invalidate the decision, and so enforcement of the decision does not involve a departure from the strict principles of *ultra vires*. The distinction between mandatory and directory requirements is a vague one and depends to some extent on all the circumstances of the case.[10] This flexibility enables the courts, by classifying procedural requirements as being merely directory, to evade the doctrine of *ultra vires*, without actually having to create exceptions to it.

It can be seen that this second exception deals with a rather different situation from the first. Here the issue is not one of the authority of an

---

[6] See n. 5 above.
[7] [1967] 1 WLR 1000.
[8] [1981] 2 All ER 204.
[9] See p. 121 above.
[10] See de Smith, *Judicial Review of Administrative Action* (4th edn., 1980) pp. 142–6.

officer acting on behalf of the authority, but the more immediate issue of the validity of the authority's decision. The first exception assumes that the only defect in the decision is that it was made by the wrong person, and that, if it had been made by the authority itself, it would have been valid. On the other hand, it should be noted that, in the case of each exception, the ground of invalidity in issue is a procedural one. There is no suggestion in the cases that the doctrine of estoppel can be used to prevent an agency from asserting the invalidity of a decision which is bad in its substance (for example, which is unreasonable). The problems associated with too wide a power to dispense with the doctrine of *ultra vires*, are much more acute in relation to substantive *ultra vires* than they are in relation to procedural *ultra vires*.

(d) Further Exceptions?

The law, then, appears to recognize two rather limited exceptions to the doctrine of *ultra vires*. Beyond this, however, it does not go. So, for example, a local planning authority cannot be estopped from asserting that planning permission has been refused by the fact that a clerk has mistakenly issued a notice saying that permission has been granted,[11] or has issued a notice of grant of permission in order to forestall litigation against an authority which has, in fact, refused permission; or by the fact that the signature of a local authority clerk has been forged on a fake notice of grant of permission; or by the fact that a notice of grant has been signed by a subordinate official without authority.[12] It may be possible for the aggrieved citizen to sue the clerk responsible personally, if he has been fraudulent or negligent (or sue the council vicariously; or personally, if it has been negligent or fraudulent) but, to succeed, it would not, of course, be enough for him to show that he had been injured by a false appearance of validity. He would have to show that this was the result of fraud or negligence on the part of the authority or its agents.

A possible explanation for this unwillingness to extend the doctrine of estoppel is that public officials might become overcautious in dealing with the public if they thought that any statement or decision they made would bind their agency, even if it turned out to be wrong. Public officials should be encouraged, to some extent at least, to be creative and spontaneously helpful, rather than always going exactly 'by the book'.

[11] *Norfolk County Council* v. *Environment Secretary* [1973] 1 WLR 1400.
[12] *Co-operative Retail Services Ltd.* v. *Taff Ely BC* (1980) 39 P & C R. 223.

234

(e) Detriment

A third point to make at this stage is that there is authority[13] for the rule that an estoppel will only operate against a public authority, either in respect of an *ultra vires* decision, or in respect of the alteration or revocation of an *intra vires* decision, if the plaintiff has acted *to his detriment* on the false appearance of validity or finality.

(f) A Balancing of Interests Approach

There is a quite different approach which could be taken to these cases. Instead of adhering to the doctrine of *ultra vires* as the benchmark of enforceability of decisions, it would be possible to go to the heart of the matter and recognize that what these cases involve is a conflict between individual interests, on the one hand, and government policy and public interest, on the other.

The basic question to be answered would be whether, balancing the various interests involved, the authority should be allowed to assert the invalidity and unenforceability of its decision, or whether, on the other hand, it should be required to stand by its decision or that of its officer, despite its invalidity. A governmental decision would be enforceable by a citizen, despite the fact that it was *ultra vires*, if not to enforce it would inflict injury on the individual, without any countervailing benefit to the public (apart from the fact that an *ultra vires* decision would not be enforced). On the other hand, if enforcement of the decision would damage the public interest in a significant way, this would justify allowing the authority to plead its illegality, despite the fact that the plaintiff would be injured by the non-execution of the decision. For example, in *Robertson* v. *Minister of Pensions*[14] the plaintiff sought to enforce against the defendant an *ultra vires* assurance that he was entitled to a pension. Clearly the impact on Robertson of not receiving the pension would be very considerable, whereas the impact on the public purse involved in paying it would be imperceptible. By contrast, the interests of particular third parties, and of the public generally, will often be significantly injured if *ultra vires* grants of planning permission are allowed to stand. Furthermore, such third parties will have no chance to put their side of the story if the disappointed landowner seeks to enforce an estoppel by court action.

It appears to be implicit in this approach that it would only apply in what might be called 'estoppel situations', that is situations in which an

---

[13] *Norfolk* case, [1973] 1 WLR 1400.   [14] [1949] 1 KB 227.

individual, who has acted to his detriment in reliance on an *ultra vires* decision, seeks to enforce the decision against the maker of it. It does not seem to be contemplated that a governmental body, whose decisions are directly challenged by application for judicial review, should be entitled to appeal to the balancing of interests approach to argue that its decision, though *ultra vires*, ought not to be quashed because it inflicts no appreciable injury on the person challenging it. (It will be recalled, however, that there are natural justice cases in which just such an approach has been adopted by the courts in favour of public bodies; cases in which a breach of natural justice has been held not to invalidate a decision, because no substantial injustice to the applicant has resulted from the decision).

Unlike the approach in *Western Fish*, which seeks to mitigate the harshness of the *ultra vires* principle by creating two narrow 'procedural' exceptions to it, this approach contemplates a 'substantive' exception to the principle: it involves looking at the substance of the decision in order to decide whether it ought to be allowed to stand or not. An important implication of this approach is that it may not be enough to ask whether the authority's decision ought to be executed or not. There is another theoretically possible remedy for an aggrieved citizen who has suffered loss by reliance on a false appearance of validity: monetary compensation for his loss. So, even if a court decides, as a result of balancing the interests involved, that a particular decision ought not to be allowed to stand, there may be no reason of public policy why the aggrieved citizen ought not to be compensated out of public funds for his loss. Conversely, it may be that if an *ultra vires* decision (for example, an *ultra vires* planning decision as in *Lever*) is allowed to stand, third parties who have to put up with the existence of the unauthorized development should be compensated for having to do so, for in that case they will have suffered injury as the result of an *ultra vires* decision.

There are two major problems with this approach. In the first place, the task of balancing public and private interests in the unstructured way which the approach contemplates, is not one which the courts are likely to be willing to undertake. Is a court likely to be prepared to decide whether the loss to a developer, who has to abandon a development for which *ultra vires* approval was given, is greater than the loss which would be suffered by his neighbours if the development went ahead?

Secondly, when would this balancing approach be used? Would it only be appropriate where the decision in question was *ultra vires* on one of the two procedural grounds discussed in the *Penwith* case? Or would it apply in any case where an individual sought to enforce an *ultra vires* decision against a public authority? Suppose, for example, that a grant of planning permission is successfully challenged by a third party on the ground that it was made as the result of taking into account an irrelevant consideration. The person to whom the grant was made could surely not then argue that, despite the fact that the decision was in substance (as opposed to procedurally) *ultra vires*, nevertheless the balance of public and private interests was such that the decision ought to be allowed to stand. The very decision that the grant was *ultra vires* means that, in some sense, it was not in the public interest. If the decision is *ultra vires* for substantive reasons, then it must be quashed. Otherwise the whole doctrine of *ultra vires* would be subverted. Estoppel should only apply where the ground of *ultra vires* in issue is procedural: many such cases involve unmeritorious insistence, by government bodies, on the strict technical letter of the law in a way that cases of substantive *ultra vires* usually do not.

Once this restriction is stated, however, it appears difficult to justify. Why should balancing of interests justify dispensing with the doctrine of *ultra vires* in some cases, but not in others? Why *not* substitute balancing of interests for the heads of *ultra vires* as the test of legality and enforceability in public law? The answer was given earlier, in stating the first objection to the balancing of interests test. Once balancing of interests is made the test of enforceability in some cases, there seems no reason why it should not be the test in all cases; and not just where an individual seeks to have a decision enforced, but also where he seeks to have it invalidated. For this very reason, the courts are unlikely to be prepared to adopt a test which threatens to subvert the whole doctrine of *ultra vires*, since that doctrine embodies a principle of judicial restraint in reviewing administrative action, which the balancing of interests test does not.

3. ESTOPPEL AND INTRA VIRES DECISIONS

All of the cases so far considered involved an attempt by a public body to rely on the illegality of some action or decision, taken by it or by one of its officers. The other context in which the language of estoppel appears, is where a plaintiff, who has relied to his detriment (and detriment is essential)[15] on an *intra vires* decision, attempts to prevent the agency which made the decision, from changing it to one which deprives the plaintiff of some benefit to which the original decision entitled him. The basic rule is, of course, that *intra vires* decisions are legally effective and binding on the body which makes them. This rule is sometimes put in terms of the principle of *res judicata*: once a matter has been determined, it cannot (subject to some statutory exceptions) be reopened before the same body, or before another body of equivalent status. But the use of this phrase is apt to mislead because it applies, basically, to judicial decisions. In relation to decisions made in exercise of statutory discretionary powers, it seems to be recognized that a certain amount of flexibility has to be allowed in the exercise of such powers, to take account of the fact that the demands of public policy may change over time in a way which would justify revoking a lawful decision to the detriment of a private citizen. The public policy defence to actions for breach of contract is a sort of application of this idea.

On the other hand, the basic and usual rule must be that lawful decisions are binding and irrevocable, and in Chapter 4 we considered a number of cases in which public bodies were held to have acted unlawfully in going back on some undertaking made by them.[16] For example, in *R. v. Liverpool Corporation*[17] the council was held to have acted unfairly in not abiding by an undertaking not to issue more taxi licences before certain legislation was passed, without giving a hearing to opponents of the issue of more licences. In *A.-G. of Hong Kong v. Ng*[18] it was held unlawful for immigration authorities to go back on an assurance that illegal immigrants would be given a hearing before being deported. By contrast, in *R. v. IRC, ex parte Preston*[19] it was held that the Revenue had not acted unlawfully in going back on a promise, made by it, not to investigate further the applicant's tax affairs for a particular tax year, because new information had emerged in the mean-time.

These cases show that it is not *per se* unlawful for an agency to change its mind about what it will do in exercise of a discretionary power. But it is objectionable if an applicant is led to expect, by the agency's words or conduct, that it will act in a particular way, but then the authority, without any particular good reason, changes its mind and

---

[15] *Rootkin* v. *Kent CC* [1981] 1 WLR 1186.
[16] pp. 73–4 above. [17] [1972] 2 QB 299.
[18] [1983] 2 AC 629. [19] [1985] 2 WLR 836.

decides to act in the contrary way. Presumably, good reason would consist of some consideration of public policy or interest which, in the light of changed circumstances, would justify disappointing the expectations of the applicant. The court has to decide, therefore, whether the public interest in changing the decision outweighs the interest of the applicant in not having it changed; or, in the words of Lord Denning, MR in *Laker Airways Ltd.* v. *Department of Trade*[20] whether the change inflicts injury on the applicant, without any countervailing benefit to the public.

It might be asked why balancing of interests is acceptable in this context, but not in the previous one. The answer might be as follows: since unfairness is a head of *ultra vires*, then the revocation of a lawful decision will be held to be *ultra vires* only if it is unreasonable, in the strict sense in which that word is used in the context of *ultra vires*. So, the balancing of interests required of the court here, is no greater than that required by the doctrine of *ultra vires* generally. It is a different thing, it might be thought, to give a court the power to *dispense* with the doctrine of *ultra vires* on the basis of a balancing of interests.

There are at least two cases in which it has been held that an authority could not be estopped from changing its mind. In *Laker*[21] it was said, incidentally, that a department of central government cannot be estopped from changing policy previously adopted. The court had in mind, particularly, the position of a government department after an election which brought the Opposition to power, and the case concerned a matter of high policy, namely, international civil aviation licensing. It would seem reasonable that a government of one political persuasion should be able to change at least some of the policy directives of a previous government without passing legislation; and it would seem inevitable that the more highly contentious (in a political sense) an undertaking is, the less likely it is that the courts will prevent an administrative body changing its mind in response to political pressures on it.

But the right to change earlier decisions is not limited to such cases. In *Rootkin* v. *Kent CC*[22] the council changed its mind about whether the applicant's daughter was entitled to a free bus pass. The Court of Appeal held that since the decision to give the pass was a discretionary one—the child had no right to a pass, even if she lived the requisite distance from school—the council could not be estopped from going

---

[20] [1977] QB 643, 707; cf. *HTV Ltd.* v. *Price Commission* [1976] ICR 170, 185.
[21] Ibid.   [22] [1981] 1 WLR 1186.

back on its decision. As a general rule, it was said, a public authority cannot be estopped from exercising its powers from time to time, as it sees fit. But this statement seems to be too wide; the courts are sometimes prepared to act to reverse particularly unfair and unjustifiable changes of mind. The present case was weak from the applicant's point of view, because the pass was withdrawn only after it was discovered that the child did not, in fact, live the requisite distance from the school. At all events, it was held that no detriment had been suffered (apart from the obvious one engendered by the revocation of the earlier decision) by withdrawal of the pass.

It is clear that, in this class of case, the word 'estoppel' is used in a rather different sense from that which it bears in the context of creating exceptions to the doctrine of *ultra vires*. It seems clear, too, that, in this context, the courts are aware that they have to be careful, for constitutional reasons, not to go too far in preventing governmental bodies from changing their mind in a way that is open to them by virtue of the discretionary nature of their powers. It is true, of course, that a power to choose between alternative outcomes does not entail a power to alter the choice once it has been made. But, sometimes, such an additional power is necessary. Nevertheless, the power to reverse a decision should be dependent on the authority adducing very strong reasons for doing so. If the change of mind was based on delicate political considerations which the court is unwilling to adjudicate upon, then it should allow the reversal of the decision to stand, *not* on the ground that authorities must be allowed to change their mind, but on the ground that the case raises non-justiciable issues.

19

Discovery and Public Policy

I. INTRODUCTION

DISCOVERY of documents is what is called an interlocutory procedure. By means of discovery a party can, before trial of an action, obtain access to documents in the possession or custody of the other party, which are relevant to his case. A related interlocutory procedure is that of serving interrogatories, that is, a list of questions addressed to the other party to the action, designed to elicit information known to the other party or to which he has access, which is relevant to the interrogator's case. Both of these procedures are essentially pre-trial evidence-gathering mechanisms. They are designed to save time at the oral trial, and to enable a party to know, as fully as possible in advance, the case which may be presented against him, and to prepare his own case as effectively as possible.

The rules of evidence in our system include rules about when a person giving evidence is entitled not to answer a question or to provide information requested. For example, a professional man, such as a doctor or solicitor, is entitled, in certain circumstances, to refuse to divulge information given to him in confidence, in his professional capacity. There are analogous rules relating to discovery and interrogatories. One of these rules is that, in certain circumstances, a party may decline to give evidence, or disclose documents, or answer interrogatories, if he can establish that the demands of public policy justify or require non-disclosure of the evidence or documents. In relation to actions against governmental bodies, the issue of non-disclosure of evidence more often arises in the pre-trial than in the trial context, because in such actions the evidence is usually given in written (affidavit) form. Of the two pre-trial procedures, discovery is, in practical terms, the more important and so, for the sake of simplicity, this topic will be discussed with reference to discovery, even though it is relevant to oral evidence and interrogatories as well.

2. CROWN PRIVILEGE OR PUBLIC INTEREST IMMUNITY?

The rule that disclosure of documents can be resisted on the ground of public interest, used to be referred to by the phrase 'Crown privilege', signifying that the Crown had a privilege against disclosure. The word 'privilege' was derived from the private law rules of evidence; for example, the right of a solicitor not to disclose certain information is called 'legal professional privilege'. The nature of this right as a 'privilege' has two corollaries in private law. First, the right of silence attaches not to the information but to the witness asked to give it. So, if some other person who does not enjoy such a right, can be found, who can give the required information, there is nothing to stop his being asked the relevant questions and answering them. Secondly, a party who enjoys the right of silence has a choice whether he will claim it or not. If he chooses not to exercise the privilege, then there is nothing to stop the evidence being given. Only the witness can raise the issue of privilege. It has never been entirely clear whether either or both of these corollaries also attached to the use of the term 'privilege' in the public law context.

The term 'Crown privilege' is now thought to be misleading and incorrect in a number of respects. First, although the cases are not entirely unanimous on the point, it appears that, in many cases, public interest immunity from disclosure attaches to the information and not to the witness (that is, the Crown or other body from which information is sought). So, in theory, if the public interest demands silence, the right to silence cannot be waived. In practice, if the right to silence is not claimed, the evidence is unlikely to be withheld. In one type of case it might be argued that there is no reason why the immunity ought not to be waivable, even though it protects a public interest in non-disclosure. In a number of cases, bodies such as the Customs and Excise Commissioners and the NSPCC have successfully claimed immunity from disclosing the sources of their information on the ground that, if confidentiality was not maintained, their sources of information would dry up. In such cases, there seems no reason why the particular source being protected should not waive the immunity, because people will not be discouraged from coming forward if they know that it is only by their own choice that their identity may become known.

A second reason why the term 'Crown privilege' is now thought to be misleading is that it is not up to the government whether the immunity is claimed or not. Any party to the litigation can raise an issue of public policy immunity, and the court can raise it of its own motion. If the court decides that the evidence in question should not be disclosed, the government may not then waive the immunity. Thirdly, the term 'Crown' is inaccurate because it used to be taken as implying that public policy immunity only attached to documents generated by the activities of departments of central government. But it is now clear that the demands of public policy can justify non-disclosure of material generated by local government, or even by such non-official bodies as the National Society for the Prevention of Cruelty to Children.

3. INSPECTION TO DETERMINE RELEVANCE

To understand the law in this area properly it is necessary to draw a distinction between two different questions: what might be called 'the discovery question', on the one hand, and 'the immunity question', on the other. In the present context, the discovery question is essentially a private law question, because the fact that the information has been generated by a public body does not, in theory, affect the issue of whether the conditions laid down in the Rules of the Supreme Court for the availability of discovery, are satisfied. The immunity question, on the other hand, is often a public law question, in that the argument for non-disclosure turns on the public nature and responsibilities of the body which generated the document the discovery of which is sought.

The basic rule governing the discovery question is that documents should be disclosed if they are relevant to questions in dispute, and their disclosure is necessary for the saving of costs, or the just disposal of the case. So, for example, it has been held that, if a document is 'confidential', it should not be subject to discovery if the relevant information it contains can be found in another non-confidential source.[1] Only if the discovery question is answered in favour of disclosure does any question of immunity arise. There is, however, a difficulty here, because, in order to know whether a document contains information relevant to an issue, it is necessary to know exactly what it does contain. But if a claim of immunity is made, it may turn out, if the claim is justified, to be improper to reveal what it contains in order to

---

[1] *SRC* v. *Nasse* [1980] AC 1028.

determine its relevance. A solution to this problem might be to allow the court to examine the documents in private to ascertain whether they contain relevant material. But, it has been held by the House of Lords[2] that a judge should inspect documents for which immunity is claimed, only if he is satisfied that they are more likely than not to contain material which would give substantial support to the contentions of the party seeking disclosure. This is a high standard and it imposes a considerable restriction on the power of the court to inspect documents.

The importance of this restrictive attitude to inspection is not limited to the discovery question. If a claim of public interest immunity is made, then the only way the court can judge the strength of the claim, without actually allowing the contents of the documents to be disclosed, is to inspect the documents in private. If inspection is not allowed, because the plaintiff has not passed the 'relevance threshold' for inspection, then the court has no alternative but to accept the claim of immunity; otherwise it risks causing exactly that damage to the public interest which the government alleges will flow from the disclosure. Thus an unwillingness to inspect for relevance leads to an inability to question claims of immunity. It is important to realize that the upshot of a denial of discovery may not just be that some relevant documents are unavailable. If the essential elements of the plaintiff's case are buried in documents which the court refuses to inspect or refuses to allow the plaintiff to see, then his case may never get off the ground and a wrong may go uncorrected.

4. INSPECTION TO DETERMINE IMMUNITY

At one stage, the courts took the view that if a suitably senior administrative officer (usually a Minister) certified that the interests of the State required non-disclosure, such a certificate would be treated as conclusive by the court.[3] But since *Conway* v. *Rimmer*[4] the courts have been much less prepared to accept the views of the executive as conclusive of the question of immunity. Hence the practice of inspection in private by the court, this being the only way to adjudicate properly on a claim of immunity, without revealing the contents of the documents. This change of attitude effected a significant shift of power from the executive to the courts. The courts took upon

---

[2] *Air Canada* v. *Trade Secretary* [1983] 2 AC 394.
[3] *Duncan* v. *Cammell Laird* [1942] AC 624.   [4] [1968] AC 910.

themselves the task of deciding exactly what the demands of public policy were, in respect of the disclosure of government information. The position now appears to be that no government document, however exalted in origin (e.g. Cabinet documents) is necessarily entitled to immunity, although the higher the origin of the document, and the closer its connection with matters of high policy (as opposed to routine government administration), the less likely are the courts to question any claim for immunity made in respect of it.[5]

The task of the court, when it inspects documents in order to adjudicate on a claim of immunity, is to balance the alleged public interest in non-disclosure against the *public* interest in the due administration of justice (which, in an adversarial system, requires the disclosure of all information having more than marginal relevance to the case), and to decide, on the basis of this balancing, whether the documents ought to be disclosed or not.

It is important to note that what is weighed against the alleged public interest in non-disclosure is not the interest of the individual litigant, but the public interest in the due administration of justice. This is not to say that the interests of the litigant are not relevant: the public interest can only be measured with reference to the strength of the plaintiff's case as a matter of law and fact, and the importance of the interest he seeks to vindicate by his action. But, at the end of the day, what the courts are seeking to uphold is the integrity of the legal process. This explains why the courts are prepared, in this area, to do the sort of balancing exercise which they are not generally prepared to do: the courts are, in a special sense, guardians of the legal process, and their responsibility to protect it from encroachment by administrative action is greater than their responsibility to protect purely private interests from such encroachment.

As is the case with any balancing operation which requires detailed reference to the facts of particular cases, not all decisions will necessarily sit easily with one another. A distinction, which seems of doubtful value, has been drawn between disclosure of documents relating to the behaviour and treatment of a child in the care of a local authority (the child, now an adult, sought to sue the authority for negligent maltreatment while he was in care) and documents relating to the behaviour of a delinquent schoolboy, not in care, who assaulted a teacher, who then sought to sue the local authority in negligence. In

---

[5] *Burmah Oil Ltd.* v. *Bank of England* [1980] AC 1090.

the former case,[6] it was held that the proper functioning of the care services demanded that their records be kept confidential and should not be inspected by the judge, while, in the latter case,[7] it was held that the court was right to inspect the documents and decide, on the basis of their significance, whether the demands of justice outweighed the desirability of confidentiality of the records of education authorities on individual problem children.

A close reading of these two cases suggests that the court was unsympathetic to Gaskin's claim but sympathetic towards Campbell's. We have noted that there is an unavoidable link between the strength of the plaintiff's case and the propriety of allowing discovery. This is true in relation to the immunity question, as well as in relation to the discovery question, because the former question involves a balancing exercise in which one of the factors weighed (that is, the interest in the due administration of justice) inevitably raises the issue of the strength and importance of the plaintiff's case. But it is important that rules of discovery should not be used to prejudge the merits of the case. It may be undesirable that complaints against care authorities, of the relatively nebulous character of Gaskin's (he claimed that he had suffered psychological injuries and anxiety neurosis as a result of maltreatment) should be made in the courts, given the complex nature of the relationship between child and care authority. But if such actions are to be countenanced, they should not be frustrated by denying the plaintiff access to records about himself.

5. CLASS AND CONTENTS CLAIMS

Unwillingness to accept official certificates that the public interest requires non-disclosure is also reflected in a greater scepticism of claims of immunity made on the basis that the documents in question belong to a class of documents which ought not to be disclosed (class claims), than of claims made on the basis that the documents in question contain sensitive material (a contents claim). The leading case is *Conway* v. *Rimmer*[8] which involved an action for malicious prosecution by a former probationary constable against his one-time superintendent. The Home Secretary objected to the production of a number of internal reports on the conduct of the plaintiff during his probation, but this claim of immunity was rejected. The claim in this

---

[6] *Gaskin* v. *Liverpool CC* [1980] 1 WLR 1549.
[7] *Campbell* v. *Tameside MBC* [1982] QB 1065.   [8] [1968] AC 910.

case was important because it was a class claim and the main argument for non-disclosure was a candour or confidentiality argument: that internal reports on individual policemen would be less frank if the writer feared disclosure to the subject. The House of Lords asserted the right of the court, in all but the clearest cases, to assess for itself any claim of immunity, especially where the claim was a non-specific class claim, and it encouraged scepticism towards the candour argument. On the other hand, the history of the distinction between class and contents claims has been somewhat chequered, and not all judges take the same sceptical attitude to class claims. In *Air Canada*,[9] for example, Lord Fraser suggested that the court might be *less* well equipped to controvert a class claim than a contents claim, because the court would not be in a good position to judge the importance of the particular class of documents to public administration as a whole.

One area in which the courts are likely to be prepared to accept without question a claim of immunity, even if it is a class claim, is that of defence and foreign affairs. Thus in *Duncan* v. *Cammell Laird*[10] a claim for immunity was upheld, in respect of certain documents and plans relating to a submarine which sank during sea trials. Although the approach of deference to executive claims of privilege in this case has been in some degree departed from, the actual decision seems to be accepted as correct.

6. CONFIDENTIALITY

Another litmus-paper test of the changing attitude of various courts and judges to the sanctity of executive claims of immunity, is the attitude taken to the issue of confidentiality. A claim of immunity often rests partly on the argument that desirable frankness in the administration of government business will be discouraged, if officials are aware that they risk disclosure of internal departmental documents. Lord Upjohn in *Conway* v. *Rimmer*[11] was dismissive of such arguments and could 'not believe' that Civil Servants would be influenced by such a consideration. This approach gave rise to the conventional wisdom that confidentiality *as such* is not a ground of immunity. But the idea of confidentiality *as such* is a very doubtful one. Confidentiality is always in aid of some end, and if the end is important enough and is likely to

---

[9] [1983] 2 AC 394, 436.
[10] [1942] AC 624.   [11] [1968] AC 910, 993–4.

be jeopardized by lack of frankness, then it can be said that immunity is protecting the end, not the confidentiality.

Anyway, not all claims of candour and confidentiality are treated with equal suspicion. In *Alfred Crompton Amusement Machines Ltd.* v. *Commissioners of Customs and Excise*[12] a claim of immunity was upheld in respect of a class of documents containing, amongst other things, information given voluntarily by third parties, about the commission of excise offences. This was done in part so as not to discourage third parties from giving information, for fear of being later identified. The same argument was important in *D*. v. *NSPCC*[13] in which the House of Lords upheld a claim of immunity in respect of the identity of a person who had provided information to the Society. The claim for disclosure arose in connection with a claim for damages in negligence against an officer of the society, for failure to investigate a complaint properly before confronting the plaintiff about it, thus causing her nervous shock.

With the *Crompton* and *NSPCC* cases can be contrasted *Norwich Pharmacal Co.* v. *Commissioners of Customs and Excise*[14] in which the applicant sought an order of discovery for disclosure of the names of illicit importers of a compound over which they had a patent. In this case the litigant's interest in the disclosure was strong and clear—to enforce his legal patent rights—and the argument for non-disclosure was weak because the identity of the importers was revealed by ordinary commercial documents supplied in the ordinary course of business, and not some sensitive or confidential source. So there was no reason not to order disclosure.

Just as the courts have been prepared to protect the activities of gaming licensing bodies from close scrutiny by means of a claim that the rules of natural justice have been breached,[15] so, too, they have been prepared to protect documents relating to applications for licences from discovery, even in the face of allegations that the informant of the body has criminally libelled the applicant.[16] The feeling that the gaming fraternity is one of doubtful probity, and that there is a great need to protect informers generally from possible consequences of candour, serve to support the arguments for secrecy

---

[12] [1974] AC 405; cf. Contempt of Court Act 1981 s. 10 on which see *Defence Secretary* v. *Guardian* [1984] 3 WLR 986.
[13] [1978] AC 171.   [14] [1974] AC 133.
[15] *R.* v. *Gaming Board for Great Britain, ex parte Benaim & Khaida* [1970] 2 QB 417.
[16] *R.* v. *Lewes Justices, ex parte Home Secretary* [1970] AC 388.

for the records of police and related bodies. This is clear in recent cases concerning inquiries under section 49 of the Police Act 1964, which establishes an internal complaints procedure. In *Neilson* v. *Laugharne*[17] and *Hehir* v. *Commissioner of Police*[18] it was held that demands of candour and public interest in the proper investigation of complaints against the police would generally support a claim of immunity against disclosure of records of a section 49 inquiry, in a civil action against any of the police officers involved. It is significant that the claim of immunity was made in respect of a particular class of documents (regardless of their actual contents) and was upheld as such. One gets the uneasy feeling, from the readiness of the courts to accept class claims and the candour argument in these cases, that courts are rather too willing to use the law of discovery to deny proper access to information to persons of whom they disapprove. This is a misuse of the law of discovery.

At the end of the day, all claims to immunity are claims of confidentiality, and the issue is whether there is a sufficient public interest in non-disclosure (and hence, by implication, in confidentiality) to justify immunity from discovery. Some judges have certainly shown themselves more sympathetic to the candour argument than Lord Upjohn. In *Burmah Oil* v. *Bank of England*[19] Lord Wilberforce said that he thought the candour argument had received an 'excessive dose of cold water'.

7. FREEDOM OF INFORMATION

Beneath this area of the law lies the idea that discovery of truth is not an absolute value in our legal system, and that, sometimes, truth has to be sacrificed to other social interests. One way of resolving the conflict between truth and the disclosure of information, on the one hand, and the public interest in secrecy, on the other, is for Parliament to enact legislation regulating access to governmental and other official and semi-official records. In the absence of such legislation, the common law of public interest immunity assumes great importance. In fact, one explanation for the explosion of case-law in this area in recent years, is that it is a response on the part of the courts and litigants to the failure of Parliament to legislate on freedom of information. It can be seen,

---

[17] [1981] QB 736.   [18] [1982] 1 WLR 715.
[19] [1980] AC 1090, 1112.

therefore, that the law of discovery is not a minor by-way of administrative law, but raises issues of fundamental importance concerned with the openness of government processes.

And, as in other areas where private law rules are applied to governmental bodies, the courts are being asked to make decisions (which are often difficult and politically contentious) about what modifications to those private law rules, public interest and public policy justify and demand. We must ask, therefore, whether in this area the courts are being asked to do things which it would be better for Parliament to do. Which would be politically and constitutionally preferable: a clear and quite precise Freedom of Information Act, or a general principle, developed and applied by the judges, that the government is entitled to immunity from disclosure if public interest so demands? There is no obviously correct answer to this question. Much depends on one's own political views. What is important is that the impact of the work that the courts are being asked to carry out, on the authority and legitimacy of the judicial process, should not be ignored.

There are some cases which throw light on the attitude of the courts to issues of freedom of information, not only in terms of access to information generated by governmental bodies and other bodies performing functions of public importance, but also in terms of the free flow of information in society generally. The most famous is *BSC* v. *Granada Television Ltd.*[20] in which Granada claimed immunity from disclosure for the name of a mole inside BSC, who had leaked confidential documents to Granada, which was making a programme about a steel-workers' strike. It was held that the media had no general immunity (based on a public interest in the free flow of important information) from disclosing the sources of their information, which would justify keeping the name of an informant secret lest future potential informants should be discouraged from coming forward. In this case, too, the House of Lords felt that the interests of BSC, in identifying and taking action against the mole, were of such importance that disclosure was required. Section 10 of the Contempt of Court Act 1981 now provides that no court may require the disclosure of sources of information, unless such disclosure is necessary in the interests of justice, or national security, or the prevention of disorder or crime.[21]

[20] [1981] AC 1096.
[21] On the interpretation of this section see *Defence Secretary* v. *Guardian* [1984] 3 WLR 986.

In *Birmingham City DC* v. *O.*[22] a city councillor, who was not a member of the social services committee, sought access to committee documents about a particular adoption application, because she had reason to believe that the adoptive parents were unsuitable persons to be allowed to adopt a child. It was held that, although the councillor had no *right* to see the documents, it was ultimately up to the council, as a whole, to decide whether a councillor, who was not a member of the committee, should have access to its papers; and that the decision to allow access to the files was not an unreasonable one because, despite the sensitivity and confidentiality of the information, the councillor had made out a case for being allowed to see the documents. This case gets closer than any of the others we have looked at, to issues of open government, since here the question of disclosure did not arise in the context of litigation involving the person seeking disclosure. The action was an application for judicial review of the council's decision to allow access, and the issue was not whether the due administration of justice required disclosure, but whether the public interest in the due administration of the adoption service did. This case might open the way for other cases in which ordinary citizens could, subject, of course, to any statutory provisions regulating access to government documents, challenge government decisions to allow or refuse access to files.

Related issues arise where a person, sued for breach of confidence as a result of the publication or threatened publication of (non-governmental) confidential information, pleads a defence of public interest, that is, pleads that a public interest in disclosure justified publication of the material. For example, it has been held that the public interest might justify publication of confidential information about the reliability of intoximeters (breathalyser machines).[23]

These latter cases illustrate how far beyond the original idea of 'Crown privilege' the law in this area is developing. The notion of the public interest, and the distinction between the public and the private spheres of social life, are being used to develop sets of rules about when information of general social interest and importance may, or must, be kept secret, and when it may be made public.

So far as disclosure of government documents is concerned, the Official Secrets Acts 1911–39 impose wide-ranging restrictions on the disclosure by government employees of information which they acquire in their official capacity. These restrictions are enforced by the criminal law.

[22] [1983] 1 AC 578.   [23] *Lion Laboratories Ltd.* v. *Evans* [1984] 3 WLR 539.

PART III

NON-JUDICIAL SCRUTINY
OF ADMINISTRATION

20

Parliamentary Scrutiny

THE CONSTITUTIONAL FUNCTIONS OF PARLIAMENT

(a) Legislation

IN order to understand the role of Parliament in scrutinizing administrative action, it is necessary to draw a distinction between two different functions which Parliament performs. In the first place it is a legislative body. Parliament, of course, legislates on a great many matters, a lot of which have nothing directly to do with the powers of government. But many Acts of Parliament are concerned with conferring and defining the administrative and legislative powers of central and local government and of public bodies, such as nationalized industries.

The most striking feature of our parliamentary system is the extent to which the legislative process (from the first stages of formulation of policy, through the drafting stage, and right up to the final stage of voting on the third reading of a Bill) is under the control of the government. This is not to say, however, that Parliament plays no part at the policy-formulation stage. Debates initiated by the opposition, or debates on Green or White Papers issued by the government, do allow policies to be aired before the proposals reach an advanced stage. But equally important in the policy-formulation process is the well-established practice of all governments of engaging in extensive consultation with interest groups outside Parliament, affected by the proposed legislation. Groups, such as trade unions, employers' organizations, consumer and environmentalist groups, are constantly in touch with government, seeking to influence the formulation of legislation which affects them. (This is as true in relation to delegated as to primary legislation). It is well known, too, that many MPs are 'sponsored' by extra-parliamentary interest groups and put forward views and interests of these groups in debates. In the House of Lords, where party loyalties are less important, and which is manned by many life peers who are chosen specifically because of their knowledge of particular areas of social and economic life, the practice of putting forward the views of sectional interests is common.

Once the legislation is drafted and is before Parliament, the ability of peers and MPs to get the substance of the Bill changed is strictly limited. This is not to say that the government is never defeated when the Houses of Parliament vote on proposed amendments to a Bill, although, if the government has a comfortable majority in the House of Commons, defeats in that House are extremely unlikely—such defeats are more likely in the Lords. Nor is it true to say that the government is never persuaded to alter a Bill as a result of opposition, although, once again, if it has a comfortable majority, such changes are more likely to be prompted by opposition from the government's own back-benchers than from the official opposition. But, given that debates, both in standing committees (to which many Bills are referred at the committee stage) and on the floor of the House, are conducted in an adversarial spirit rather than in a spirit of co-operative effort to achieve a good result, and given that voting is on party lines, the impact which Parliament can have on the shape of a Bill is, at most, marginal.

Does all of this have any relevance for administrative law? At first sight the answer must be negative. In English law there is a sharp distinction between primary and secondary legislation: the courts can invalidate the latter on certain limited grounds, but the validity of the former cannot be questioned. And this is so, regardless of the fact that there are many elements in the parliamentary process which might be thought to fall short of the ideal of representative democracy: the part played by the House of Lords, the degree of control of the government over the legislative process, the fact that, in practice, specialized interest groups have much more to say at the drafting stage than do the elected representatives of the people, the strength of the party system in the House of Commons which operates as a hindrance to searching bipartisan examination of proposed legislation. It might be argued, for example, that not only in the case of delegated legislation, but also in the case of primary legislation, the courts ought to be prepared to ensure that all interested groups get a chance to have their say in respect of the drafting of legislation. On the other hand, the introduction of judicial review into this context would involve the injection of a further non-democratic element into what should be a highly democratic process. Much more desirable would be reforms of the legislative process itself in such a way as to increase the power of the House of Commons over the preparation and scrutiny of proposed legislation. If power over the legislative process is to shift from the government, it ought to shift to the legislature, not to the courts.

Another point worth making in this context is that, under British constitutional arrangements, certain governmental activities must be supported by empowering legislation in order to be lawful. For example, taxation must be authorized by legislation. In theory, then, and subject to what was said above, the government is forced to obtain parliamentary approval for some of its actions (which are, therefore, subject to parliamentary scrutiny and control), and is, in this way, made accountable to Parliament for what it does. It should be remembered, however, that there are many activities which the government can engage in without seeking parliamentary approval in the form of legislation. In Chapter 16 we noted the use of the government's economic power in awarding contracts, to enforce economic policies without parliamentary approval. Again, a government Minister recently intimated that government contracts might not be awarded to employers who did not employ enough black people.[1] The government also exercises a great deal of regulatory power over the economy through the activities of the Bank of England; this does not involve the use of legislative coercion of financial institutions, but the exercise of *de facto* economic power. Even in cases where legislation is needed, for example, to authorize public expenditure, the legislation is often purely formal, and the real decisions about spending are subjected to scrutiny by non-legislative parliamentary procedures.[2]

Finally, it is worth noting that, although most governmental administrative and legislative powers are conferred by legislation, such powers are often couched as broad discretions, and in very vague terms. One frequent result of this, it is often alleged, is that politically contentious issues, as to how the powers will be exercised, and to what ends, do not surface and are not debated. In this way parliamentary control over governmental activity is weakened.

We can see, then, that, in theory, legislative activity provides Parliament with important opportunities for scrutinizing and controlling government activity. But, in practice, Parliament's position is weakened by the fact that the government can, in a variety of ways, bypass the legislative process; and by the fact that, even when it is used, it is too formalized to provide any real check on governmental policies and activities.

[1] *Guardian*, 14 October 1985.
[2] See Daintith (1976) 92 LQR 62.

(*b*) *Scrutiny of Government Activity*

(*i*) *Ministerial responsibility*

The other function of Parliament is that of controlling the day-to-day activities of government. The constitutional linchpin of this activity is the doctrine of ministerial responsibility. But this doctrine means little more than that a Minister must be prepared to answer questions in the House on the activities of his department. Very rarely does the doctrine by itself lead to a ministerial resignation. More potent in this respect is whether the conduct in question will cause the government embarrassment in the country at large. The pressure to resign is more likely to be effective if it emanates from the Prime Minister, than if it comes from the House of Commons. In a way this is not surprising. Departments of central government are so large that no one man can be expected to keep an eye on all or even a fraction of the matters which are dealt with within it. Administrative law recognizes this by allowing that ministerial powers may be delegated. On the other hand, a main reason, in traditional constitutional theory, why the Minister was to take responsibility for what his Civil Servants did was in order to maintain the anonymity and independence of Civil Servants, who are meant to be non-partisan *servants* doing the will of their political masters. A consequence of taking pressure off Ministers ought to be that pressure is put on Civil Servants to be more efficient. To some extent the Ombudsman does this, as we will see; and internal management procedures are aimed at achieving efficiency. It must be to such non-legal methods, rather than to the courts, that we look to ensure that government runs efficiently and that citizens are not prejudiced by bad administration.

(*ii*) *Questions*

Parliamentary questions have two main functions: to elicit information about the activities of government and to ventilate policy issues which arise out of the day-to-day running of government. By far the majority of questions receive written answers and this is the best medium for obtaining detailed information. Oral questions tend to be designed for political purposes, rather than for the getting of information. Even if Ministers rarely resign as a result of revelations elicited by parliamentary questions, it is nevertheless true that governments can be embarrassed by questions and can be prompted to do something about the matters raised. Important, too, is the fact that the question is really the only parliamentary procedure which has remained under the complete control of the back-bencher, and for this reason, if for no other, questions remain an important counterweight to government power and a constant, if minor, irritant.

A major theoretical limitation on the usefulness of questions is that a Minister can only be asked and need only answer questions on matters over which he has control. By and large this prevents Ministers from being questioned about the activities of nationalized industries and other governmental bodies which are independent of ministerial control and direction. In practice this limitation is generally, but not rigidly, observed. It is obvious that, if questions were really a tool of enforcing ministerial responsibility, then it would not be right to make a Minister answer for activities over which he had no control. Also, it is often said that because nationalized industries are meant to operate commercially, political scrutiny of their day-to-day activities is inappropriate. But neither of these arguments seems to provide a good reason why Ministers should not be a channel of information about the activities of independent governmental bodies which are funded wholly or partly by public money.

(iii) Select committees

Unlike standing committees, which consider legislation at the committee stage and operate in an essentially adversarial way, as a microcosm of the Committee of the Whole House, the select committees are more investigative and usually less partisan, their membership consisting of back-benchers who are particularly interested in the area of operation of the committee. The number of these committees was increased considerably in 1979, so that all of the major departments of state now have a committee. The function of these committees, which have wide powers to summon persons and papers, and to initiate inquiries, is to maintain continuing scrutiny over the day-to-day running of government. Sometimes the committees investigate large policy issues, and sometimes they probe more detailed current problems in the administration of government programmes. The terms of reference of the select committees are wide and enable them to investigate the activities, not only of government departments, but also of 'fringe bodies',[3] such as nationalized industries and other non-departmental agencies.

The select committee system is, potentially, a very important tool in

---

[3] See Bowen, *Survey of Fringe Bodies* (1978).

scrutinizing governmental activity. It can provide much more thorough and systematic investigation than can questions, which are haphazard and often ill-informed. The back-bencher asks his question from a position of ignorance, whereas the select committee can fully inform itself on the topic of its investigation. How effective the committees turn out to be depends partly on what is done with their reports. At the moment reports are presented to the House, but are rarely specifically debated. Publicity is the committees' main weapon. Much will depend, too, on whether the committees operate in a properly investigative and non-partisan way and on the willingness of the government to accept criticisms made by committees.

(*iv*) *Control of delegated legislation*

Most statutory instruments have to be laid before Parliament before they come into effect. In some cases, the statute under which the legislation is made only provides that the legislation shall be laid before the Houses (or the House of Commons only); in other cases, the statute provides that an instrument shall expire or not come into effect unless approved by resolution of the House(s) (the affirmative procedure); in yet other cases, the statute provides that, after laying, the instrument will automatically come into operation unless either House (or the House of Commons only) resolves to the contrary (the negative procedure). Statutory instruments can be subjected to both technical scrutiny and scrutiny on the merits. The latter is concerned with the substance of the legislation and whether it is acceptable in policy terms; the former is more concerned with ensuring that the instrument does not exceed the powers of the maker (i.e. that it is *intra vires*) and that it is clearly and effectively drafted to achieve its stated purpose.

Views differ about the value and effectiveness of parliamentary scrutiny of delegated legislation. The main theoretical advantages of parliamentary control of delegated legislation, compared with judicial review, are that it takes place before the legislation actually comes into force (but only after it has been drafted and the policies underlying it have been settled), or at least very soon after it comes into effect; and that it can concern itself much more with the substance of the legislation than the courts are prepared to do. In relation to the first point, the fact that judicial review of legislation may take place a long time after the instrument has come into operation, and despite the fact that it has been laid before and approved by Parliament (if the instrument is subject to the affirmative procedure),[4] probably acts as a disincentive to the courts to declare delegated legislation invalid, since this will mean that any acts done under it will be legally ineffective or unlawful. The courts can lessen the impact of such invalidation in some cases. For example, it has been held that failure to consult a body required by statute to be consulted before legislation is made, invalidates the legislation only as against that party;[5] and it has also been held that, if only one part of an instrument is invalid and can be easily severed from the rest of the instrument, then the remainder can be allowed to stand.[6]

Nevertheless, since delegated legislation usually affects very many people, it is a distinct disadvantage if, after it has been in operation for a long time, it can be struck down at the suit of an individual. The importance of this should not, however, be exaggerated. If the purpose of judicial review is to protect individuals, it cannot be a conclusive argument against invalidating delegated legislation, that it has been in operation for some time and has had wide effects. In legal systems, such as that of the USA, in which statutes can be struck down because they are in conflict with a written constitution, people are much more used to the idea of invalidating legislative acts of wide importance in order to protect individual rights.

The second advantage of parliamentary scrutiny—that it can concern itself more with the substance of the legislation—raises the central dilemma in this area. One of the main reasons why so much rule-making is done by delegates of Parliament is that parliamentary time is limited: the business of government is simply too multifarious and extensive to be regulated entirely by Parliament. And, although the scrutiny of rules made by someone else may not take as long as making the rules in the first place, the parliamentary timetable would simply not permit every instrument of major importance to be debated. This is why the affirmative procedure is relatively little used, as it necessitates a debate.

So, whatever the defects of the actual procedures used in Parliament for scrutinizing instruments, it is unlikely that the level of scrutiny will ever be such as to make parliamentary scrutiny an important organ of control. The position of Parliament is also weak because there is no

---

[4] *F. Hoffman–La Roche & Co. AG* v. *Trade Secretary* [1975] AC 295, 354 *per* Lord Wilberforce.
[5] *Agricultural Training Board* v. *Aylesbury Mushrooms Ltd.* [1972] 1 WLR 190.
[6] *Dunkley* v. *Evans* [1981] 1 WLR 1522.

requirement that Parliament be consulted when delegated legislation is being drafted; nor is Parliament in fact normally consulted.

It should probably, therefore, be recognized that Parliament does not and never will play a significant part in scrutinizing delegated legislation, or participating in its preparation. We should concentrate on increasing the power of Parliament in scrutinizing primary legislation, and develop other methods for increasing the democratic input into the making of delegated legislation.

21

Ombudsmen

THE basic idea of the Ombudsman is a simple one: he is an official independent of the administration with power to investigate citizens' complaints of maladministration. There are three types of Ombudsmen in England. The Parliamentary Commissioner for Administration (PCA) is concerned with central government departments, the Health Service Commissioners (HSC) (there are three posts all held by the PCA) with the National Health Service, and the Commission for Local Administration (CLA) with local government. In Northern Ireland there is a Parliamentary Commissioner and a Commissioner for Complaints who deals with local authorities and other public bodies.

I. THE FIRST OMBUDSMAN

The first Ombudsman office to be created in England (in 1967) was that of the PCA. The office was conceived, in part, as a way of making up for the deficiencies and gaps in judicial and parliamentary mechanisms for reviewing administrative activity. Thus the PCA was seen as having two main functions: the redressing of genuine grievances; and, conversely, legitimizing the administrative process in cases where complaints were found to be unwarranted, and enabling Civil Servants accused of maladministration to clear their names.

As with judicial review, the volume of complaints handled is very small, given the number of administrative decisions made every year. Between 1967 and 1982 complaints properly received through MPs (through whom complaints have to be channelled) never exceeded about 1300, and in some years were less than 600. Of these only a small proportion are formally investigated in full, the rest being rejected because the PCA decides that they fall outside his jurisdiction, or that they ought not, for some other reason, to be investigated. Formal investigation produces a result favourable to the complainant in an average of somewhat less than half of the cases examined. The departments which are most frequently the subject of complaint are the Inland Revenue and the DHSS.

The PCA can deal with decisions made personally by Ministers as well as with decisions made by departmental officers. This happened, for example, in 1967 when the Foreign Secretary refused to allow certain compensation claims by ex-servicemen; and in 1974 when the Industry Secretary made misleading statements about the financial soundness of a tour operator.

The PCA deals with a wide variety of complaints: for example, about delays in making refunds of tax overpaid as a result of errors in calculation made by the Inland Revenue; about agencies which give false or misleading advice about citizens' rights; about failure to inform people properly of changes in administrative practice or about newly available benefits; about discrimination in the provision of social welfare or other benefits; about failure to apply properly departmental guidelines for reimbursement of costs to successful objectors at public inquiries; about refusal and allowing of planning appeals; about failure to pay compensation for injustice or loss inflicted by administrative action. Conduct complained of ranges from mere arrogance, inefficiency, or incompetence to deliberate misconduct such as lying, personal bias, and suppression of information.

2. THE PCA AND PARLIAMENT

The Parliamentary Commissioner, as his name implies, is seen very much as an adjunct of Parliament. The Commissioner makes frequent reports to Parliament (he must report at least annually) and there is a select committee on the PCA, which monitors his work, and can investigate for itself and report to Parliament on matters arising from the reports of the PCA. These activities of the committee can give extra impact to the work of the PCA in cases where the additional publicity given by a report of a parliamentary committee is thought to be useful in securing compliance with recommendations of the PCA by a resistant department, or in prompting some change in administrative policy or practice. Another function which the select committee has exercised, is to review the powers and operation of the PCA institution. But whereas the committee has been very successful in helping the PCA to enforce his recommendations against departments, it has been notably unsuccessful in persuading governments to extend the jurisdiction and powers of the PCA.

It is ultimately the complainant's MP who decides (either when he receives it direct or when it is referred to him by the PCA) whether the

PCA will be asked to investigate a particular complaint, or whether the member himself will take some action, such as writing to the Minister or telephoning an official. This is because, constitutionally, the primary responsibility for defending the citizen against the executive is seen as resting with MPs. In fact, MPs deal personally with vastly more complaints than are referred by them to the PCA.[1] Generally, only cases which are somewhat difficult, complex, or out of the ordinary are referred to the PCA. A high proportion of MPs refer at least one complaint a year to the PCA. The PCA receives some complaints direct which, when referred to the appropriate MP, are not referred back to the PCA. He also receives a lot of complaints which are not referred to MPs because they do not seem prima facie investigable.

From one point of view, therefore, the role of the PCA is to make up for some of the inefficacy of other parliamentary procedures, such as questions and select committee investigations, as means of monitoring and provoking changes in administrative practice. However, whereas these parliamentary methods operate via the doctrine of ministerial responsibility, in that they do not generally seek to uncover the exact point in the government machine where the defect is, the PCA goes behind the screen which ministerial responsibility throws up in front of the anonymous public service, and looks at the administrative machine itself, seeking to identify exactly where things have gone wrong. He seeks to put things right, whereas the traditional parliamentary methods tend to tell the Minister to put things right.

Like select committees the Ombudsman has very wide powers to call for and examine documents and persons. The PCA's investigations are protected by the law of contempt in that any act or omission which would be a contempt of court, if the PCA's investigation were a court proceeding, can be treated as a contempt of the PCA's investigation.[2] So far as documents are concerned, the PCA is, in one respect, in a *stronger* position than a court, in that public interest immunity cannot be pleaded in respect of documents to which he has access, nor do statutory limitations on disclosure of information avail against him. On the other hand, the PCA has no access to Cabinet papers, while the courts, as we have seen, claim the power in theory to inspect even

[1] See Page [1985] PL 1; in the year 1976–7 in New South Wales (where complaints can come direct from a member of the public *or* via an MP) only 20 out of 2209 complaints came via an MP (Annual Report of the NSW Ombudsman, 1976–7, para. 4). The fact that in England MPs are very active in dealing with complaints probably accounts,to some extent, for the fact that the PCA deals with so few complaints.

[2] Parliamentary Commissioner Act 1967 s. 9(1).

Cabinet papers. The PCA must conduct his investigations in private, but subject to that he has very wide discretion as to how he will proceed. Select committees, on the other hand, normally conduct their inquiries in public. The PCA's procedure can be more flexible than that of a select committee which, because of its nature and composition, is more or less restricted to formal interrogation of Ministers and senior Civil Servants. The PCA can conduct much more personalized inquiries which get much closer to the exact seat of specific problems.

3. THE PCA'S JURISDICTION

The PCA has a discretion, unreviewable by the courts, as to whether he will investigate any particular complaint or not. His jurisdiction is, in its terms, very wide: it covers any action taken by, or on behalf of, the government departments and other authorities listed in Schedule 2 to the Parliamentary Commissioner Act 1967, in exercise of administrative functions of the department or authority. Thus, it is wide enough to cover actions of independent governmental bodies to which the performance of administrative functions of departments has been delegated (including public local inquiries[3] but not tribunals because tribunal members are not Civil Servants; and because tribunals are seen as being more like courts than like administrators, so that to allow the PCA to investigate them would be to jeopardize their 'judicial independence'). It would not, however, cover activities of bodies which are not ultimately under ministerial control. In this way the PCA is as limited in his operations as MPs are in asking questions about bodies such as the nationalized industries. In fact these public corporations seem to fall through almost every investigatory net that exists (except, to some extent, select committees), even though they consume large amounts of public money, affect the daily lives of individuals more than most government departments, and are major tools of government economic policy. It has recently been announced that the jurisdiction of the PCA is to be extended to include fifty non-departmental bodies ('quangos') including the Arts Council, the Medical Research Council, the Sports Council, and the Equal Opportunities Commission.

Certain areas are specifically excluded from the PCA's jurisdiction. These include foreign affairs, diplomatic activity, the administration of

[3] See Chapter 23.

justice, the investigation of crime, action in matters relating to contractual or commercial activities, and the conditions of service of Crown servants. Some of these exclusions have been criticized, in particular, that relating to complaints arising out of commercial transactions (especially the tendering process: we have seen how little control the common law exercises over this) and complaints about the conditions of service of Crown employees.[4]

4. THE PCA AND REMEDIES FOR MALADMINISTRATION

The PCA has no power to award a remedy and, whereas an application for judicial review[5] operates to suspend action on the matter complained of, while the application is being adjudicated, instigation of an investigation by the PCA does not in any way affect the activities of the department or authority concerned. However, this strict legal position masks a very different reality. The PCA has a great deal of persuasive power, partly *because* he has no coercive powers. Besides securing apologies, he has on numerous occasions secured financial relief for a complainant or persuaded an authority to reconsider some decision made by it. Furthermore, in cases where the particular complaint is just a symptom of a wider problem, the PCA can sometimes persuade an authority to change its general procedure for dealing with that type of case. An example is the *Ostler* case which will be discussed below. If a department proves to be resistant to the PCA's suggestions, or is guilty of repeated maladministration, the select committee will call the Minister before it and question him on the PCA's findings, thus putting considerable, unwelcome pressure on him.

Should the PCA be given coercive remedial powers? There are arguments against this. First, although the PCA is required to give bodies or persons, whose actions are the subject of complaint, an opportunity to comment on the allegations made, his inquiry is informal and essentially investigative. Only very rarely does the PCA conduct an oral hearing, in an attempt to resolve conflicts of evidence which the investigators have been unable to reconcile. The PCA is not bound by the rules of evidence and does not have to follow adversarial procedures. If he were to have power to award coercive remedies, justifiable demands could be made that his procedure should be more formalized, so as to give the body complained about a full chance to

---

[4] Annual Report of the PCA, 1983, p. 4.
[5] See Chapter 10 above.

put its side of the case. This could add to the expense and length of inquiries.

Secondly, at present all the PCA's investigations are private.[6] This is probably desirable in that it maintains the anonymity of the Civil Service, which the doctrine of ministerial responsibility is designed to protect, and which places the responsibility for the efficiency of the administration squarely on the government, rather than on individual Civil Servants. If remedies were to be available, at least some part if not all of the investigation would need to be in public. Thirdly, the PCA's decisions are not subject to review. If he had the power to give coercive remedies the possibility of review would be essential.[7]

In short, the fact that the PCA achieves quite a lot, despite his lack of formal remedial powers, is ironically a function of the fact that he operates privately and quietly. All the PCAs have felt that they can do more by persuasion than they could hope to achieve by coercion. The independence of the PCA is guaranteed—he can only be removed from office by an address from both Houses of Parliament—and the fact that he is in this way equated with High Court judges gives him, by association, much of the moral authority which attaches to the judiciary.

If, however, it were thought desirable to give the powers of the PCA some coercive support, the Commissioner of Complaints Act (NI) 1969 might provide a suitable model. It empowers the County Court to award damages, an injunction, or other relief, in cases where the Commissioner has found maladministration; and in cases where there is evidence of continuing maladministration, the Attorney-General can apply for an injunction. Perhaps this latter power could be given to the PCA.

5. THE PCA AND THE COURTS

We have noted some ways in which the work of the PCA is similar to and differs from that of select committees. It is also illuminating to compare his work with that of the courts in judicial review. Like the courts, the PCA is essentially an institution for rectifying individual complaints. Thus, for example, he declined to investigate the complaints involved in the *Fleet Street Casuals* case (see Chapter 9) on the ground that the allegations of injustice in the administration of the

---

[6] Parliamentary Commissioner Act s. 7(1).
[7] Annual Report of the PCA, 1983, p. 6.

tax system affected all taxpayers and, in a sense, the whole nation.[8] However, just as the law of standing allows individuals to be heard, provided they have a genuine grievance, even though their interest is no greater than that of many others, so the PCA would be prepared to investigate, for example, a complaint by an angling association that their fishing waters had been polluted by effluent from an M.o.D. factory. But the PCA will only investigate complaints which affect the complainant uniquely or affect him as one of a small class. As in the case of the common law rules of standing, the rationale of this approach is to draw a demarcation line between the activities of the PCA and matters which ought properly to be dealt with by the political process.

On the other hand, just as the decision of a court often has an impact beyond the actual litigants, so too the PCA can, by securing satisfaction for a single complainant, at the same time indirectly help other potential complainants or, by prompting a change in administrative practice, improve the situation for others dealing with the particular department in the future. For example, an investigation in 1977 into an individual complaint of non-payment of a war pension, led to a review of twenty-four similar cases and payment of the pension. But this wider effect is an incidental by-product of an investigation into an individual's complaint. The PCA does not perform an inspectorial function; in other words, even if, in the course of investigating a particular complaint, the PCA discovers some wider inefficiency in the administrative process, he does not investigate this himself. If he thinks that further investigation is warranted, he can refer the matter to his select committee which can inquire more generally into departmental rules and practice, and recommend wider administrative changes. Nor, of course, can he launch investigations into departmental procedures on his own initiative and without a complaint because he has some reason to suspect bad administrative practice.

There is much to be said for giving the PCA a limited power to launch a wider investigation into administrative practice, if the investigation into an individual complaint reveals some wider problem. However, a recommendation along these lines by the select committee in 1977 was rejected by the government, on the ground that the PCA's main function was investigating individual complaints and that resources ought not to be diverted from this function.

[8] Clothier (1984) 81 LS Gaz. 3108.

One particular feature of the institution of the PCA which distinguishes it from the office of judge is the essentially personal nature of the office. The volume of complaints with which the PCA deals is small enough for him to be able to supervise each one personally at some stage, and it is arguable that one of the secrets of the success of the office is that people view them as a real person to whom they can complain. If the volume of complaints increased greatly, or if the PCA's powers were greatly extended, then this individual, personalized element might be lost. A Department of Complaints would be a very different institution from the PCA.[9]

There is clearly a conflict here. It *is* probably true that the administration, as well as the public, has greater faith in the PCA institution because of its personalized nature. At the same time, it seems a poor justification for not advertising the PCA more widely, or for not extending the scope of an admittedly useful and successful institution, that thereby the number of complaints might increase above the number which one person can deal with single-handedly. Surely a number of individuals could achieve much the same effect if they were given different areas of operation, rather than arranged hierarchically under one super-Ombudsman. The important thing is that each complaint should be dealt with ultimately by an identifiable and trusted individual. As it is, most of the actual spadework is done by assistants to the PCA, as one would expect. There is no intrinsic reason why, for example, complaints against the police should not be dealt with by the Ombudsman mechanism, but it might be desirable for this work to be given to a separate police Ombudsman, rather than to the present PCA for him to delegate within his organization. The present Police Complaints Authority (chaired by a former PCA) is a step in this direction, but it only has the power to review and, in some cases, supervise inquiries by the police themselves into complaints.

The most important boundary line (in theoretical terms, at least) between the PCA and the courts is that, whereas the latter deal with questions of legality, the PCA deals with 'maladministration'. An ex-PCA has recently described maladministration as 'any departure from what the average reasonable man would regard as fair, courteous, efficient and prompt administration'.[10] The classic formulation of the meaning of this word is the famous 'Crossman catalogue' (which was formulated by the government spokesman, Mr Crossman, in the

---

[9] loc. cit. n. 7.   [10] Clothier (1984) 81 LS Gaz. 3108.

course of a House of Commons debate on the 1967 Act): 'bias, neglect, inattention, delay, incompetence, ineptitude, perversity, turpitude, arbitrariness and so on'. The PCA Act provides that the PCA shall not investigate a matter if the complainant could take or could have taken it to a court or tribunal, unless the PCA thinks that it would not be reasonable to expect the complainant to take or to have taken this course. This provision assumes, as seems to be clear from the Crossman catalogue, that some administrative defects will be capable of being described not only as maladministration, but also as *ultra vires* acts, or as an exercise of discretion such as would justify an appeal to a tribunal.

Therefore, the definition of maladministration has to be read subject to the general qualification that the jurisdiction of the PCA is residual. So, the PCA will not normally investigate complaints solely about the content of discretionary decisions, nor will he investigate complaints about delegated legislation. This restraint is reinforced by section 12(3) of the Parliamentary Commissioner Act, which provides that the PCA may not question the merits of a decision taken without maladministration. This seems to assume that maladministration is procedural, but since the distinction between substance and procedure is not always easy to draw, the PCA (on the urging of the select committee) does not interpret this restriction rigidly. If a decision was alleged to be oppressive, unjust, or unreasonable, then the PCA would be prepared to investigate it. The PCA is also prepared to investigate cases in which some administrative rule has been properly applied, but where it is argued that the rule itself is a bad one. He can recommend that the rule itself be changed; he can also recommend amendments to statutory regulations or to legislation. In this way the PCA can perform a more positive and constructive role than the courts.

As a result there are certain types of administrative 'misbehaviour' which are sometimes dealt with by a court, sometimes by the Ombudsman, for example: unfair procedure, ignoring material relevant to the decision, unfair departure from announced policy guidelines or decisions favourable to the citizen, the giving of misleading or incorrect advice.[11] There are also cases in which the Ombudsman has been able to secure (*ex gratia*) monetary compensation for an aggrieved citizen; some such cases might now fall within the rules of tort liability considered in Chapter 15 above.

[11] Bradley [1980] CLJ 304, 324, 332.

The justification for avoiding undue overlap between the PCA and courts or tribunals is clear: consideration of the same issue from different angles and in different ways, leading possibly to different results, is both wasteful of resources and undesirable, in that it creates a possibility of conflicting decisions of bodies neither of which is subject to control by the other. On the other hand, the distinction between maladministration and the legality, or substantive correctness, of decisions is not always an easy one to draw, and this justifies the PCA in taking the view that, if the complaint is such a minor one that it really does not warrant litigation, and if he judges that litigation is unlikely if he finds against the complainant, then he can investigate despite the fact that the complainant could litigate. An important point to bear in mind in this respect is that the services of the PCA are free to the complainant whereas, of course, litigation can be extremely costly. So, for example, the PCA would not expect a taxpayer, worried about delay in issuing an amended tax assessment, to go to court for an order of mandamus requiring the Inland Revenue to perform its duty. For reasons which are not clear, the PCA rarely exercises his discretion to investigate in cases where the complainant has a right of appeal to a tribunal. The explanation may be that, on the whole, tribunals are cheaper and less formal than the courts, and so the existence of a free and informal alternative is not as important in relation to tribunals, as in relation to courts.

There have been a couple of notable cases in which the same issue has been the subject both of investigation by the PCA and proceedings before a court. In one case the Home Office threatened to revoke television licences, bought by licensees before the expiry of their old licence in order to avoid an announced licence fee increase. The PCA investigated the Home Office's action on the assumption that it was lawful, and found that the Home Office had acted inefficiently and with lack of foresight in creating the situation in which people could buy overlapping licences but failing to explain the situation to the public; but he did not recommend a remedy. In later litigation by an aggrieved licence-holder, the Home Office's action was held to have been unlawful and licencees who had paid the new higher fee were given a refund.[12] This case illustrates nicely the distinction between unlawfulness and maladministration.

Another example involved a case in which a landowner (Ostler)

---

[12] *Congreve* v. *Home Office* [1976] QB 629; 7th Report of the PCA 1974–5 (HC 680).

sought to challenge proposals for a trunk road, on the grounds of breach of natural justice and bad faith, after the statutory time-limit for challenges had expired. He alleged that there had been a secret agreement between the department and a third party, and that if he had known about it earlier he would have challenged the proposals when they were being considered at a public inquiry. The Court of Appeal held that the time-limit provision was effective to bar the challenge.[13] Ostler then complained to the PCA[14] and, as a result, the Department of the Environment made an *ex gratia* payment to Ostler to cover the reasonable costs of his court action. Also, as a result of the PCA's investigations, new procedures were introduced to prevent a repetition of any such situation.

It can be seen, therefore, that sometimes the courts can provide a remedy where the PCA fails to do so, and sometimes vice versa. The *Ostler* case raises a larger issue about compensation for loss inflicted by administrative action. We have seen that in cases such as *Ostler* and in cases where authorities make *ultra vires* representations or give *ultra vires* assurances, which it is not in the public interest to enforce by an estoppel, there is a strong argument for paying the injured party compensation. It seems that the investigative techniques of the PCA (or of the CLA) would be well suited to deciding, in particular cases, whether compensation ought to be paid or not. Indeed, in a number of cases where misleading advice has been given, the PCA has secured the payment of *ex gratia* compensation.[15] On the other hand, it might be thought desirable that there should be a *right* to compensation in such cases, rather than that it should depend on persuasion by the PCA and the goodwill of the department concerned.

There is an argument which says that, since the office of the PCA was set up, the courts have become much more willing to hold that bad administrative action is illegal and to control the exercise of administrative discretion on both procedural and substantive grounds. As a result, many of the gaps in judicial review, which the PCA was set up to fill, no longer exist. Therefore, the PCA institution has to some extent outlived its purpose. The conclusion does not, however, necessarily follow, even if the premise is correct. Litigation is

[13] *R. v. Environment Secretary, ex parte Ostler* [1977] QB 122; 2nd Report of the Select Committee on the PCA 1976–7 (HC 524).
[14] 3rd Report of the PCA 1976–7 (HC 223).
[15] For a useful selection of examples see Wade, *Administrative Law* (5th edn., 1982), pp. 85–6.

expensive and slow, and judicial adversarial techniques for finding facts are not always as appropriate as the investigative techniques of the PCA. Provided the PCA and the courts are applying essentially the same principles of good administrative conduct, a sensible division of labour is possible: the PCA acting as a sort of policeman or trouble-shooter, while the courts deal with the really serious cases and those which raise important and novel issues of principle. It may be that the best way to distinguish between the courts and the PCA is not in terms of the concepts of illegality and maladministration, but in terms of their differing roles and expertise in enforcing standards of good adminis-trative conduct. The PCA can, for example, deal with a minor case satisfactorily by securing an apology. Court action to secure such an outcome would be totally wasteful and unnecessarily provocative.

6. THE OTHER OMBUDSMEN

The Commissions for Local Administration (one for England and one for Wales) perform essentially the same function, in respect of local government, as the PCA performs in respect of central government. The constitutional underpinning of this institution is slightly different from that of the PCA, in that there is no direct equivalent of ministerial responsibility at the local level. Nevertheless, local authorities are elected representative bodies and, like MPs, many members of local authorities perform a problem-solving function. So, except in a few cases where the CLA is satisfied that a councillor has refused to refer a complaint to the CLA when requested to do so, all complaints must come via a member of the authority complained about or of any other authority concerned. The CLA takes the view that the 'councillor filter' should be removed.[16]

As with the PCA, the CLA deals with a very small number of complaints relative to the number of decisions made by administrators within its jurisdiction. For example, in 1983 about 3867 complaints were received. A finding favourable to the complainant was made in about 190 of the approximately 370 cases investigated. About 800 complaints were rejected as being outside the CLA's jurisdiction, while about 1600 were settled after only informal inquiries. About one third of complaints are on housing matters, one third on planning issues, and the remaining one third on all the rest of local government services.

[16] Yardley [1983] PL 522, 528.

The Local Government Act 1974 s. 26(7) provides that the CLA may not investigate complaints which affect all or most of the inhabitants of the authority's area. The idea behind this is that such complaints really concern 'the way the country is being run' and ought to be pursued through the political process. This reasoning also lies behind the PCA's willingness only to entertain complaints by individuals or small groups of individuals, even though he is not strictly limited to doing so by statute. This limitation, which is similar to that which the courts enforce by means of the rules of standing, preserves the nature of all these institutions as essentially *ex post facto* complaint- or dispute-settling mechanisms, as opposed to quality control mechanisms, or avenues for achieving political aims which the complainants have failed to achieve through the political process. The limitation helps to preserve the independence of all these bodies from political influence.

On the other hand, the CLA has been rather more active than the PCA, in seeking to forestall complaints by improving local mechanisms for dealing with them.[17] To this end the CLA encourages the council involved to deal locally with complaints received by the CLA; it has also promulgated, jointly with the local authorities associations, a voluntary code of practice for dealing with complaints. This code concerns both procedures for dealing locally with complaints made to the CLA, and procedures for dealing with complaints made to the council in the first instance. The aim of the latter part of the code is to develop good administrative practice and clear lines of communication between councils and their constituents, so as to minimize the level of dissatisfaction with the services provided by local authorities.

As in the case of the PCA, the CLA has no coercive powers. However, whereas the PCA has great persuasive influence and can also publicize cases in which a department refuses to take action in the face of an adverse finding, by reporting to Parliament and by enlisting the aid of the select committee to investigate further, the CLA's recommendations and reports, which are made to the local authority under investigation, are much more at the mercy of the authority, which is more or less free to decide how and whether to respond. This is particularly important in cases where a report on an individual complaint has knock-on effects for other cases. For example, if the CLA finds undue delay in repairing a council house, or in dealing with an application for planning permission and recommends that the particular complainant

---

[17] There are also some statutory provisions which establish local complaints procedures: see Birkinshaw [1985] CJQ 15, 47.

be compensated or recompensed in some other way, the council might resist by saying that the individual case was just one of many and that the resources available to the council would not enable it to reduce the delay in all cases; in this light there would be no justification for giving special treatment to one isolated victim of a general shortage of resources. This sort of response raises more general issues which will be discussed shortly. In its Report for 1982–3 the CLA takes the view that persuasion is less threatening to local authority independence than coercion and, therefore, expresses the hope that the introduction of coercive powers will not prove necessary.[18]

Finally, the constitutional position of the Health Service Commissioners is different again from that of either the PCA or the CLA. Here, although the Minister is ultimately responsible for the functioning of the Health Service, the day-to-day running of it is largely in the hands of local health authorities, and there is no elected person with direct constitutional responsibility in relation to these authorities. So, complaints can be made directly to the HSCs, provided they have first been brought to the attention of the health authority. The HSCs investigate complaints about the administration of the Health Service, but not about questions of clinical medical judgment, or policy issues such as the provision of kidney machines.

It might be asked why, if the Ombudsman idea is thought suitable for the Health Service, it could not also provide a means of exercising some control over other nationalized industries. The answer would appear to be the same as that which might be thought to justify the exclusion of commercial and contractual matters from the sphere of the PCA, namely that commercial activities are not suitable subjects for review or regulation by non-market mechanisms. This point raises fundamental issues about the nature and responsibilities of nationalized industries which we cannot go into here. Let the problem simply be noted.

7. THE OMBUDSMAN IDEA

The Ombudsman idea is a very simple and adaptable one. There is no reason why it should not be extended to cover, for example, the police and nationalized industries. Although it is free to the complainant, it is not a cheap method of complaint investigation

[18] Paras. 16–25; see Yardley op. cit. 529–30.

because each complaint is investigated as fully as is necessary to resolve it. The CLA has, however, been much more prepared than the PCA to deal with simple cases by cheap informal methods, such as telephone calls, as opposed to formal investigations. At the central level MPs play an active role in handling small complaints, and the desirability of MPs continuing to see and have this as part of their constitutional function is thought to justify the division of labour between them and the PCA.

Ombudsmen provide an adjunct to the judicial and tribunal system in that they can deal with minor complaints on matters which would not fall within the jurisdiction of those bodies. As has been noted, the types of bad administrative behaviour listed in the Crossman catalogue can amount to *ultra vires* conduct, challengeable in a court. But the fact that an administrative lapse may not constitute illegal behaviour does not mean that it is not worthy of rectification, and this is where the Ombudsman can be important. On the other hand, just as conduct within the Crossman catalogue may not be illegal, the flexibility of the notion of 'maladministration' means that such conduct might be found not to fall within this concept either. It is up to individual Ombudsmen to decide whether the complainant has suffered maladministration, and in this respect the Ombudsmen, like the courts, exercise a crucial role in defining the limits of acceptable administrative behaviour. In this way Ombudsmen can perform a very important role in legitimizing governmental behaviour. Given that, on average, less than half of the complaints investigated by Ombudsmen are found to be justified, and given that the number of complaints investigated is, anyway, miniscule, the work of the Ombudsmen might be thought to show that all is basically well with the administrative machine. And the few highly publicized cases of maladministration can, ironically, contribute to this legitimization process, because they reassure people that when things go wrong they will be rectified.

One might seriously ask whether a complaints mechanism which produces results which are, on the whole, so congenial to the government is really worth having (unless, of course, one believes that all is, by and large, well with the administration). It may be that Ombudsmen are valuable, if only to keep administrators up to the mark by the very *possibility* of complaint, investigation, and publicity. On the other hand, some people initially feared that the activities of the Ombudsman might generate 'defensive administration', that is, elaborate, costly, and time-consuming precautions and procedures, designed to forestall and deflect criticism; and might discourage administrators from acting boldly and imaginatively, for fear of adverse criticism if things went wrong. There is some evidence that if Ombudsmen are too demanding they can have these negative effects. So, Ombudsmen have to strike a compromise between, on the one hand, ensuring that citizens are not maltreated and, on the other, making demands on the administration which exacerbate some of the problems being complained about.

Ombudsmen also provide an adjunct to government inspectorates, which do not investigate individual complaints of maladministration but are concerned with general questions of the quality of government services. If the Ombudsmen were given some power to launch wider investigations prompted by individual complaints, this would undoubtedly add to the value of the institution. In this way progress could be made towards developing general principles of good administration appropriate to various government agencies. Once such principles had been established, the role of the Ombudsmen in relation to individual complaints would be to ensure that authorities complied with the principles, which would constitute a sort of charter of 'citizens' administrative rights' analogous to the rules of natural justice and *ultra vires*. The Ombudsmen's investigative and inquisitorial procedures are well suited to this type of wider role. It might, however, in some cases conflict with the function of resolving individual complaints. For example, individual complaints about delay in dealing with planning applications, or about discrimination in the allocation of council housing, might appear justified when viewed in isolation, but appear less so when the total resources available to a governmental agency, or the interests of other applicants, are taken into account. This is the problem of polycentricity which we have considered before, and it does force us to ask what the main function of the Ombudsman is: to protect individuals or to promote good administration within the limits of what is feasible and practicable?

Another useful addition to the powers of the PCA would be a power to instigate litigation on behalf of a complainant, when this seemed the appropriate course. The Commission for Racial Equality and the Equal Opportunities Commission can do this. Such a power would strengthen the 'tribune of the people' aspect of the PCA's office. It would enable the Ombudsman to apply for an interim injunction to maintain the status quo, pending the outcome of his investigation (at present the instigation of an investigation by the PCA does not prevent the body under investigation taking further action on the matter), and to obtain court orders against recalcitrant authorities who refuse to act upon his report. Such a power would also enable the Ombudsman to help complainants with important cases, which he feels he cannot deal with because litigation is more appropriate (such a procedure could provide a sort of substitute for legal aid). Again, in the television licences case discussed earlier, it might have been useful if the PCA could have applied to the court for a declaration as to whether the threatened revocation of licences was lawful or not. A decision that it was not would have done away with the need for further consideration by the PCA as to whether the Home Office's action, though lawful, amounted to maladministration.

PART IV

TRIBUNALS AND INQUIRIES

22

Tribunals

1. INTRODUCTION

It is extremely difficult to define the word 'tribunal' and no attempt will be made here. It is better simply to give an account of the salient characteristics of tribunals. Tribunals play a very important part in modern government and they deal with a wide diversity of matters. For example, the Supplementary Benefits (now Social Security) Appeals Tribunals (SBATs) and the Social Security Commissioners (formerly the National Insurance Commissioners) deal with social welfare benefits; there are immigration tribunals and taxation tribunals, tribunals dealing with air and road traffic licensing and with land valuation; and rent assessment and mental health tribunals (the latter dealing with decisions to commit people to mental institutions). The case-load of the tribunals varies widely. In 1981, for example, the Transport Tribunal (which deals with transport charges and road carriers' licences) dealt with twenty-nine cases, while SBATs handled over 43,000 cases, and Local Valuation Courts (which, despite their name, are treated for many purposes as tribunals) over 134,000 cases. In sheer volume of work, therefore, tribunals greatly overshadow the courts as checkers of the administrative process.

Most[1] tribunals are appellate bodies, the function of which is to hear appeals against the substance of discretionary administrative decisions, made by administrative officers or other tribunals. Tribunals are not primarily concerned with the legality of administrative decisions—this is the function of judicial review—or with questions of maladministration—this is the province of the Ombudsmen—but with the substance of administrative decisions.

Most tribunals are concerned with disputes about the provision by government of some benefit, such as a licence or social security payment. But this is not true of all tribunals. For example, rent assessment committees decide disputes between landlords and tenants, and industrial tribunals decide disputes about unfair dismissal between

---

[1] But not all; for example, the Civil Aviation Authority has original licensing powers.

employers and employees. Here we are primarily concerned with tribunals of the former type.

2. TRIBUNALS, COURTS, DISCRETION, AND RULES

All tribunals which deal with disputes between citizens and government are concerned with the exercise of administrative powers. Sometimes administrative powers are closely defined and circumscribed by legal rules, but often administrators have a considerable amount of discretion. We have also already seen that the exercise of discretionary power can be, and often is, structured and confined by informal policy guidelines, although, by and large, the courts have taken the view that administrators should make only limited use of such policies. Since tribunals are concerned with reviewing the exercise of discretionary powers, it is worth considering the balance between discretion and rules in their activities. To what extent do and should tribunals apply rules, and to what extent do and should they exercise discretion? And do they differ from courts in the extent to which their decisions are rule-based? Is it more accurate to see tribunals as similar to administrators exercising discretionary power, or as similar to courts applying legal rules?

Clearly, one of the functions of a tribunal will be to ensure that the administrator has properly applied any statutory rules or regulations relevant to the situation. Clearly, too, if factual issues relevant to the exercise of the discretion are in dispute, the tribunal will have to decide these. In these respects the tasks performed by a tribunal are no different from those performed by a court. Indeed, a person aggrieved by an administrative decision may be able not only to question it before a tribunal, but also to challenge it by way of an application for judicial review in respect of alleged errors of law or fact, or appeal to the High Court on a point of law under section 13 of the Tribunals and Inquiries Act. We have already noted that there is a general rule that a judicial review remedy will not be awarded if there is some more convenient remedy, such as an appeal to a tribunal; and RSC Ord. 53 r. 3(8) allows an application for judicial review to be stayed while other avenues of redress are pursued.

Very often, however, a tribunal will be asked to review the exercise of a discretion. This does not, of course, distinguish a tribunal from a court, because courts, too, review the exercise of discretions by administrators. However, the power of the courts to strike down the exercise of a discretion is limited by the doctrine of *ultra vires*, whereas a tribunal, being an appellate body, can substitute its opinion on a matter of discretion, for that of the original decision-maker. In this sense tribunals are part of the administrative branch of government, in that *their* decisions on matters of discretion, like those of the administrators whose decisions are appealed against, are reviewable in the courts in accordance with the doctrine of *ultra vires*.

Tribunals, then, have the power on appeal to decide how a discretionary power ought to have been exercised; or, in other words, they can exercise, at an appellate level, administrative discretionary powers. This fact is sometimes seen as providing an important point of contrast between tribunals and courts, in the sense that courts apply rules of law, while tribunals exercise discretions. However, the position is not as simple as this. Courts, too, exercise discretions and *make* law (as opposed to simply *applying* rules). Conversely, tribunals, such as the Social Security Commissioners, administer a complex body of legal rules, in a way very similar to the way a court does. Therefore, we cannot draw a simple contrast between tribunals and discretion, on the one hand, and courts and rules, on the other. Apart from anything else, the amount of discretion exercised by a tribunal depends on the extent to which the powers, the exercise of which it reviews, are themselves subject to legal limitation. For example, there is now less unregulated discretion in the supplementary benefits system than before 1980, and this will have affected the nature of the issues with which tribunals in this area have to deal.

It is, nevertheless, true that the discretion exercised by courts is, in general, more heavily circumscribed by legal rules, than that exercised by tribunals. Judicial discretion operates only at the margin of legal rules, and the courts hold themselves to be under a general obligation to follow earlier decisions. By contrast, tribunals are not bound to follow their earlier decisions. This does not mean that, in practice, tribunals do not often follow their own previous decisions. Following precedent is just a way of acting consistently, and basic fairness requires that every decision-maker act consistently. The practice of following precedents is particularly notable in the case of tribunals which administer areas which are heavily regulated by law, such as the Social Security Commissioners; although it is really only possible to follow earlier decisions in any organized way if there is a reliable system for the reporting of decisions, which most tribunals do not have. But the less legally regulated the subject matter of the tribunal's business, the less willing are the courts to allow the tribunal, any more than administrators themselves, to develop rigid policy guidelines. It is not the function of tribunals, on this view, to structure or restrict the exercise of discretionary powers by developing and applying legal rules, but rather to ensure that the discretion was properly exercised, given the particular circumstances of the case.

The important conclusion to be drawn from the discussion so far, is that no general propositions can be laid down as to the extent to which tribunals administer legal rules, and the extent to which they make discretionary decisions. All depends on the legislative scheme under which the particular tribunal operates.

3. THE INDEPENDENCE OF TRIBUNALS

A most important point which arises out of this discussion is the following: departmental administrators are expected to exercise administrative powers in accordance with government policy: their function is to apply government policy to particular cases. Administrators are, therefore, directly subject to the control of their political masters in respect of the policy decisions they make. The amount of independence which administrators enjoy is a matter for the government to decide. To what extent is this true of tribunals? Do tribunals exist just to ensure that administrators apply government policy consistently and in accordance with the spirit of the policy, or is it their function to exercise discretionary powers as seems best to them, in an independent way?

By and large tribunals are independent of direct interference by the departments which administer the social progammes they supervise. With a couple of exceptions, notably civil aviation and land transport licensing tribunals, tribunals are not subject to policy direction by Ministers.[2] The mode of appointment of tribunal chairmen and members (often by the Lord Chancellor) and the organizational structure of the tribunal system are designed to foster independence; and the basically adversarial procedure of tribunals, in which the tribunal members act primarily as adjudicators taking relatively little part in the proceedings, helps to remove any appearance of bias towards the departmental position. This is obviously very important to

[2] However, in relation to the CAA the system of 'policy guidance' was abolished in 1979. See, on this point and the CAA generally, Baldwin, *Regulating the Airlines* (1985). *Re* land transport see e.g. Public Passenger Vehicles Act 1981 s. 4(3).

an applicant who is complaining against the department. On the other hand, tribunals are usually staffed by Civil Servants from the relevant department, and this inevitably sometimes creates an appearance if not the actuality of bias. The clerk to the tribunal often plays a considerable part in the more minor cases with which the tribunal deals. Moreover, even members of tribunals (e.g. Immigration Adjudicators) are sometimes appointed by the department whose decisions they monitor (in this case, the Home Office). However, most tribunals are *meant* to be fully independent, even if in practice they do not always appear to be (and perhaps are not) as independent as they might be.

But this assertion of independence raises a very fundamental constitutional difficulty, which needs to be faced. The problem can be brought out clearly by considering the courts. They are highly protected from political influence and interference, much more so than tribunals. But this independence has a price: it is only justifiable so long as the courts decide cases, as much as possible, on the basis of publicly announced rules which are adhered to as rigorously as possible, discretion being exercised only at the margins; and so long as the courts restrain themselves from getting involved in politically contentious areas. Tribunals can pay this price easily when they are supervising an area of administration which is heavily circumscribed by legal rules. But, if they are reviewing essentially discretionary decisions which administrators, of necessity, make in accordance with government policy, it is less clear why a tribunal, which is immunized from political influence or accountability, ought to be allowed to entertain appeals from such decisions, and apply policies not laid down by the government but decided on by the tribunal itself.[3]

The answer to this problem may be as follows: in some cases, where it is felt that individual decisions of tribunals are likely to be of considerable policy importance, the government might retain the power to give policy directions to the tribunal. But the vast majority of tribunal decisions are not individually of great policy significance. Most tribunal business involves applying legislative schemes to the facts of individual cases and, even if a tribunal develops a particular way of dealing with a particular type of case, the issues involved will usually be very small-scale, and will be matters of detail over which the

[3] Discussions of departure from government policy by the Australian Administrative Appeals Tribunal will be found in Kirby (1978) 2 U. of NSWLJ 203, 233–8; (1980) 6 Monash LR 171, 190–1; Brennan (1980) 9 Sydney LR 1, 9–10.

government is not concerned to exercise direct control. The major issues will have been dealt with in legislation. There is also considerable advantage for the government in setting up independent bodies to deal with individual grievances which are not of great public significance, because it generates in citizens a feeling that governmental power is subject to check, and provides a way in which feelings of having been treated unjustly or unfairly can be defused.

The basic idea that tribunals ought to be independent of the government departments whose activities they monitor, rests on an important political choice. There is no intrinsic reason why discretionary administrative decisions ought not to be reviewed by more senior officials within the department, or by the Minister, according to avowedly political criteria, rather than by an external and relatively independent body free from policy interference. Indeed, this is what happens in certain areas, perhaps the most notable being that of planning, where many appeals are decided ultimately by the Minister or by inspectors employed by the D.o.E. In addition to defusing feelings of dissatisfaction, as noted above, there are are least two fairly obvious political advantages for the government in setting up independent tribunals. One is that it enables the Minister to offload responsibility for certain potentially contentious decisions onto a body immune from political criticism; another is that the provision of an independent dispute-settling mechanism may make people less unwilling to accept changes in the substantive rules which they do not like.[4] These political reasons for establishing tribunals mean that the decision to do so is sometimes itself a subject of political controversy. On the other hand, there are significant areas of government activity which have not been provided with a tribunal to hear appeals, and arguments, such as the desirability of retaining ultimate ministerial responsibility for decision-making, and that a right of appeal to a tribunal causes inflexibility and delay in the dispatch of government business, have been used to resist creation of new tribunals. The decision whether or not to create a tribunal in a particular area seems to be made very much on the merits of the case, rather than according to any general principle or overall plan.

4. TRIBUNAL PROCEDURE

Procedure before tribunals is rather varied, but the Council on

---

[4] Harlow & Rawlings, *Law and Administration* (1984), pp. 74–8.

Tribunals, which has general oversight of the tribunal system and of procedural rules of tribunals, has taken the view that tribunal procedure ought to be basically adversarial. The ramifications of this are important. In the first place it assumes that the best model for tribunal procedure is the adversary contest. In many cases the applicant before a tribunal will be at a disadvantage as against the respondent department, in that he will be unfamiliar with legal proceedings. The members of the tribunal may take steps to ensure that the applicant feels at ease, but the logic of the adversary system prevents the tribunal members taking an active part to assist the complainant to put his case. It is, therefore, important that he should be entitled to be represented by a lawyer or someone else who has some experience in presenting cases before tribunals. The procedural rules of some tribunals give an unrestricted right of representation and the Council on Tribunals encourages this. As we have seen, it is unclear to what extent the common law recognizes a right to be represented.

If a right to legal representation is to be truly effective, it must be possible for the applicant to pay a representative, if necessary, particularly where his case raises legal or complex factual issues for the presentation of which legal representation is desirable, or where a great deal is at stake for the applicant. At present, whereas litigants before courts can often get legal aid, applicants before tribunals can get legal aid only to cover the cost of advice, not representation. Furthermore, most tribunals have no power to order the respondent to pay the applicant's costs. In many cases this will not matter a great deal because tribunals are relatively cheap; often, too, representation by a social worker or a trade union official may be adequate and, as some evidence shows, more effective than legal representation. But, in more difficult cases, these financial considerations may put tribunal justice out of the reach of many applicants.

A second important ramification of the adversarial model is that the tribunal itself takes very little part in the proceedings, and must make its decision on the basis of the material put before it by the parties. It might be, however, that in some cases, particularly in cases where the applicant is a private individual not represented by a competent advocate and not used to legal proceedings, it would be a good thing for the tribunal itself to have some powers which would enable it to help the applicant in the presentation of his case, and to make inquiries for itself to gather relevant information. This might go some way to redress the imbalance between the parties. On the other hand, the disadvantages of this are as clear as the disadvantages of tribunals being staffed by Civil Servants from the department being challenged (tribunal members might well be 'administration-minded'), and the better approach would be to ensure that proper facilities were made available, so as to enable every applicant to be properly represented.

The discussion so far has accepted the basically adversarial nature of tribunal procedure. However, we have already seen that there are alternatives to adversarial procedure, such as investigation, mediation, and conciliation, and it might be thought that some of these alternative techniques would be particularly appropriate ways of dealing with disputes between citizens and the government in some of the areas with which tribunals deal. For example, it could be argued that disputes over entitlement to supplementary benefit could most suitably be dealt with by some non-adversarial technique of investigation and compromise.

5. THE DIFFERENCES BETWEEN TRIBUNALS AND COURTS

As compared with courts, tribunals tend to be relatively cheap and expeditious, and their procedure is relatively informal, or, at least, it is conducted in a relatively informal atmosphere. The word 'tend' has been used because the procedure of some tribunals is considerably more formalized than that of others. The more legalized the issues with which a tribunal deals, the more formal its procedure tends to be, with lawyers playing an important part in presenting cases, and with parties standing on their legal rights. But even the procedure of very formal tribunals is not as complex, nor usually as time-consuming and expensive, as that of the High Court.

Tribunals are more specialized than courts, both because they are usually set up to deal with just one sort of issue (for example, rent control or national insurance); and because their membership usually includes non-lawyers who have special expertise in the subject matter of the tribunal's jurisdiction (for example, the Industrial Tribunals include representatives of employers' and employees' associations). Courts, on the other hand, deal with a very wide range of matters, and judges tend to be specialists in no more than a couple of areas of the court's jurisdiction. The introduction of the Crown Office List for applications for judicial review[5] will produce a certain amount of specialization in administrative law matters, but this will be specialization more in the general principles of administrative law, rather than in particular subject areas of public law.

The main advantages of specialization are seen as being greater consistency in decision-making and a greater ability to give effect to the social policy behind the legislation, in a way which really makes sense of the realities of the matters regulated by the legislation. We also noted earlier, when discussing decisions on questions of fact and law, that such decisions may often be more rational and sensible if made with a thorough understanding of the area in which the questions arise.[6]

There is, however, another side to the issue of specialization. The expertise of lay members of tribunals is in the *non-legal* aspects of the tribunal's work. But, even in areas where tribunals are reviewing discretionary powers not heavily structured by legal rules or formal policy guidelines, they operate within a framework of legal rules, and it is important that tribunal members understand these rules. Training of lay tribunal members is important in this respect, but, in practice, lack of legal expertise often forces tribunals to rely heavily on their clerk for legal guidance (as in the case of magistrates). Because the clerk is an employee of the department under investigation, this practice jeopardizes the independence of tribunals.

Another technique for overcoming problems caused by lack of legal expertise is to provide for appeals to the High Court on points of law, and to require tribunals to state reasons for their decisions, so that the appellate court knows exactly the basis on which the decision was made.[7] But this solution is expensive and cumbersome. It is much more desirable to improve the quality of tribunal decision-making in the first instance. However, once increased emphasis is put on legal correctness, at the tribunal hearing stage, pressure almost inevitably builds up to formalize procedure and to make it more adversarial. Lawyers get more involved in representing claimants, and tribunal proceedings become more lengthy, expensive, and intimidating for the ordinary applicant. It seems that the price of informality is a certain amount of legal inaccuracy, and it may be that some conscious effort

[5] See p. 181 above.
[6] See p. 48 above.
[7] See Tribunals and Inquiries Act 1971 ss. 12 and 13.

has to be made, if informality is to be preserved, not to insist on the observance of strict legal niceties. The trouble is that, once legal rights are defined, the beneficiaries of those rights usually want to insist on their strict observance, rather than just using them as bargaining counters in informal negotiations. This tendency often has an ideological underpinning. For example, many see it as important, in order to preserve the dignity and individual worth of welfare claimants, that they should have clearly defined rights, and not be subject to the discretion and mercy of the government, or of tribunals which might be inclined to take an establishment view of matters.

Finally, tribunals are not as tied by precedent as courts. They are more concerned than the courts to apply the sort of flexible standards of decision-making which administrators strive for, and less concerned to develop and apply rigid rules. But this difference ought not to be exaggerated, because every decision-maker comes under pressure to be *consistent* in his decision-making.

These differences between tribunals and courts are usually seen as being advantages of tribunals, and as reasons for establishing a tribunal rather than a court; both because cheapness, speed, and so on, are good in themselves; and because, in some areas at least, many applicants before tribunals are poor and ill-educated, and so would find a traditional court very intimidating. Tribunals can be seen, therefore, as having both technical and social advantages over courts. Indeed, the creation of a new court is an extremely rare event.

If tribunals possess such advantages over courts, we might well ask why the courts continue to be involved in administrative law and the legal control and review of the exercise of discretionary power. The answer lies in a recognition that tribunals and courts are not alternative candidates for the same jobs, but perform different functions. Tribunals are chiefly concerned with the day-to-day administration of government programmes and policies, and with the substance of administrative decisions. Courts, on the other hand, are more concerned with establishing the broad legal and constitutional framework within which the business of government is carried on, with protecting legal rights from undue encroachment in the name of the public interest, and with establishing standards of procedural justice. For these tasks the more elaborate procedures of the courts, their specialist legal personnel and their elaborately protected independence from political influence or control, are both necessary and desirable.

6. THE STRUCTURE OF THE TRIBUNAL SYSTEM

There are a large number of tribunals and they have come into existence in a piecemeal and unsystematic way. The Council on Tribunals plays some part in advising on the setting up of new tribunals, but attempts by it to persuade the government to simplify and rationalize the tribunal system have been unsuccessful. As a result, tribunals vary considerably in their membership, procedures, and relationship with the departments whose activities they monitor.

One way of injecting some uniformity into the tribunal system would be to set up a general administrative appeals tribunal (such as exists at the federal level in Australia) with power to hear appeals from any first instance tribunal. At the moment the appellate structure is complex, and in some cases there is no appeal at all; in other cases there is an appeal from one tribunal to another (as in the case of social security tribunals) and in a few cases there is an appeal from a tribunal to a Minister. The advantage of a general appeals tribunal would be that it could develop general principles of administrative discretion. On the other hand, the advantages of specialization and expertise, which tribunals are designed to possess, would, to some extent, at least, be put in jeopardy.

Mention has been made of the Council on Tribunals.[8] This is an advisory body which performs three functions: dealing with complaints about the operation of tribunals, participating in the drafting of procedural rules for tribunals, and advising on the setting up of new tribunals and on the structure of the tribunal system as a whole. In the third of these areas the Council has had very little impact. There is reason to believe that the Council has had an important impact in the second area, in reinforcing the adversary model as the appropriate one for tribunal procedure. In relation to the first function, it is important to remember that tribunals do not fall within the jurisdiction of the PCA. This is partly because tribunals are conceived of as being somewhat analogous to courts, so that the substance of their decisions ought to be monitored by means of appeals or judicial review. But this reasoning does not deal with complaints about the functioning and operation of tribunals. The Council receives a few of these, but it does not have the resources to entertain a significant number of complaints. (So far as courts are concerned, the position is even worse: there is *no*

---

[8] Wade, *Administrative Law* (5th edn., 1982), pp. 799–800; Harlow & Rawlings op. cit. chapter 6.

formal mechanism for making complaints about the operation of the judicial system). It might be argued that an Ombudsman dealing with tribunals (and courts) would threaten the independence of these bodies. But this argument would not be of great force if the Ombudsman restricted his attention to the operation of courts and tribunals, and did not deal with the substance of their decisions. Of course, as we saw when we considered the Ombudsmen, this distinction between substance and procedure is not always easy to draw; but it is not sufficiently difficult to draw as to justify dismissing out of hand the idea of an Ombudsman for tribunals and courts.

23

Inquiries

1. INTRODUCTION

PUBLIC inquiries are an important feature of the British administrative process. Their most significant, but by no means their only, use is as part of the process preliminary to a decision by central government as to the use of land for such things as new towns, housing developments, roads, schools, playing fields, and so on. When we examined the process of making delegated legislation, we found that there were very few formal procedural requirements. By and large it is up to the legislator to decide whom he will consult before he legislates.[1] By contrast, the administrative decision-making process relating to land use is highly organized, and allows citizens to have a say before decisions are made that will affect their rights and interests. Other areas in which public inquiries play a part include housing, agriculture, health, and aviation.

Three thousand or more inquiries are held each year; most are run by the Department of the Environment. The largest group of inquiries concerns planning applications, but a significant number deal with compulsory acquisition of land. Inquiries are conducted by 'inspectors', most of whom are employed by the D.o.E., although independent persons (e.g. a QC or judge) are sometimes engaged to conduct large and contentious inquiries. There are about three hundred D.o.E. inspectors.

2. APPELLATE INQUIRIES

Public inquiries concerning land use perform two main functions. First, they play an important part in the planning appeal process. If, for example, a landowner appeals to the Minister against a decision of a local authority refusing planning permission, or making a compulsory purchase order, the public inquiry performs the function of ascertaining the relevant facts, hearing objections from interested third parties, and

---

[1] See p. 135 above.

assessing the local conditions relevant to the particular decision. In such cases, the inquiry will usually be concerned essentially with establishing facts relevant to assessing the strength of objections to the local authority's decision. The issue will often not raise important matters of national policy, but will involve a small-scale dispute between a particular landowner and a local authority.

When the main aim of the inquiry is to gather facts, it seems only reasonable and fair that the Minister should not be entitled to take account of factual material which did not come out at the inquiry, and which the applicant has not had a chance to challenge. And this is the basic legal position embodied in statutory procedural rules. In such cases the Minister performs essentially the same function as an appellate tribunal, and it is only a matter of organizational detail that it is the Minister, rather than tribunal, who makes the final decision. The task of gathering facts (and in many cases making the final decision itself) is committed to an inspector, simply because the Minister has more pressing things to do.

3. LARGE-SCALE INQUIRIES

In other cases, however, the function of an inquiry is very different. The classic example is a motorway inquiry; in such cases the Minister's role is not appellate. The Minister is both the initiator of the scheme involving the proposed land use and also the person with whom lies the power of decision as to whether the scheme will be put into effect. Here the inquiry performs the function of allowing local views to be expressed about a national programme which affects many millions of people in a variety of ways. The ultimate decision about whether the motorway will be built or not must be taken at the central government level because it affects so many people in so many areas, and is of such general economic and social importance.

Planning appeals also sometimes raise issues of national importance and questions of relevance to many groups and interests. A good example is an appeal in relation to planning permission to build a nuclear power station or fuel reprocessing plant. Such an appeal raises ecological, economic, and energy-policy questions of very deep and wide significance.

In one sense the decision whether or not to build the motorway or to allow a nuclear power station to be built is a legislative one, in that it affects a very large number of people, and has wide and long-term effects. It is to some extent a question of technique, although a very important question of technique, whether such decisions are made by means of primary legislation, delegated legislation, or administrative decision (involving local inquiries). It is a curious feature of our administrative system that there appear to be no general political constitutional principles relevant to deciding which decision-making technique will be used, even though the choice has important ramifications for the way decisions are made. What is clear is that proposals for such mammoth schemes of development ought ideally to be subjected to a considerable amount of public scrutiny before the final decision to proceed or not is made.

It is a matter of considerable debate exactly what the function of public inquiries is in relation to large-scale developments of national importance. One view is that inquiries are designed to ensure that the best possible decision is made *in the public interest*. This aim requires that local objections to the development should be aired, so that they can be weighed against the public benefit to be achieved by the scheme in a sort of cost–benefit analysis. Associated with this idea is the notion that inquiries are designed to 'inform the mind of the Minister', as to relevant local conditions and views. This conception of the function of local inquiries perhaps lines up with the public interest view of the function of administrative law and judicial review. It leads to the idea that the procedure at local inquiries is not designed to protect individual rights, but rather to maximize the sources of information available to the Minister. So, for example, the right of objectors at an inquiry to cross-examine witnesses need not be as extensive as in a court of law, because the aim of the exercise is not to give them a right to challenge every point adverse to them.

A second approach says that the local inquiry is a statutory and institutionalized version of the fair hearing required by natural justice. This approach sees public inquiries in terms of the protection-of-the-individual view of administrative law. It would obviously have important ramifications for the sort of *procedure* which ought to be followed at inquiries: in general it would dictate that judicialized procedures should be adopted as much as possible. It might also suggest a quite strict division of labour between the inquiry and the Minister, the former being concerned with justiciable questions of fact, and the latter with questions of policy. This distinction is, to some extent, present in the law, but recent dicta in the House of Lords have stressed that a public inquiry ought not to be seen as being like a piece of civil litigation. So, it is unclear to what extent an inquiry ought to be seen as a formalized version of the fair hearing.

A third view would see public inquiries as designed to inject an element of public *participation* into administrative decision-making. The optimistic version of this view sees inquiries as giving citizens a real opportunity to influence the mind of the government, even if they give no *guarantee* of any particular outcome. The pessimistic version treats public inquiries as no more than a public relations exercise (and often a very lengthy one, costly in time and money for both government and objectors) designed to assuage and defuse the strong feelings of the objectors.

There is considerable room for doubt as to whether local inquiries perform a useful function, whichever of these views of their role is preferred. In the first place, since the project under consideration will usually be of national significance, the views and objections of people living in one particular area can only be of limited importance or impact; at the end of the day the national interest will prevail over the local interest. Secondly, even in relation to questions which are of mainly local significance, such as the exact route of the motorway, so much planning will have gone into the question of the route, before the inquiry is even held, that it is likely that only the most compelling arguments will sway the decision-makers, even on such issues. It is unlikely that they will not have contemplated most of the objections in advance and the inquiry will do no more than provide the objectors with a chance of airing their views, without any real hope of influencing the outcome. Inquiries occur too late in the decision-making process in such cases to have any very significant impact.

A second and related problem arises out of the fact that, in relation to large-scale national projects, the Minister not only makes the final decision as to what will be done, but also initiates the proposals which the inquiry considers. This is inevitable, given the nature of the issues at stake, but it does mean that the Minister will usually be so committed to his initial proposals that departure from those proposals, as a result of what is said at an inquiry, is rather unlikely.

Thirdly, the law itself draws a distinction between matters of national policy and matters of local concern. Inquiries are not to be used as a forum for discussing matters of national policy. This is a rather difficult distinction to maintain in practice, and large-scale inquiries often tend to focus as much on broad as on local issues. However, the distinction does provide a tool for limiting the participation which inquiries allow to citizens in the decision-making process.

Finally, even at the local level, the issue of the building of a motorway, for example, is a classic example of a multipolar or polycentric issue. Environmentalist groups, traders' associations, inhabitants of nearby villages and towns, motorists' associations, British Rail, truckers' associations, and so on, might all have different arguments (apart from considerations of cost) for and against particular routes. It may well be that it would be impossible to find a solution which would meet the desires and objections of all these groups.

For all these reasons, there is some ground for thinking that the public inquiry system, in this type of case, is unlikely to be very satisfying for those opposed to the proposals. This view is confirmed by the amount of dissatisfaction, in certain quarters, about the public inquiry system.[2] Dissatisfaction is particularly strong amongst environmentalist groups. The basic problem is that objectors have unrealistic expectations about the functions and possibilities of public inquiries. Although inquiries have the appearance of injecting an element of participation and consultation of interest groups into the decision-making process, they do not in fact do this, because there is no necessary relationship between what the interest groups say at the inquiry and the final decision. In these cases, most of the material put forward at the inquiry will be of a technical and expert nature, of which the government is already aware, or the validity of which is contested; or else it will consist of contestable assessments of the balance between various uncontested but opposing factors. So, it is unlikely that the inquiry will actually produce material which the government feels is such as to compel a change of decision. Interest groups are allowed to participate, but only by making their views known. True participatory democracy involves participation in *making* decisions; but our public decision-making system is basically representative, not participatory, and the inquiry system has not led to any significant shift in the allocation of decision-making power.

Furthermore, this dissatisfaction with inquiries on the part of objectors, should be set alongside the point of view of the government and those who favour the proposed development. Large-scale inquiries are often extremely expensive and time-consuming. For

---

[2] See, for example, Lucas, *Democracy and Participation* (Harmondsworth, 1976), pp. 276 ff.

example, the inquiry into the building of Britain's first pressurized water reactor at Sizewell cost about £2.5 million, lasted 340 days, and took evidence from 120 witnesses. Another example is the inquiry in *Bushell* v. *Environment Secretary*[3] which lasted for 100 days; and, by the time the proceedings had been through the court system, the decision-making process lasted about five years. Such delay is bound to generate frustration and opposition to the whole inquiry process amongst the government officials involved and amongst private citizens who will benefit from the planned development, and contractors who will be involved in its construction. The length and cost of many major inquiries also means that it is difficult for individuals or unorganized groups of objectors, with limited resources, to participate. Even organized pressure groups have difficulty in raising the large sums needed to employ the staff and legal advisers necessary to make effective contributions to large public inquiries. In some cases, Ministers have power to pay the costs of the parties involved in inquiries, and the costs of successful objectors are usually met as a matter of administrative practice. But this only deals partially with the problem. Taking public participation seriously means that it should be made financially possible, even if it does not result in a change in the proposed plan, provided it is not frivolous.

The fact that inquiries give people the opportunity to be heard, but very little prospect of affecting the substantive result (that is, they are a procedural device, not a substantive one) provides the key to another reason why inquiries are unsatisfactory. Many of the land-use decisions which inquiries precede, relate to projects which are in themselves highly contentious. There is a great deal of opposition, in general, to the building of motorways and nuclear installations, two of the major types of land use which inquiries concern these days. When the goals to which decision-making mechanisms are directed are very contentious, it is unlikely that basically adjudicatory procedures, which give objectors a say but no vote in the substantive outcome, will satisfy these objectors. The choice of the public inquiry mechanism pushes these contentious land-use issues out of the political arena, and forces the *political* debate into the forum of the supposedly non-political public inquiry. But the law has set its face against the use of inquiries for political purposes; and, anyway, even if political debate could be conducted at inquiries, the fact that they are no more than forums for debate, and that they give the objectors no vote in the substantive

[3] [1981] AC 75.

outcome, means that no matter how extensive the opportunities are for objectors to put their case at inquiries, they are bound to be an unsatisfactory substitute for the political process.

As for the procedure at inquiries into large-scale projects, in practice it tends to be formal and to incorporate many features of court procedure. It could be argued that, because of both the essentially local nature of public inquiries and of the polycentric nature of the issues they raise, there is little point in insisting that the procedure at such inquiries conform closely to an adversarial judicial model. The procedure is largely in the hands of the inspector, and the courts have shown reluctance, for example, to require him to allow cross-examination of departmental officials on technical matters or matters of national policy.[4] It is a waste of time and money to insist that elaborate adversarial procedures (which are designed for a situation in which there is a direct relationship between the cases the parties make and the outcome) should be adopted in situations where the ultimate decision need not be tied to the material presented to the adjudicator. What is undoubtedly important in big public inquiries, is that objectors should be given access to all relevant information and documentation, and be given the chance to speak and comment on that material. Statutory procedural rules governing the conduct of inquiries, make detailed provision about the giving of notice that an inquiry is to be held and about the steps that parties must take to inform other parties of the case that will be put at the inquiry.

It is clearly desirable that the basis of government decisions should be open to scrutiny and examination, and the attitude of the courts to cross-examination (for example) may involve, not a denial of the desirability of openness, but a concern lest inquiries become too cumbersome, expensive, and long. This is a problem for objectors as much as for the government, in that public inquiries are very expensive, not only for the government (which can afford the expense), but also for the objectors, who often cannot afford a protracted, trial-like inquiry.

Other aspects of inquiry procedure worth noting include the fact that the report of the inspector is invariably published, even when this is not required by law. The Tribunals and Inquiries Act 1971 s. 12 requires reasons to be given for the Minister's ultimate decision. These features of inquiry procedure have contributed to the 'judicialization'

---

[4] *Bushell* v. *Environment Secretary* [1981] AC 75.

of the system. The law concerning standing to appear before inquiries is not entirely clear, but, in practice, not only the proponents of and objectors to the proposed development, but also all genuinely interested third parties are allowed to appear and present their views. Legal representation is always allowed. Pursuant to the 1971 Act, statutory procedural rules have been made in respect of the most important classes of inquiries, including compulsory purchase, planning, and motorway inquiries. In other cases, similar procedures to those set out in such rules are often voluntarily followed by analogy. The activities of inquiries can, of course, be the subject of applications for judicial review to the High Court. The Council on Tribunals and the PCA also have oversight of the inquiry system. The CLA, by virtue of its jurisdiction over local authority planning decisions, is also involved with inquiries.

4. INSPECTORS

Finally, a word should be said about the inspectors who conduct inquiries. As we have already noted, most inquiries are conducted by inspectors employed by the D.o.E. The main argument for this is that D.o.E. employees are likely to be more in touch with governmental policy than are independent inspectors. This argument rests on the view of inquiries which sees them as administrative machinery for informing the mind of the Minister prior to his making a policy decision. In contrast to tribunals, inquiries are not seen as independent machinery for adjudication. And yet, in the case of many planning appeals, the inquiry does perform an essentially adjudicatory function. The inspector arbitrates between the local authority and the landowner; often there are no third party objectors and no issues of national policy are at stake (which would give the D.o.E. a direct interest in the outcome); the inspector makes the final decision in the majority of such cases (about seventy per cent). It is not clear why there should not be a planning appeal tribunal to deal with such cases. It does not, of course, follow from this that procedure in such cases should be essentially adversarial. Questions of planning might be thought particularly suitable to resolution by negotiation and compromise, with the help of an independent third party conciliator or mediator.

The cases in which independent inspectors are appointed tend to be those involving large-scale inquiries into projects of national importance, where the final decision will be made on policy grounds, and where the

D.o.E. or other department is directly interested. The contentious nature of many such inquiries clearly means that it is in the interest of the department which has proposed, and will ultimately decide the fate of the development under consideration, to distance itself from the outcome by appointing an independent inspector. On the other hand, the political nature of the ultimate decision really makes such distancing impossible, and the attempted appearance of impartiality is a sham. This is the essential dilemma of the large public inquiry: it is a non-political mechanism for dealing with essentially political issues.

PART V

ADMINISTRATIVE LAW AND ADMINISTRATION

24

Administrative Law and the
Administrative Process

I. JUDICIAL REVIEW AND GOOD ADMINISTRATION

THE bulk of this book has been concerned with judicial review of administrative action. We have seen that different views can be held of the role of judicial review, but all these views have one thing in common: they see the prime functions of judicial review as essentially negative: the controlling of governmental power to ensure that governmental bodies do not overstep the proper bounds of their powers, and protecting the rights of individuals, and the interests of groups and the public, against undue encroachment by government agencies. The courts do not see it as their function to ensure, in a positive way, that administration is well conducted and the country well run. Put another way, the judicial function is complaint or grievance handling rather than complaint avoidance mechanism.

There are, indeed, two features of judicial review which make it less than ideally adapted to the function of ensuring administrative efficiency and securing that the policy goals, which the powers of the administration are designed to effectuate, are achieved as thoroughly as possible. The first is the unsystematic nature of judicial review: the courts will review the activities of government only when asked to do so, within time, by an applicant with the required interest in the outcome of the review. So judicial review cannot be used to conduct wide-ranging and co-ordinated investigations into the conduct of government business. Secondly, judicial review is essentially retrospective: it is primarily concerned with righting a wrong done to an individual in the past, and its effect on the future conduct of the administration is incidental to this main concern. The importance of this point should not, however, be overestimated. Judicial decisions in individual cases often have a direct knock-on effect in many other similar cases, and a widespread indirect effect if they establish rules and principles for dealing with particular types of case or situation.

The Ombudsmen share with judicial review this emphasis on the individual, and their activities are similarly unsystematic; although, as we have seen, the PCA's investigations can often have a wider impact, by suggesting that a department alter the way it deals with a particular type of problem or organizes some section of its work, or by recommending changes to administrative rules, or to regulations or legislation. It has also been suggested that there can be gleaned from the reports of the PCA, over the years, certain principles of good administration (e.g. that matters should be dealt with reasonably speedily), which could provide guidance to administrators as to how to behave, and which constitute a sort of citizens' charter of rights to good treatment at the hands of the administration.[1] But still the PCA is seen as primarily concerned with correcting the effects of maladministration and not with promoting good administration. On the other hand, in Chapter 21 we saw that the Commission for Local Administration has been quite active in encouraging local authorities to accept voluntarily a code of good administrative practice, in an attempt to minimize the grounds for justified citizen dissatisfaction with local authority administration.

There is, then, an important distinction between retrospective control of administrative action, and prospective regulation to improve the quality of administrative decision-making and to minimize the number of complaints about it. But this distinction is not a sharp one because techniques of retrospective control, in particular judicial review, also generate rules and principles of general application to the future conduct of administrators. In this respect it is useful to draw a distinction between judicial review for procedural shortcomings, and judicial review for substantive errors, such as error of law or fact and abuse of discretion. Clearly, the rules of natural justice, which have been developed by the courts, provide the administration with a general procedural blueprint which they would be wise to consider when deciding how to deal with the public. However, of course, the application of those rules is often unclear. In some cases a challenge on the ground of breach of natural justice will not be of much general importance in guiding the administration in how to conduct its affairs because the dispute is simply one of fact as to what procedure was actually followed, or because it concerns the application to the facts of that particular case of an undisputed procedural requirement. But

---

[1] Bradley [1980] CLJ 304, 310–12.

some cases lay down important general principles of procedural propriety, which are bound to have an effect on the way a body conducts its affairs in the future. And there is no doubt that, in moulding these principles, the courts often have an eye on the future impact of their decision. For example, in *Payne* v. *Lord Harris of Greenwich*[2] in which it was decided that the Parole Board was under no duty to tell a prisoner why his application for release on licence had been refused, Lord Denning, MR, although of the view that, in the interests of the prisoner, reasons ought to be given, felt that the interests of society at large and the due administration of the parole system counted against disclosure. All the judges saw the case as raising an issue not confined to the particular case, but having an impact on the running of the parole system generally.

As far as review for substantive error is concerned, the picture is somewhat more complex. Clearly, particular cases of review for error of fact will usually not have any direct impact, beyond that case, on the conduct of administrators. But there may be indirect effects. For example, the decision in *R.* v. *Home Secretary, ex parte Khawaja*[3] in which it was held that the court should exercise tight control over findings of fact by immigration officers on which the personal liberty of immigrants depended, may have the effect of making immigration officials more careful in investigating the cases which come before them. Regarding review for error of law, one of the chief justifications for the expansion in recent years of the courts' control over decisions of law is that, in this way, uniformity can be achieved in cases where a large number of bodies or officers throughout the country are confronted with the same issue. This is clearly desirable, but the indirect effects may not be so desirable. The more prepared the courts are to intervene and to lay down legal rules to control, for example, the dispensation of social security benefits, the more important legal expertise becomes in deciding entitlement to such benefits, and this is not necessarily a good thing, because it might lead to increasing judicialization of the tribunal appeal system which, in turn, could make the proceedings of these tribunals more formal, lengthy, and expensive.

The general principles according to which the courts exercise control over the exercise of discretionary powers are not particularly useful in guiding the future conduct of administrators. Concepts such

---

[2] [1981] 1 WLR 754.
[3] [1984] AC 74.

308 Administrative Law and Administration

as unreasonableness, improper purposes and irrelevant considerations, and the principle that discretionary powers must not be fettered are, when stated abstractly, important chiefly as organizing categories for analysing the decisions of the courts and for assessing their constitutional role in controlling the administration. But when these concepts are given concrete content in the light of particular legislative provisions and particular facts, they *can* provide useful guidance for administrators dealing with similar cases under the same statutory provisions. For example, there is a very considerable body of law on the question of what conditions can be properly attached to the grant of planning permission, given the aims of the planning legislation and the planning system. The interest of the administrator is in the detailed application of the concepts rather than with their general nature. When a body of case-law develops in a particular area, providing administrators with guidance as to how their powers ought properly to be exercised, the rules and principles so established are analogous to policy guidelines formulated by administrators for their own guidance (with the important difference that they are legally authoritative). Like policy guidelines, they will not *dictate* the way in which powers are to be exercised, because the powers are *discretionary* by nature and so their exercise must be moulded to the facts of particular cases. So, even when there is a considerable body of case-law concerning a particular power, it will not always be possible to say for certain, in advance, whether any particular exercise of the power would be held by a court to be lawful. But the principles laid down in the cases will provide useful guidance. This process of creating bodies of guiding principles is sometimes called 'rule-making through adjudication'. It can be seen at work, not only in judicial review, but also in the activities of some tribunals such as the Immigration Appeals Tribunal.[4]

In summary, we can say that the decisions of the courts in applications for judicial review often contain rules and principles which can provide administrators with guidance as to the proper exercise of their powers. But the importance of judicial review, in this respect, is reduced by its unsystematic nature and by its emphasis on remedying past grievances of the applicant. The impact of judicial review is further lessened by the fact that the government can, and often does, reverse or neutralize judicial decisions, which it does not like, by statute or regulation; or it can confine them within narrow

---

[4] Harlow & Rawlings, *Law and Administration*, pp. 517 ff.

bounds by issuing administrative policy guidelines as to how particular decisions are to be applied in practice.[5] This fact emphasizes the point that judicial review operates in a political environment.

The basic justification for judicial review, then, is not that it structures administrative decision-making in advance, but that it checks its exercise after the event. This emphasis on retrospective checking is often considered a grave defect in the institution of judicial review; but structuring and checking are quite different techniques for controlling decision-making, and it is at least arguable that neither is in all circumstances and for all purposes superior to the other. There is room for both.[6]

Before we go on to consider other techniques which could be used to promote good administration prospectively, it is worth asking by what criteria we judge whether the administration is working well.

2. WHAT IS GOOD ADMINISTRATION?

An obvious criterion of success is provided by the level of citizen satisfaction with the administrative machine. The number of errors made, and the number of complaints lodged with grievance-solving bodies, give an important guide as to how well the administrative system is working. If citizens are happy with the way the system is operating, then administrators have some ground for satisfaction. Other criteria of success could also be suggested. In particular, two issues seem important: first, is the administration achieving the policy goals, which the government wants it to achieve and which Parliament has set for it in legislation? Secondly, assuming that the administration is working well both from the citizen's and the government's points of view, is it doing so efficiently, or could the same results be achieved at less cost?

This last yardstick is of particular importance in relation to nationalized industries for, although such enterprises must be subject to legal and political control, such control has to be tempered by the need for financial planning and discipline in the day-to-day running of industrial concerns, and also by reason of the fact that some nationalized industries are subject to competition from private industry.

---

[5] See Prosser, *Test Cases for the Poor* (1983), chapter 5.
[6] Baldwin & Hawkins [1984] PL 570.

3. PROMOTING GOOD ADMINISTRATION

(a) Good Procedure

One obvious way of promoting customer satisfaction, at the level of procedure, is to lay down codes of procedure in advance. This has been done extensively in relation to the activities of tribunals and inquiries, and it is noticeable that the amount of litigation about the procedure of such bodies is very small, given their number and volume of activity. Most of the significant natural justice cases of recent years have concerned bodies whose activities are not governed by a comprehensive procedural code. The drafting of a procedural code in advance also has the advantage that the procedure can be moulded to the tasks which the body has to perform. We have seen that the quasi-judicial procedures embodied in the rules of natural justice are not always the most appropriate, and the courts have not shown themselves particularly able or willing to develop different procedural models. Bodies such as the Council on Tribunals could do much to develop appropriate procedural codes for different administrative activities. It is clearly important that some body independent of the administration should have a say in the drafting of such rules, to ensure that they maintain a proper balance between the interests of citizens and government. But, at the end of the day, good procedure, which makes citizens feel that they have been justly treated, is as much in the interests of the government as it is to the benefit of the citizen.

(b) Sound Decisions

A second major area where there is considerable potential for providing prospective guidance, is that of the exercise of discretionary powers. In Chapter 4 we discussed the relationship between discretion and rules. We saw that rules can be used to structure and confine discretion, and that such rules yield advantages of uniformity and predictability in decision-making. Rules benefit citizens because they create entitlements to be treated in defined ways. This promotes customer satisfaction. Rules also enable the political arm of government to ensure that administrators pursue sound and acceptable policies. We have also seen, however, that the courts are unwilling to allow informal rules of thumb and policies to be used extensively to restrict the breadth of the administrator's discretion. We noted, too, in Chapter 7, that, in many areas of governmental activity in Britain, as compared with the United States, the system of administration makes much more use of discretion than of rules.

Clearly there is a case, in certain circumstances at least, for defining the scope of discretion in advance, rather than controlling abuse of discretion or excesses of power retrospectively. A major question which must be faced, however, if rules are to play a larger part in the administrative process, concerns who is to make these rules and by what procedures they are to be made. To the extent that primary and delegated legislation lays down rules governing the exercise of governmental powers, we have an established system for making such rules. But we have seen that there are many *informal* rules which regulate the exercise of governmental powers. In fact, it is almost inevitable that holders of discretionary powers will develop policies about their exercise, both in order to save time in dealing with similar cases, and in order to be seen to be acting fairly. Obviously, once it is known that rules are being used to regulate the exercise of powers, legitimate demands can be made to expose those rules to scrutiny. Judicial review is a very inefficient mechanism for such scrutiny because of its unsystematic and retrospective nature. It is much more satisfactory for the rules to be subjected to scrutiny before they come into force.

Apart from the fact that such early scrutiny is expensive of time and money, two other important points arise in connection with it. The first concerns the issue of at whose behest the scrutiny would take place. Judicial review concentrates on the individual and the way acts of the administration affect him, whereas rule-making is usually concerned with classes of situations and persons. As a result, the consultation process preliminary to the making of rules gives the opportunity to be heard primarily to groups and interests, rather than to individuals. Groups tend to differ widely in their resources and degree of organization and, unless weaker and poorer groups are given some assistance to put their views, the interests of the better organized and wealthier groups may be disproportionately represented. This fact might at first sight make consultation seem unattractive, as compared with judicial review. However, two comments should be made. First, at least since the introduction of the 'sufficient interest' test of standing, the judicial review process is arguably just as available to interest groups as it is to individuals. Secondly, individuals also differ considerably in their resources and, in the absence of generous legal aid, the judicial review process is much more open to the wealthy than to the poor.

The other point which would arise out of an increased emphasis on rule-making (if this was coupled with a formal system of entitlements to be consulted and to make representations, before the making of the rules) is that it would introduce into our law-making system a significant participatory element. Traditionally, our law-making system has been primarily representative. It is, of course, open to our elected representatives to consult whomever they choose before they make law, but there is no constitutional obligation on them to do this. So, it might be thought that a greater emphasis on administration according to general rules would bring about significant change in the fundamental nature of our polity.

However, there are several features of the modern governmental system which suggest that this representative model is somewhat outdated. First, it assumes that the effective law-makers are elected Members of Parliament who, by acting collectively as such, make the laws under which we live. But the degree of executive control of the law-making process and the importance of party loyalty in the life of the modern MP, lessen the representative role of the individual MP and, also, lessen the function of the House of Commons as an effective law-making body. Secondly, the representative picture of law-making is inappropriate to delegated legislation, even that made by Ministers, because MPs who become Ministers are not elected as representatives of anyone to make law in their own right, but to make law as MPs. Furthermore, the representative picture has nothing to say about delegated law-making by non-political bodies, such as nationalized industries. Local authorities (which make by-laws and regulations) are representative bodies, but they are not necessarily representative of the ratepayers and so the law imposes on them a special duty to consider the interests of ratepayers. Further, to the extent that local authority by-laws follow models provided by central government, the representative justification for law-making by local authorities is further weakened.

When all these considerations are coupled with arguments about the relatively unrepresentative nature of a system of non-proportional representation, it can be argued that a participatory element in law-making is highly desirable and constitutionally justified, in order to overcome some of the defects and shortcomings in the representative system. Therefore, if one believed that it was desirable to reduce the discretionary element in the administrative process, this might profitably be done by means of rules made by a process to which interested groups and parties were entitled by law to contribute. On the other hand, there is no doubt that such consultative procedures would add considerably to the expense of government, and would slow down the rate of development and change in the way government power is exercised.

(c) Value for Money

The third yardstick of success mentioned above was economic efficiency: is the administration achieving the policy ends set for it in the most efficient way? This is related to the two other yardsticks of success, in that efficiency is bound to be an incidental policy goal set by any government for its administration, whatever political goals it is required to achieve; and, also, because customer complaints often arise from inefficiency as much as from dissatisfaction with the values being pursued. The problem of ensuring value for money in government administration is particularly important, because the government is a monopoly supplier of certain services and so is not subject to the discipline of the competitive market.

There is a very large body of theoretical and empirical literature concerned with various aspects of efficiency.[7] Some of this literature is concerned with the structure and operation of *organizations* (organization theory); some of it is concerned with *human behaviour* and the relations between those who make up organizations; and some of it is concerned with the way *decisions* are made in practice, and ought best to be made in theory (decision theory). A lot of the literature is concerned with private organizations, but a good deal has also been written on public administration.

Administrative *law* is essentially concerned with specifying ends for administrators to aim at and respect. The models of administrative law suggested in Chapter 1 embody those ends in very general terms: the protection of individual rights and group interests, and the furtherance of the public good. Administrative law is not concerned with making sure that those ends are achieved efficiently. It does not follow from this, however, that studies of organizations and decision-making are of no relevance to administrative law. Although the law is concerned with specifying ends, that is, values to be achieved in the administrative

---

[7] See Brown & Steel, *The Administrative Process in Britain* (2nd edn., 1979) Part II.

process, some of these values relate to the *way* in which decisions are made, as opposed to the content of the decisions or the policy objectives which the decisions are designed to effectuate. The law is concerned, *inter alia*, with ensuring that certain normative procedural standards are observed in the decision-making process. Sometimes, these decision-making norms will conflict with the demand for efficiency. For example, the requirement of compliance with the rules of natural justice, which is designed to secure the rights of the individual and the appearance of fairness, may well make the administrative decision-making process more costly and time-consuming, without any 'improvement' in the ultimate decision, because the ultimate decision would have been the same even if a hearing had been given. In other words, the most efficient means to a particular end may be different from that means which the law requires for reasons of justice.

The basic question which this raises is the extent to which the law should mould its requirements in the light of considerations of 'efficiency'. It is, of course, clear that when 'justice' and 'efficiency' conflict, justice does not by any means always win. To give some obvious examples: there are strict time-limits on applications for judicial review so as not to hamper the administrative process unduly; the interest of litigants in full disclosure of information is tempered, to some extent, by the demands of candour and confidentiality within government departments, when this is desirable in the interests of good administration; and the demands of natural justice are sometimes watered down for the sake of promoting good decision-making, for example, in the context of the licensing of gaming establishments. So, not only do the courts play an important part in laying down values for the administration to observe, but they also decide how these normative requirements are to be fitted in with the demands of efficient administration. The reason for this is not hard to find: efficiency in administration is itself a virtue and the credibility of the courts would suffer greatly if they were to make demands of the administration which conflicted too strongly with this desirable end. So, the courts cannot ignore the demands of administrative efficiency. It is, therefore, important for lawyers and courts to be aware, at least, of this aspect of administrative activity, so as not to impose on the administration unrealistic standards of conduct.

To give this general argument a finer point, it is worth looking at what the law has to say about three of the central questions with which organization and decision theory are concerned: who decides what; by what procedures; and on the basis of what material?

(i) *Who decides what?*

The law's basic answer to the first question is that, if a discretionary power is given to *X*, it must be exercised by *X* and by no one else. This rule against delegation appears to be more strictly applied in relation to powers to make rules than in relation to other powers. It does not, however, prevent the delegation of tasks within departments of central government. The rule is enforced quite strictly in relation to the activities of local authorities, although *Western Fish Products* v. *Penwith DC*[8] does recognize that, in certain circumstances, a decision may be enforced, despite the fact that it is *ultra vires* because made by an unlawful delegate. A related rule is that against the fettering of a discretion by accepting dictation, as to the manner of its exercise, from some third party. This second rule prevents formal compliance with the first from masking an effective transfer of the power of decision to someone else. The law, therefore, imposes a certain limitation on the freedom of the administration to organize its internal decision-making structure in the way it chooses. But the law does recognize that delegation is necesary when individuals or bodies are given so many powers that they could not possibly make all the decisions, which their functions require of them.

On the other hand, when a power is given to a particular person or body, in order that the person or body might bring its particular skills and point of view to bear on the making of the decisions required of it, then it is arguable that the demands of good and efficient decision-making, as well as the demands of justice, require a rule against delegation. Of course, the legislature might be mistaken in thinking that the power-holder *is* the best person to make the decision, but it would not be proper for the courts to question the allocation of power. It would seem, therefore, that the principles which the law enforces, relevant to the question of who decides what, are sensible ones, and that they do not unnecessarily conflict with the demands of efficiency.

(ii) *By what procedure?*

The procedural question is more complex. There is often perceived to be a conflict between the demands of natural justice, and the

[8] [1979] 77 LGR 185.

demands of efficiency and good decision-making. Hearings take time and money and may not, at the end of the day, improve the quality of the final decision; the same decision might have been reached without a hearing. One of the main motivations of the courts, in watering down the requirements of natural justice in recent years, has been a desire not to hamper the administrative process unduly. On the other hand, unless one is absolutely sure that the person entitled to a hearing can have nothing to say which might improve the decision, then it is wise to work on the assumption that giving a hearing might lead to a better decision.

It was also argued, in Chapter 5, that compliance with the rules of natural justice may not only be expensive and time-consuming, but also that it may not necessarily guarantee the best result, because the rules are best suited to deciding certain types of questions on the basis of limited material. In cases where it is thought desirable that more sources of information and argument should be tapped before the decision is made, or where the nexus between the information and argument and the final result is not intended to be direct, some other procedure of decision-making might be more suitable, as well as more efficient. On the other hand, the rules of natural justice are designed to preserve and give effect to the right of individuals to be treated in a certain way when their rights are affected. The courts *ought* to see themselves as guardians of individual rights, but at the same time to recognize that the rights afforded by the rules of natural justice may not always achieve the best balance between efficiency and the interests of individuals. The courts are in a position of strategic power to strike a balance between the demands of efficiency and the interest of individuals in being heard.

(iii) Using what materials?

Regarding the third question (on the basis of what material decisions ought to be made) it has long been recognized by theorists of decision-making that all decisions are made on the basis of only a selection of the material which might be thought relevant to the making of the decision, both because the gathering of material is an expensive and time-consuming activity and, also, because the human mind can only deal with and absorb a limited amount of material. Further, part of the function of delegation and specialization in the decision-making process, is to divide up and, therefore, make more manageable the processing of material relevant to the making of particular decisions. One person in the decision-making chain will rely on another to have reached a conclusion on a particular issue relevant but subsidiary to the ultimate question to be decided. This interim decision will have been made on the basis of some material relevant to the ultimate issue, which the decision-maker higher in the chain need not consider himself.

As we have noted, the rules of natural justice, being based on the adversary model, in fact serve to limit the sources of relevant information by focusing on two parties. But this limitation is justified in terms of justice, rather than efficiency. The other legal rule relevant to this issue is that which requires *all* relevant considerations to be taken into account and *no* irrelevant consideration. On its face, this rule might be thought to run counter to the insight of decision-making theory that there is a limit, imposed by human ability and resources, on the amount of information which can be considered. But, in fact, the rule does not operate so as to make unrealistic demands of the administration. Rather, it is designed as a way of enforcing the 'information parameters' which the empowering statute expressly or impliedly lays down. Administrators are not given a free hand to consider what to take into account and what to ignore. Statutes will often give express guidance on the matter, and, even if they do not, the policy goals embodied in the statute will enable a court to decide, although not always easily or uncontroversially, what factors are relevant. In other words, a major determinant of what information is taken into account in the decision-making process, is which policy objectives are being pursued. The courts see their role as being to define those policy objectives clearly, and to decide what informational inputs those objectives require and justify.

The legal rule, in fact, contains an implicit recognition that there are limits to the amount of information to be considered. But these limits are not fixed by what is possible, but by what is desirable or required in policy terms. So, for example, the fact that particular information is difficult or expensive to acquire or evaluate will not necessarily be a reason not to require it to be taken into account, even though the administrator, concerned with costs and benefits, might think that the gain to be had from collecting the information was not worth the costs. On the other hand, the fact that information is very difficult to gather, or interpret, may provide a reason or justification for saying, as a matter of policy, that it ought to be ignored.

4. CONCLUSION

Put crudely, we might say that organization and decision theories are concerned with how to secure policy objectives in the cheapest and most efficient way. The courts, on the other hand, are concerned with setting policy objectives for the administration. The courts are not the primary policy-setting mechanism. The legislature provides the basic policy objectives, but the courts play a role in refining and defining the limits of those policies, and in putting certain constraints on the pursuit of policy. But this dichotomy is not sharp. Efficiency in public administration is itself a policy objective of every government, because every government wants to get its policies into operation as cheaply as possible. So, the courts cannot afford totally to ignore the requirements of efficiency, nor do they. Sometimes, other values have to be sacrificed to the need for efficiency and cost-effectiveness. But the very nature of judicial review, and the training and expertise of judges, makes the courts unsuitable as bodies to lay down efficiency objectives for the administration. This is the job of Civil Servants themselves and of management experts. Good management and efficiency in organizations is not achieved by coercive and inflexible rules, but by flexible and adaptable techniques which take account of the realities of the administrative process. All the courts can do is to ensure that they do not impose on the administration requirements which conflict too severely with the demands of getting the job done.

But it would be quite unrealistic to think that courts could, or should, ignore efficiency considerations, and it is much better that these be brought out into the open and discussed. At the same time, there is a great deal of disagreement amongst experts in organization and decision-making theory as to how to achieve maximum efficiency, and a great deal depends on the particular organization in question. The most we can expect of the courts is that they be aware of the problems, and attempt not to burden the administration with impossible management tasks. Beyond that it must be for the administrators to cope, as best they can, with the normative demands of the law.

Index

Index

321

delegation and agency distinguished
  231
exception to doctrine of *ultra vires*
  228 ff.
organization theory 315
representations/decisions by officials
  230–2
revocation of lawful decisions 236–9
types of 227
waiver of formalities 232–3
evidence
  see discovery
  record 53
expertise
  illegality 43
  natural justice 107–8
  remedies 154, 181
  tribunals 288–9

fringe bodies 7–8

general principles of administrative law
  9–10

Health Service Commissioners 274

illegality
  factors relevant to determining 42–4,
    47–8
  jurisdictional theory 49, 55, 56–7,
    58–9
  meaning of 39 ff.
  public law and private law 39–40
  illegality and wrongness distinguished
    41–2, 51–2
  voidness and voidability 55–6, 145–6
independence of judiciary
  judicial restraint 18, 82
  political decisions 17–18, 33
  separation of powers and 17
individuals
  natural justice 122
  protection of rights of 30–1
  rights and remedies 142–3
inquiries
  adjudicatory model 295–6, 299
  appellate inquiries 293–4
  costs 298
  expense 297–8
  functions of 293, 295
  inspectors 300–1
  large-scale inquiries 294–300
  natural justice 295–6, 299

participation 296–7
policy issues 296–7, 298–9
polycentricity 297
procedure 299
reports of inspectors 299
interest groups
  administrative functions of 26
  control of 27
  consultation of 26, 28
  influence on political process 26–7, 28
  judicial review and 27–30
  standing 30, 165

judicial functions
  contrasted with quasi-judicial functions
    19
  natural justice 96–100
  remedies 149–52
judicial review
  autonomy of 13–15
  exclusion of 187–90
  interest protection view 27–30
  legitimacy of 33–5
  procedure and substance 29
  protection of individual view 30–1
  public interest view 32–3
  retrospective nature of 66, 122
  scope of 18, 42–4, 52, 187–90
  theories of 27 ff.
  undemocratic nature of 34
  uniformity of result 43–4
  unsystematic nature of 305–6, 311
justiciability
  balancing of interests 235
  Crown immunity 199
  implied ouster of remedies 188–9
  natural justice 96–102
  polycentricity 100–2, 149–52
  remedies 149–52
  tort liability 205

legal representation
  natural justice 117–19
  tribunals 287
legitimate expectations
  natural justice 111–13
  policy guidelines 73–4
  public law rights 169
  standing 164
lobby groups
  see interest groups
local authorities
  central government and 22–4